Foucault and political reason

Foucault and political reason

Liberalism, neo-liberalism and
rationalities of government

Edited by

Andrew Barry
Goldsmiths College, University of London

Thomas Osborne
University of Bristol

Nikolas Rose
Goldsmiths College, University of London

London and New York

First published in 1996 by UCL Press

Reprinted 2001
by Routledge
11 New Fetter Lane
London EC4P 4EE

Routledge is an imprint of the Taylor & Francis Group

British Library Cataloguing in Publication Data
A catalogue record for this book is available from the British Library.

ISBNs: 1-85728-431-3 HB
        1-85728-432-1 PB

Typeset in Baskerville.
Printed and bound by
LSL Press Ltd, Bedford, Bedfordshire, England

Contents

Acknowledgements

We would like to thank Lisa Blackman and Ian Hodges for their help in organizing the 1992 Foucault and Politics Conference at Goldsmiths College, University of London from which many of these chapters derive. The conference was supported by *Economy and Society*, which initially published a number of the chapters, and we would like to thank that journal, and particularly Grahame Thompson, for supporting this project.

Chapters by Burchell, Cruikshank and Hindess first appeared in a special issue on liberalism and governmentality, *Economy and Society* **22**(3), 1993. An earlier version of the chapter by Rose first appeared as "Government, authority and expertise in advanced liberalism" in *Economy and Society* **22**(3), 1993, 283–99. An earlier version of the chapter by O'Malley first appeared as "Risk, power and crime prevention" in *Economy and Society* **21**(3), 1992, 252–75. We are grateful to Routledge for permission to publish these papers. An earlier version of the chapter by Gordon first appeared as "Foucault en Angleterre" in *Critique* **471–2**, 1986, 826–40. The chapters by Barry, Bell, Dean, Hunt, Hunter and Osborne appear here for the first time.

Contributors

Andrew Barry is a lecturer in the Department of Sociology, Goldsmiths College, University of London. He is currently working on a study of the history of networks.

Vikki Bell is a lecturer in the Department of Sociology, Goldsmiths College, University of London. She has written a number of articles on and around the work of Foucault and is the author of *Interrogating incest: feminism, Foucault and the law* (London: Routledge, 1993).

Graham Burchell is a freelance writer and translator. He was an editor of the journals *Ideology and Consciousness* and *Radical Philosophy*. He is an editor of *The Foucault effect: studies in governmentality* (Hemel Hempstead, England: Harvester Wheatsheaf, 1991) and a translator of Gilles Deleuze & Felix Guattari's *What is philosophy?* (London: Verso, 1994).

Barbara Cruikshank is Assistant Professor of Political Theory at the University of Massachusetts at Amherst. She is completing a book manuscript titled *Democratic subjects*, which is a study of governmentality and democratic welfare reform in the United States.

Mitchell Dean is Senior Lecturer at Macquarie University, Sydney. He is currently working on a book on governmentality.

Colin Gordon is the editor of *Power/knowledge* (Brighton: Harvester, 1980) and the author of a number of articles on Foucault's work. His essay on governmentality appeared in *The Foucault effect: studies in governmentality* (Hemel Hempstead: Harvester Wheatsheaf, 1991).

Barry Hindess is Professor of Political Science in the Research School of Social Science at the Australian National University, Canberra. His previous books include *Politics and class analysis* (Oxford: Basil Blackwell, 1987), *Choice, rationality and social theory* (London: Unwin Hyman, 1988) and *Discourses of power: from Hobbes to Foucault* (Oxford: Basil Blackwell, 1996).

Alan Hunt is Professor in the Departments of Sociology/Anthropology and Law at Carleton University, Ottawa. His most recent books are *Foucault and law* (London: Pluto, 1994) (with Gary Wickham) and *Governance of consuming passions* (forthcoming).

Ian Hunter is an Australian Research Council Fellow in the Faculty of Humanities at Griffith University. He is the author of *Culture and government: the emergence of literary education* (London: Macmillan, 1988), *Rethinking the school* (Sydney: Allen & Unwin, 1994) and (with David Saunders & Dugald Williamson) *On pornography* (London: Macmillan, 1992).

Pat O'Malley is Professor of Law and Legal Studies at La Trobe University. Most of his research at present concerns models of individual responsibility and enterprise in classical vs. current liberalisms. As part of this he is examining changing relations in the life, accident and property fields over the last 150 years.

Thomas Osborne has published widely in social theory and the sociology of knowledge. He is a lecturer in the Department of Sociology, University of Bristol.

Nikolas Rose is Professor of Sociology at Goldsmiths College, University of London, and author of a number of studies of political power, the human sciences and the regulation of personal identity, including *The psychological complex* (London: Routledge, 1985), *Governing the soul* (London: Routledge, 1990) and *Inventing ourselves* (Cambridge: Cambridge University Press, 1996). His current work is on changing strategies of government.

Introduction

Andrew Barry, Thomas Osborne, Nikolas Rose

The essays in this book propose some new ways of anatomizing political reason, ways that may operate upon and through history, but which do so in order to gain a purchase upon our present and its politics. Contemporary political reason seems troubled and uncertain. The death of State socialism as a viable political doctrine has been accompanied, not by an uncontested triumph of liberal democracy and free-market individualism but by a proliferation of political doctrines and programmes that are unstable and difficult to classify in conventional terms. In the name of empowering both individual and community, parties of both right and left advocate the removal of aspects of welfare and security from State control and supply. A revived communitarianism couples an emphasis on individual responsibility with a critique of the all-powerful State and finds converts from all parts of the political spectrum. Campaigns for citizenship link demands for certain political and legal rights with projects to reform individuals at the level of their personal skills and competencies. Ecological politics seem to be so attractive to many because of the simultaneous demands for action by public authorities and changes in the conduct of private companies and individuals. Feminist arguments have gone beyond the twin options of total destruction of patriarchy or simple campaigns for equality to take on issues raised by the new reproductive technology, the right to life, sexual abuse and sexual harassment to engage with a range of other issues such as the organization of work and child-care that call both for action by political authorities and ethical transformations across a population. If one thing unites these different aspects of political thought, it is the ways in which they seek a form of politics "beyond the State", a politics of life, of ethics, which emphasizes the crucial political value of the mobilization and shaping of individual capacities and conduct.

But if political reason itself is mutating, analysis of politics lags some way behind. It has proved difficult and painful for much political theory and political sociology to abandon the oppositions that have sufficed for so long: State and civil society, economy and family, public and private, coercion and freedom. Yet contemporary movements in politics show just how clumsy and inept such oppositions are: each, in different ways, demands a form of government that combines action by political and non-political authorities, communities and individuals. And the relations of force, of power, of subordination, of liberation and "responsibilization", of collective allegiance and individual choice that are brought into being in these new configurations are difficult to visualize, let alone to evaluate, in the language of orthodoxy. Indeed, in a very real sense, it is liberalism itself that is at stake in these new forms of political reason – the peculiar sense in which, for liberalism, freedom was simultaneously the antonym, the limit and the objective of government, and the ways in which these relations of liberty and authority were thought through and enacted in Western societies over the subsequent 150 years.

The studies that follow do not emerge from any shared political position, nor do they propose a new politics. Rather, their objective is the analysis of political reason itself, of the mentalities of politics that have shaped our present, the devices invented to give effect to rule, and the ways in which these have impacted upon those who have been the subjects of these practices of government. Their "analytics" thus lie somewhere between a history of political ideas and a sociology of technologies of government. Their aim is modest but important at this time when political inventiveness, especially from those who consider themselves radicals, is undoubtedly required. They will have served their purpose if they help enhance the "thinkability" of the relations of force that shape our present; for surely thought itself must play some part in evaluating and contesting these relations.

Writing the history of the present

How should one write the history of the present? The remarkable rebirth of so-called "grand theory" in Britain and America in recent years has seen the formulation of numerous ambitious theses about our world, its nature, its pasts and its futures. In this style of work, the social theorist becomes a kind of philosopher *manqué*, retaining the armchair proclivities of the philosopher, yet adding a frisson of empirical observation, usually of a "historical" order. Perhaps the key category has been that of *modernity*. Modernity takes on the status of a comprehensive periodization: an epoch, an attitude, a form of life, a mentality, an experience. The analysis of modernity is thus placed at the heart of the identity of social theory. And retrospective light is cast back upon the still-revered "founding fathers" of the discipline of sociology in order to reveal that their concerns were also fundamentally with modernity, or rather with the difference made by modernity. In these terms, Weber's concern with rationalization, Marx's analysis of the internal contradictions of capitalism and Durkheim's notion of organic solidarity were all contributions to this consideration of modernity as difference. Modernity here, takes the form of a 300-year historical bloc, which is today, and has always been, the main object of a social theory that has thus always been inseparably bound up with a "discontinuist" notion of history. Even historical analyses themselves, when undertaken from within the purview of particular sociological perspectives, are frequently concerned with constituting not novel theories of historical transformation, but the exact characteristics of the modern.

This concern with the present as modernity inevitably runs into certain problems as a result of an inherent impetus to totalization. Where are the limits – geographical, social, temporal – of modernity (Giddens 1990)? Is modernity a type of society, or an attitude or a mode of experience (Osborne 1992)? Is modernity a functionalist, a realist, or an idealist concept? Where is modernity heading? What comes after modernity? Or perhaps – the greatest iconoclasm – we have yet to reach modernity at all (Latour 1991)? In any case, the predictable consequence of these problems has been to formulate a repertoire of supplements to modernity to characterize *our* difference – postmodernity, late modernity, high modernity. These notions aspire to continuity with modernity at the level of the concept, whereas they are defined in opposition to it at the level of their object. Hence, as has often been observed, in spite of the obsession with difference so frequently displayed by the proponents of such supplementary notions – the postmodernists in particular – such concepts tend towards a reciprocal totalization; these too become concepts to grasp the essence of an epoch.

Now, it cannot be denied that the contributions in this value are also concerned with diagnosing the differences of the present. Indeed, they are instances of what has become known broadly, if a trifle grandly, as exercises in the "history of the present". But the contributors do not presume to have provided some general account of modernity or postmodernity;

3

indeed they share a certain explicit or implicit scepticism about the will to know that animates such endeavours. Nor do they seek to package and market another brand of authority under whose auspices historical investigations are to take place. For if these essays have drawn upon the work of Michel Foucault in conducting their investigations, this has not been with an eye to setting up some rival new and improved theory of modernity and its fate. Instead, a range of more local conceptual devices have been utilized: strategies, technologies, programmes, techniques. These concepts do not serve to sum up the present historical "conjuncture"; rather they are tools for understanding some of the contingencies of the systems of power that we inhabit – and which inhabit us – today. As such, perhaps the spirit of these contributions owes as much to an *empirical* as it does to any theoretical tendency in historical sociology. In place of the generalities of much grand theory, the contributions allocate theorizing a more modest role; concepts are deployed to demonstrate the negotiations, tensions and accidents that have contributed to the fashioning of various aspects of our present.

The conception of the present at stake in this work thus does not relate to some mythical Foucauldian "worldview". The "Foucault effect" can more accurately be characterized in terms of two kinds of rather local influence. In the first place, there is at work here a general *ethos* with which the study of the present is approached. In the second place, there is a concern with the vicissitudes of *liberalism* in the shaping of the political contours of this present. It is here that the analytic grid deployed by Foucault, and centred on the concept of governmentality is of some importance.

Foucault might be said to approach the question of the present with a particular *ethos* but not with any substantive or *a priori* understanding of its status. His concern is not to identify some current, perhaps definitive, "crisis" in the present. Foucault makes no reference to concepts such as post-fordism, postmodernity, "McDonaldization" or late capitalism that have often been used to characterize a certain kind of break with the past. Nor is he concerned simply with a blanket denunciation of the present. No political programmatics follow automatically from his work in this field. Foucault once argued in an interview, that one of the "most destructive habits of modern thought . . . is that the moment of the present is considered in history as the break, the climax, the fulfilment, the return of youth, etc." – confessing that he had himself found himself at times drawn into the orbit of such a temptation (Foucault 1989c: 251). But if it is the case that, for example, the closing pages of *Madness and civilization* are unquestionably apocalyptic in their pronouncements on the present, and that Foucault himself was to regret the adoption of such apocalyptic tones, in a sense, the conception of the present does retain a certain stability across his work. Above all, one might say, Foucault was concerned to introduce an "untimely" attitude in our relation towards the present. Untimely in the Nietzschean sense: acting counter to our time, introducing a new sense of the fragility of our time, and thus acting on our time for the benefit, one hopes, of a time to come (Nietzsche 1983: 60, cf. Rose 1993b: 1, Bell 1994: 155).

Our time, that is to say, is not presumed to be the bearer or culmination of some grand historical process, it has no inevitability, no spirit, essence or underlying cause. The "present", in Foucault's work, is less an epoch than an array of questions; and the coherence with which the present presents itself to us – and in which guise it is re-imagined by so much social theory – is something to be *acted upon* by historical investigation, to be cut up and decomposed so that it can be seen as put together contingently out of heterogeneous elements each having their own conditions of possibility.

Such a fragmentation of the present is not undertaken in a spirit of poststructuralist playfulness. It is undertaken with a more serious, if hopefully modest, ambition – to allow a space for the work of freedom. Here, indeed, the place of ethics is marked in Foucault's thought. Analyses of the present are concerned with opening up "a virtual break which opens a room, understood as a room of concrete freedom, that is possible transformation"; the received fixedness and inevitability of the present is destabilized, shown as just sufficiently fragile as to let in a little glimpse of freedom – as a practice of difference – through its fractures.

These concerns with the present and its contingency do not partake in the relativism that has become so fashionable; their approach is not so much "relativist" as "perspectivist". The angle they seek does not attempt to show that our ways of thinking and doing are only the habits of a particular time and place. Rather than relativize the present, these perspectival studies hope to "destabilize" it. Destabilizing the present is "perspectival" in that it does not seek to define the geographical and temporal limits of a culture, but to bring into view the historically sedimented underpinnings of particular "problematizations" that have a salience for our contemporary experience. Hence the nonsensical nature of those claims – in praise or condemnation – that Foucault's work seeks to found a new global "approach" on a par with, for example, historical materialism; or that it can be "applied" to any issue from advertising to nuclear

physics. Foucault's work always fails these tests of its universal "applicability", but such failure is not necessarily a *failing*. Further, Foucault's emphases are best put to use, not in those areas where we are so clearly the
inheritor of a history, but in those domains where an untimely analysis
seems *least* possible; above all, in those domains that emphasize psychological and anthropological constants or the immutability of nature.

The effect of such perspectival analysis is not intended to be solely an
"intellectual" one. Rather what is at stake is the production of a certain
kind of experience, a refiguring of experience itself. At their best, what is
produced in such investigations is a shattering of conventional thought
that strikes at the heart of our most taken-for-granted motivations. Here,
the sense of an assault upon our ethical certainties, of coming up against
obstacles that prevent one knowing immediately "what is to be done", has
a positive function. What occurs is a potentially productive uncoupling of
experience from its conditions. In an interview, Foucault talks of bringing
about a kind of paralysis in his readers; "But paralysis isn't the same thing
as anaesthesia – on the contrary. It's in so far as there's been an awaken-
ing to a whole series of problems that the difficulty of doing anything
comes to be felt" (Foucault in Burchell et al. 1991: 84, Burchell in ibid.:
119–20 and 146, cf. Osborne 1994: 496).

Although these "histories of the present" address themselves to our
political reason, then, this is not in the sense that any specific political prescriptions or proscriptions flow. This does not condemn historians of the
present themselves in any way to be without politics or "beyond politics".
For there is certainly an ethos of engagement tied to this way of conceiving of the present, one that may itself be historical but should not be
despised for that. In his essay on Kant and the Enlightenment, Foucault
insists that if modernity connotes anything it is not a period or a mode of
experience but an "ethos", a way of orientating oneself to history. Kant's
distinction was hardly to have inaugurated this modernity itself, so much
as to have posed the question of the present as an issue. Here we find
some hints as to Foucault's own understanding of the necessary ethos of
the intellectual in the present. Foucault highlights Kant's "pragmatic
anthropology", so different from the medium of the three Critiques,
which opened up a space for Enlightenment not as certainty but as a
kind of permanent questioning of the present, indeed a "commitment to
uncertainty" (Gordon 1986: 74). As Colin Gordon emphasizes, for
Foucault this commitment entailed a novel version of critique itself: not so
much to establish the limits of thought, but to locate the possible places of
transgression (ibid.: 75). This understanding of the present does not take

the anti-Enlightenment stance of other grand genealogies of the present moment. Gordon cites the work of Cassirer, Hayek, Adorno and Horkheimer as instances of genealogical thought linked to a "semiology of catastrophe". But as Foucault himself notes, one "does not [have] to be 'for' or 'against' the Enlightenment" (Foucault 1986: 43). Rather, the style of Foucault's histories of the present owes something to the classical orientation of Tocqueville or Weber, where "the analysis addresses the hazards and necessities of a system, not the unrecognized invasions of an alien, pathological mutation" (ibid.: 78, see also Owen 1994).

Liberalism and neo-liberalism

The names of Weber and Tocqueville lead us felicitously to the second domain in which Foucault's influence has been influential on the analyses in this volume: the analytics of liberal political reason. In the late 1970s Foucault initiated a range of researches on what he termed arts of government or political rationality. This work was never brought together in a single volume and Foucault's remarks on it are scattered across a number of interviews and essays, as well as his lectures at the Collège de France (Foucault 1989a, see Gordon 1991 for a lucid introduction to this work). For Foucault, political rationalities are more than just ideologies; they constitute a part of the fabric of our ways of thinking about and acting upon one another and ourselves. Foucault's concern with the history of political rationality also raises, as does Weber's work in a different register, the question of the relation between the mutations of politics and the history of systems of expertise. Indeed what it throws into question is precisely the nature and limits of "the political", the political as itself a transactional space, a historically variable zone of rationalization and division. But why this concern with government, and with liberalism in particular? Does a focus on liberalism, coupled with the focus on ethics and freedom in Foucault's later work, represent a retreat into the categories and dreams of political philosophy, when set against the images conjured up by the themes of surveillance, discipline and normalization that marked the analyses of power in *Discipline and punish* and the first volume of the *History of sexuality*?

It would be a mistake to think that Foucault exchanged a vision of a society dominated by discipline with a vision of a society dominated by a form of government based around the exercise of freedom. In Foucault's account, disciplinary power and government have historically co-existed.

7

"We need to see things not in terms of the replacement of a society of sovereignty by a disciplinary society by a society of government; in reality one has a triangle, sovereignty-discipline-government" (Foucault 1991: 102). Indeed, part of the attractiveness of the idea of government is that it makes it difficult to sustain the common perception – derived from Weber, the Frankfurt school as well as from Foucault – that society has become dominated by routine, discipline and rationalization (Burchell, this volume). On the contrary. The possibilities for liberal forms of freedom may historically depend upon the exercise of discipline. Freedom, in a liberal sense, should thus not be equated with anarchy, but with a kind of well-regulated and "responsibilized" liberty. The task, according to Foucault, was not to denounce the idea of liberty as a fiction, but to analyze the conditions within which the practice of freedom has been possible. Freedom is thus neither an ideological fiction of modern societies nor an existential feature of existence within them; it must be understood also and necessarily as a formula of rule. Foucault's concern here might be characterized as an attempt to link the analysis of the constitution of freedom with that of the exercise of rule; that is, with the extent to which freedom has become, in our so-called "free societies", a resource for, and not merely a hindrance to, government.

It is clear that Foucault means something rather different by liberalism than do political philosophers. He does not speak of a liberal "period", nor is he concerned principally with writing the history of the philosophical ideas of liberty or of rights. From Foucault's perspective, liberalism is more like an *ethos* of government. Liberalism is understood not so much as a substantive doctrine or practice of government in itself, but as a restless and dissatisfied ethos of recurrent critique of State reason and politics. Hence, the advent of liberalism coincides with the discovery that political government could be its own undoing, that by governing over-much, rulers thwarted the very ends of government. Hence liberalism is not about governing less but about the continual injunction that politicians and rulers should govern cautiously, delicately, economically, modestly (Rose 1993a, Osborne 1994). Thus, liberalism represents, in a certain sense, a cautious and self-critical – if not necessarily "enlightened" – approach to the problem of government.

The emergence of liberal mentalities of government in the early nineteenth century was, according to Foucault, of critical historical significance. In brief, it was only with the emergence of liberalism that it was possible for a domain of "society" to emerge (Foucault 1989a: 112). In effect, society was the product of a mutation in the demands of govern-

mental rationalities. Why is this so? One way of understanding the connection between liberalism and the historical emergence of society is to
contrast liberalism with the political rationality of police; a form of rationality that sought to govern, so to speak, *in toto*, down to the minutiae of
existence. Liberalism emerges where this question of totalized government becomes turned around:

> It seems to me that at that very moment it became apparent that if
> one governed too much, one did not govern at all – that one pro-
> voked results contrary to those one desired. What was discovered at
> that time – and this was one of the great discoveries of political
> thought at the end of the eighteenth century – was the idea of *society*.
> That is to say, that government not only has to deal with a territory,
> with a domain, and with its subjects, but that it also has to deal with
> a complex and independent reality that has its own laws and
> mechanisms of disturbance. This new reality is society. From the
> moment that one is to manipulate a society, one cannot consider it
> completely penetrable by police. One must take into account what
> it is. It becomes necessary to reflect upon it, upon its specific char-
> acteristics, its constants and variables. (Foucault 1989b: 261)

Liberalism is thus delivered to the social sciences in a double way. On the
one hand, liberal political reason is the historical condition of the very
object of their disciplines – "society". On the other hand, liberal political
reason establishes a field of concerns that are as much *technical* as they are
political or ideological. The social sciences provide a way of representing
the autonomous dynamics of society and assessing whether they should
or should not be an object of regulation. In effect, the social sciences can
act as a kind of technical solution to all the anxiety that, for liberalism,
marks the relations between society and the public authorities. Far from
seeing liberalism as an absence of government, or of a lessening of political concern with the conduct of conduct, histories of the present draw
attention to the intellectual and practical techniques and inventions via
which civil society is brought into being as both distinct from political
intervention and yet potentially alignable with political aspirations. The
supposed separation of State and civil society is the consequence of a particular problematization of government, not of a withdrawal of government as such.

Inscribed within the very logic of liberal forms of government is a
certain naturalism: the social domain to be governed is a natural one,

sensitive to excessive intervention (Osborne, this volume). As government cannot override the natural dynamics of the economy without destroying the basis on which liberal government is possible, it must preserve the autonomy of society from State intervention. At the same time, it must ensure the existence of political spaces within which critical reflections on the actions of the State are possible, thus ensuring that such actions are themselves subject to critical observation. In brief, the activity of rule must take care to observe and maintain the autonomy of the professions and the freedom of the public sphere from political interference. Thus, in the process in which intellectuals and scientists act as critics of the State, they can none the less serve to act in the interests of good government.

Foucault's account of liberalism thus directs our attention to the technical means with which the aspirations and ideals of liberal political rationalities might have been put into practice. This is not a matter of deconstructing the internal logic or contradictions within liberal political philosophy; rather it is to attend to the relations of the *ethos* of liberalism and its *techne*: its organization as a practical rationality directed towards certain ends. This emphasis upon *techne* gains further significance when one comes to consider the way in which liberalism has been refigured in its neo-liberal incarnation. As Graham Burchell argues, neo-liberalism replaces the naturalism of liberalism with a certain kind of constructivism (Burchell, this volume). In the styles of neo-liberal political reason that began to be formulated after the Second World War, it was the responsibility of political government to *actively* create the conditions within which entrepreneurial and competitive conduct is possible. Paradoxically, neo-liberalism, alongside its critique of the deadening consequences of the "intrusion of the State" into the life of the individual, has none the less provoked the invention and/or deployment of a whole array of organizational forms and technical methods in order to extend the field within which a certain kind of economic freedom might be practised in the form of personal autonomy, enterprise and choice (Rose, this volume).

There have been, of course, other sociologies of neo-liberalism; most particularly those addressed to the rise to political power of the New Right in the 1980s. In Britain it is the work of Stuart Hall and his colleagues that immediately springs to mind in this context. This neo-Gramscian perspective sought to show how an ideological bloc – prototyped by the Thatcherite phenomenon in Britain – sought more or less successfully to gain a hegemonic position within the political conjuncture of the late 1970s. For Hall, there was a crucial structural ambiguity about Thatcherism, evidenced in its mixture of authoritarianism and populism.

Thatcherism embodied a "highly contradictory strategy"; "simultane-ously dismantling the Welfare State, 'anti-statist' in its ideological repre-sentation, *and* highly State-centralist and dirigiste in many of its strategic operations" (Hall 1988: 152). There were many merits to this position – not least the empirical sensitivity that it espoused, and the refusal simply to treat the Thatcher phenomenon as a monolithic bloc of class-derived "interests". Nevertheless it will serve briefly to mark some differences from the style of the analyses that follow. Although Hall's analysis certainly does not reduce Thatcherism to the realm of ideology, the insist-ence that part of its function was to permeate "common sense" within civil society made its ideological impulse of considerable importance. But what Hall misses by way of this ideological perspective is any sense of Thatcherism as a positive – in the technical not the ethical sense – art of government; that is, of an inventive and constructive alignment of inter-ests, powers, objects, institutions and persons (cf. Laclau & Mouffe 1985, Barrett 1992: 64–8). Hall's analysis of the New Right in terms of the constitution of hegemony and the specificity of national context, remains instructive, if not entirely born out by subsequent events. None the less, the focus of the essays collected here is on the "ethical" and "technical" character of neo-liberalism as an art of government, not upon the "ideo-logical" conditions under which it may or may not be able to operate. In a certain sense, then, we return to something of enduring value in the work of Max Weber. The material conditions of particular regimes of authority, of economic action, of social regulation, are to be located, at least in part, through an analysis of their technical methods such as accounting and auditing: and this is equally, indeed particularly, true of government in its "neo-liberal" form (Miller 1992, Power 1994).

Above all, it is a mistake to see neo-liberalism as simply a negative political response to the welfarism or corporatism of previous decades. Hall retains this emphasis in his contention that Thatcherism embodies a fiscal retreat by the State, even if this is countermanded by an enhance-ment of repressive powers. This is to impose too reductive, reactive and univocal an interpretation upon the variety of phenomena embraced under the designation of Thatcherism; a consequence, no doubt, of the obsession with the question of the State that has dominated so much recent thinking in this area. This "retreat from the State" is also itself a positive technique of government; we are perhaps witnessing a "degovern-mentalization of the State" but surely not "de-governmentalization" *per se*. Rather, these studies suggest, that what has been at issue has been the fabrication of techniques that can produce a degree of "autonomization" of entities of government from the State: here the State, allying itself with a range of other groups and forces, has sought to set up – in Latourian language – chains of enrolment, "responsibilization" and "empowerment" to sectors and agencies distant from the centre, yet tied to it through a complex of alignments and translations.

The technical and the political

The theme of expertise and the relation between expertise and politics has been an important one in social theory. It was central to the work of Weber, and to the development of Weber's analysis in the critical theory of the Frankfurt school and in the work of Jürgen Habermas. More recently, many sociologists of science have become increasingly concerned, both at a theoretical and political level, with the relation between expertise and politics, and expertise and law. What connections are there between the approach to the study of expertise developed from the work of Foucault and these other related traditions in sociology?

In common with Weber and Habermas, Foucault emphasized the historical relation between the technical and the political; however, the nature and consequences of this connection were thematized very differently. For Habermas, this relation has taken a particular form. On the one hand, science and technology have become increasingly divorced from politics. They have been constituted as a domain autonomous from and impervious to the critical gaze of the public sphere and, even, to the control of the State itself. On the other hand, according to Habermas, political decisions themselves have increasingly been transformed into technical ones. In short, argues Habermas, there has been a "scientization of politics" (Habermas 1971). Crucially, Habermas, like so many other social theorists, poses a certain antinomy between aspirations to the full realization of human potential and the rise and domination of the technological, with its instrumental reasoning, its rationalizations and "objectifications", its specialists and its bureaucrats, its dreams of order, predictability and control.

This opposition hampers thought about our present and its ethical character – it must be refused: this is one of the most distinctive features of the histories of the present represented here. To speak of the conduct of conduct as being made thinkable under certain rationalizations and practicable through the assembling of technologies is not, thereby, to subject these endeavours to a critique. The introduction of the theme of technology here thus does not encourage one to dream of an alternative – an anti-technological future of the full realization of humanity – any more than it licenses one to participate in the dream of those who see technology as leading to human emancipation from the demands of toil, the constraints of time and space and even of human finitude. Further, to recognize that subjectivity is itself a matter of the technologizing of humans is not to regard this process as amounting to some kind of crushing of the human spirit under the pressure of a corset of habits, restrictions and injunctions. Human capacities are, from the perspective of these investigations, inevitably and inescapably technologized. An analytics of technology has, therefore, to devote itself to the sober and painstaking task of describing the consequences, the possibilities invented as much as the limits imposed, of particular ways of subjectifying humans.

Rather than conceiving of the relation between the technical and the political as an opposition, the authors of these studies highlight the variable ways in which expertise plays a part in translating society into an object of government. One implication of this is that instead of viewing technology or expertise as distinct from politics, "technical" terms themselves – such as apparatus, machine or network – best convey a sense of the complex relays and linkages that tie techniques of conduct into specific relations with the concerns of government. These notions of technology, in the sense of complex and heterogenous relations amongst disparate elements, stabilized in particular ways, enables us to reconnect, in a productive way, studies of the exercise of power at the "molecular" level – in schools, prison cells, hospital wards, psychiatric diagnoses, conjugal relations and so forth – with strategies to programme power at a molar level in such "centres of calculation" as the Cabinet Office, the War Office, the Department of State, the party manifesto, the Government White Paper or the enactment of legislation (Latour 1987: 232–57, Rose & Miller 1992: 185).

These investigations of the relations of the political and the technical, like those conducted under the auspices of the Frankfurt school and its successors, come to bear upon the question of politics itself. Here, the limits of the political are not defined in terms of the boundaries of an apparatus – the State – or in terms of the fulfilment of certain necessary functions – repressive and ideological State apparatuses – but as themselves discursive. Rather, politics has itself to be investigated genealogically, in terms of the ways of coding and defining or delimiting the possible scope of action and components of an apparatus of rule, the strategies and limits proper for rulers, and the relations between political rule and that exercised by other authorities. Such a perspective is useful, for it enables us to analyze, without prior commitments, what is entailed in the shifting boundaries of the political and the technical. This is required not only to give intelligibility to the implications of, for example, the introduction of budgetary disciplines into domains previously directed by decisions of elected politicians, but also to understand what is at stake in the deployment of such slogans as "the personal is political" or in current demands within political discourse itself for an end to "big government" in order to give back "liberty to the people". Here we see different variations on the theme that politics should or should not be conceived of as a particular sort of endeavour conducted by specific persons and institutions and under particular mandates, distinct from the exercise of authority by priests over parishioners, teachers over pupils, parents over children, men over women and so forth. In denaturalizing politics and making it a possible object for genealogy, this approach therefore establishes the conditions for investigating what is at stake in the contemporary rise of anti-political themes at the heart of controversies about the exercise of power (cf. Hindess 1996).

These essays address the problem of expertise in a further sense, through their concern with the role of expertise in what has been termed, following Bruno Latour's use of this phrase, "action-at-a-distance" (Latour 1986). As Nikolas Rose argues, public authorities seek to employ forms of expertise in order to govern society at a distance, without recourse to any direct forms of repression or intervention (Rose, this volume). Of key importance to neo-liberalism, for example, is the development of techniques of auditing, accounting and management that enable a "market" for public services to be established autonomous from central control. Neo-liberalism, in these terms, involves less a retreat from governmental "intervention" than a re-inscription of the techniques and forms of expertise required for the exercise of government. The "distance" over which liberal government is exercised is, however, real as well as metaphorical. As Andrew Barry argues, liberalism has had particular use for electrical communication technologies in increasing the quantity and rapidity of the flow of information between spatially dispersed points without the need for the development of an extensive system of surveillance controlled by the State (Barry, this volume). Indeed, although the focus of the majority of genealogies of expertise has been on the social and human sciences, and of the "human technologies" made possible by such mathematical inventions as statistics and calculation, Barry's study shows us the productivity of this approach when directed towards the rise of those forms of knowledge and intervention with a "higher epistemological profile" such as physics and chemistry.

But this stress on the relations between expertise and politics does not imply that it is one of functionality or of co-optation. Rather, the relations established, although "functionalizable", are contingent. As Foucault himself argued, the discipline of architecture acquired particular political significance in relation to the political rationality of police as it did for Jeremy Bentham in proposing a practice of reformatory incarceration. This does not mean either that architecture is inevitably to be understood, let alone explained, in terms of its functioning within modern forms of political power, or that "similar" styles and forms of architecture might not be articulated with quite different political projects. Likewise, if particular technologies such as auditing and accountancy have a particular utility to neo-liberalism, this does not mean that there is an intrinsic relation between the techniques and the politics, such that they must be discarded by those who seek an alternative art of government. In any case, it is never in these analyses merely a question of being either for or against the technological. Humans' relations to technology are not merely those of a passive "reduction"; rather, technology is an aspect of what it is to be human (Canguilhem 1994). And if technology is political, it is because technology always carries with it a certain "telos" of operations, a certain directive capacity. In other words, technology – both in terms of the human side of technology and of the technology of what it is to be human – is integral to those relations of authority and subjectivity that insert our selves into the space of the present, giving us the status of living beings capable of having "experience" of the present. In short, technology neither is, nor could be either ,"outside" politics or corrosive of politics; it is tied irrevocably to our political self-understanding and our understanding of the political.

Conclusions

The essays collected here do not attempt to provide a comprehensive analysis of liberalism and neo-liberalism. A whole series of quite legitimate questions concerning the history of our contemporary political rationality are not addressed. Most notable among these omissions are the "vital" rationalities of nation and race, of sexuality, territory and blood, of nationalism, colonialism and militarism, which have been so important both to liberalism and neo-liberalism. Further, despite the best intentions of their authors these essays no doubt suggest a degree of coherence, interconnectedness and homogeneity to the various components of liberalism and neo-liberalism that would need to be interrogated further (Foucault 1972: 149). We have made little attempt to explore some of the key differences between the various traditions of liberalism or the meaning of liberalism within different national contexts. So the analyses included here represent only a beginning; albeit a beginning that – as Deleuze might say – begins in the *middle*.

But such limitations and omissions notwithstanding, we believe these essays together map out an approach to our present that has a certain productivity, not least because the analytical tools that are demonstrated at work here are capable of development and deployment in relation to a whole range of significant contemporary problems concerning government, expertise and conduct. Further, we believe that this approach promises certain, modest benefits in relation to the thinkability of politics itself. These perspectives on governmentalities deliver, we think, real and immediate gains, conferring a new kind of intelligibility upon the strategies that seek to govern us, and the ways in which we have come to understand, embrace or contest such strategies. This is not because they will help us know if we should be "for" or "against" the present; such judgements must be left to other, perhaps more immediate, contexts and occasions. But because one of the most important questions on the agenda of those who are concerned about our present is to start to write the genealogy of liberty itself, so that we might begin to find inventive ways of evaluating, enhancing and generalizing the possibilities for practices of freedom.

References

Barrett, M. 1992. *The politics of truth: from Marx to Foucault.* Cambridge: Polity.

Bell, V. 1994. Dreaming and time in Foucault's philosophy. *Theory, Culture and Society* **11**, 151–63.

Burchell, G., C. Gordon, P. Miller (eds) 1991. *The Foucault effect: studies in governmentality.* Hemel Hempstead, England: Harvester Wheatsheaf.

Canguilhem, G. 1994. *A vital rationalist.* New York: Zone Books.

Foucault, M. 1972. *The archaeology of knowledge* (trans. A. Sheridan). London: Tavistock.

Foucault, M. 1986. What is enlightenment? In *The Foucault reader*, P. Rabinow (ed.), 32–50. London: Penguin.

Foucault, M. 1989a. *Résumé des cours.* Paris: Juillard.

Foucault, M. 1989b. An ethics of pleasure. In *Foucault live*, S. Lotringer (ed.), 257–76. New York: Semiotext(e).

Foucault, M. 1989c. How much does it cost for reason to tell the truth? See Lotringer (1989), 233–56.

Foucault, M. 1991. Governmentality. See Burchell et al. (1991), 87–104.

Giddens, A. 1990. *The consequences of modernity*. Cambridge: Polity.

Gordon, C. 1986. Question, ethos, event: Foucault on Kant and Enlightenment. *Economy and Society* **15**(1), 71–87.

Gordon, C. 1991. Governmental rationality: an introduction. See Burchell et al. (1991), 1–52.

Habermas, J. 1971. *Towards a rational society*. London: Heinemann.

Hall, S. 1988. *The hard road to renewal*. London: Verso.

Hindess, B. 1996. *Discourses of power: from Hobbes to Foucault*. Oxford: Basil Blackwell.

Laclau, E. & C. Mouffe 1985. *Hegemony and socialist strategy*. London: Verso

Latour, B. 1986. Visualisation and cognition: thinking with hands and eyes. *Knowledge and Society: Studies in the Sociology of Culture, Past and Present* **6**, 1–40.

Latour, B. 1987. *Science in action*. Milton Keynes, England: Open University Press.

Latour, B. 1991. *We have never been modern*. Hemel Hempstead, England: Harvester Wheatsheaf.

Miller, P. 1992. Accounting and objectivity: the invention of calculating selves and calculable spaces. In A. Megill (ed.) Rethinking objectivity, *Annals of Scholarship* **9**(1/2), 61–86.

Nietzsche, F. 1983. *Human, all too human: a book for free spirits* (trans. R. Hollingdale). Cambridge: Cambridge University Press.

Osborne, P. 1992. Modernity is a qualitative, not a quantitative concept. New Left Review **192**, 65–84.

Osborne, T. 1994. Sociology, liberalism and the historicity of conduct. *Economy and Society* **23**(4), 484–501.

Owen, D. 1994. *Maturity and modernity: Nietzsche, Weber, Foucault and the ambivalence of reason*. London: Routledge.

Power, M. 1994 *The audit society*. London: Demos.

Rose, N. 1993a. Government, authority and expertise in advanced liberalism. *Economy and Society* **22**(3), 283–300.

Rose, N. 1993b. Towards a critical sociology of freedom. Inaugural Lecture delivered 5 May 1992, London: Goldsmiths College.

Rose, N. & P. Miller 1992. Political power beyond the state: problematics of government. *British Journal of Sociology* **43**(2), 173–205.

Chapter 1
Liberal government and techniques of the self

Graham Burchell

Defining it in general as "the conduct of conduct", Foucault presents government as a more or less methodical and rationally reflected "way of doing things", or "art", for acting on the actions of individuals, taken either singly or collectively, so as to shape, guide, correct and modify the ways in which they conduct themselves (Foucault 1988a).[1] Thus understood, the notion of government has a fairly wide sense and it may be helpful for what follows to pick out certain elements.[2]

First, government understood in this wide sense may refer to many different forms of "the conduct of conduct", the particular objects, methods and scale of which will vary. For example, it may, as in the sixteenth century, refer to the government of oneself, to the government of souls and lives, to the government of a household, to the government of children, and to the government of the State by a prince (Foucault 1991). There may also be interconnections and continuities between these different forms of government and, in particular, between local and diverse forms of government existing at the level of interpersonal relations or institutions dispersed throughout society on the one hand, and political government as the exercise of a central, unified form of State sovereignty on the other, or between forms of government existing within microsettings like the family or the school and the macropolitical activities of government directed towards individuals as members of a population, society or nation.

Secondly, the general idea of government is used by Foucault in a sense that is clearly in continuity with his analysis of power in *Discipline and punish* (Foucault 1977). On occasions Foucault refers to government as a way in which power is exercised over individuals. Government seems to be used as a synonym or preferred alternative for the use of power to identify a general field of analysis. Part of the word's attractiveness to Foucault could well have been that it makes it more difficult to sustain a lurid "iron

19

cage" type of interpretation of the analysis of disciplinary techniques. We may recall that government in general is understood as a way of acting to affect the way in which individuals *conduct themselves* (Foucault 1988a). All the same, Foucault's analysis prior to the introduction of the idea of government does not sanction the illusion of what might be called "the all-powerfulness of power". Part of the point of describing the disciplines as a technology of power is to distinguish them from the land of technologies that involve a simple and direct physical determination of their objects: as techniques of power, the disciplines presuppose the activity, agency or the freedom of those on whom they are exercised (Foucault 1982).

Government, though, is not merely a synonym that signals the extension of the analysis of power from the microphysical to the macropolitical or that corrects possible misunderstandings of an earlier use of the word power. For example, Foucault makes it clear that "technologies of domination", like the disciplines, only ever constitute one side of the practical systems through which individuals are governed. Government, Foucault suggests, is a "contact point" where techniques of domination – or power – and *techniques of the self* "interact", where "technologies of domination of individuals over one another have recourse to processes by which the individual acts upon himself and, conversely, . . . where techniques of the self are integrated into structures of coercion" (Foucault 1980).[3] We might say that whereas in *Discipline and punish* Foucault emphasized the subjectification of individuals through their subjection to techniques of power/domination, the perspective of government establishes an essential relationship between these and other techniques of the self in the subjectification of individuals.

> I think that if one wants to analyze the genealogy of the subject in Western societies, one has to take into account not only techniques of domination, but also techniques of the self. Let's say one has to take into account the interaction of these two types of techniques. (Foucault 1980)

Thus, within the perspective of government, the introduction of the idea of techniques of the self, of arts or aesthetics of existence, etc. seems to imply a loosening of the connection between subjectification and subjection. A loosening but not a severing of all connections, as should be clear from Foucault's analysis of the relationships between particular practices of the self and relations of domination in ancient Greek and Roman societies (Foucault 1985, 1986).

Foucault speaks of the interactions of these two types of technique. There is no simple determination of techniques of the self (either of governed individuals or of those governing) by techniques of domination. Rather, in particular cases it may be that the latter are presupposed by, or are conditions for the possible existence of, the former. Moreover, the irreducibility of one to the other implies that their relationships and interactions are not necessarily always harmonious or mutually reinforcing. Hence, part at least of the interest in this field: if techniques of the self are more than the insubstantial complement or effect of technologies of domination, if they are not just another way of securing ends sought through technologies of domination, then the study of their interaction with these technologies would seem to be highly relevant to the ethical problems of *how* freedom can be practised.[4]

It is these interconnections, continuities and interactions between techniques of domination and techniques of the self that I want to begin to explore.

Liberal government – old and new

Foucault adopts a distinctive approach towards the analysis of liberalism. This consists in analyzing it from the point of view of governmental reason, that is from the point of view of the rationality of political government as an activity rather than as an institution. On this view, liberalism is not a theory, an ideology, a juridical philosophy of individual freedom, or any particular set of policies adopted by a government. It is, says Foucault, a rationally reflected way of doing things that functions as the principle and method for the rationalization of governmental practices (Foucault 1989). Liberalism is described as a particular way in which the activity of government has been made both thinkable and practicable as an art. Above all, Foucault emphasizes the *critical* and *problematizing* character of liberalism. The point may be made clearer by crudely contrasting two different kinds of liberalism widely separated in time.

Foucault describes early, or "classical", liberalism as emerging in relation to a problem of how a necessary market freedom can be reconciled with the unlimited exercise of a political sovereignty. This problem already implies a kind of criticism of a characteristic form of government in the early modern period – the "police state" associated with *raison d'état*. The assumption of *raison d'état* was that the State was able to have an adequate and detailed knowledge of what had to be governed – that is to say, a knowledge of itself – on the basis of which it could act to direct and shape that reality in accordance with its, the State's, own interests; increasing its wealth and strength *vis-à-vis* other States, for example. According to Foucault, the decisive point of liberalism's critique of this view is its scepticism about the State and *its* reason, about the possibility of it, or of anyone, being able to know perfectly and in all its details the reality to be governed, and about its capacity to shape that reality at will on the basis on such a knowledge.

The Anglo-Scottish school of early liberalism sets limits to the State's capacity to know and act by situating it in relation to the reality of the market or of commercial exchanges, and more broadly of civil society, as quasi-natural domains with their own intrinsic dynamic and forms of self-regulation. On this view, interventions by the State in these domains are liable to produce effects that, as well as being different from those intended, are also likely to be positively harmful. Commercial exchanges will not produce the benefits demanded from them by the State unless the State secures the conditions necessary for them to be able to function freely and naturally to optimum effect. *Laissez-faire* is here both a limitation of the exercise of political sovereignty *vis-à-vis* the government of commercial exchanges, and a positive justification of market freedom on the grounds that the State will benefit more – will become richer and more powerful – by governing less.

Now for modern forms of liberalism – those generally referred to as neo-liberalism or as economic liberalism or economic rationalism – it is still a question of a critical reason concerning the limits of government in relation to the market. For the German school of *Ordoliberalen* that developed during and after the Second World War, and many of whose members played a significant role in the early years of the Federal German Republic, the problem is not one of how a space can be found within an existing State for a necessary market freedom, but of how to create a State on the basis of an economic freedom that will secure the State's legitimacy and self-limitation. The problem is especially marked by the experience of National Socialism. An essential part of the Ordo-liberal argument was historical and involved the claim that National Socialism was not some monstrous aberration but the quite inevitable outcome of a series of *anti-liberal* policies – national protectionism, the welfare policies of Bismarckian State socialism, wartime economic planning and management, and Keynesian interventionism. Each of these policies entails the other three in a vicious circle, the inevitable outcome of which is the kind of exorbitant growth in the State witnessed in National Socialist

Germany. In a sense, the Ordo-liberals argued somewhat like those who say that socialism has not failed because nowhere has it been truly practised. There has been, they suggest, a constant retreat from liberalism in the face of what were perceived to be its unpalatable consequences.

The Chicago school of economic liberalism, some of whom established strong contacts with members of the Ordo-liberal school just after the Second World War also functions as a criticism of the consequences of too much government. The historical references naturally differ from those of the Ordo-liberals, but in each case the general form of argument is very similar. What they have in common, putting it very crudely, is a question concerning the extent to which competitive, optimizing market relations and behaviour can serve as a principle not only for limiting governmental intervention, but also rationalizing government itself. Both are looking for a principle for rationalizing government by reference to an idea of the market. Where they differ from earlier forms of liberalism is that they do not regard the market as an existing quasi-natural reality situated in a kind of economic nature reserve space marked off, secured and supervised by the State. Rather, the market exists, and can only exist, under certain political, legal and institutional conditions that must be actively constructed by government.

This rough contrast between early and modern forms of liberalism can be continued in a related area that will return us to our main focus. Both forms of liberalism set out a schema of the relationship between government and the governed in which individuals are identified as, on the one hand, the *object* and target of governmental action and, on the other hand, as in some sense the necessary (voluntary) *partner* or accomplice of government.

For early liberalism, to govern properly involves pegging the principle for rationalizing governmental activity to *the rationality of the free conduct of governed individuals themselves*. That is to say, the rational conduct of government must be intrinsically linked to the *natural*, private-interest-motivated conduct of free, market *exchanging* individuals because the rationality of these individuals' conduct is, precisely, what enables the market to function optimally in accordance with its nature. Government cannot override the rational free conduct of governed individuals without destroying the basis of the effects it is seeking to produce (Burchell 1991). Of course, this is not the whole story and I will add to it below.

By contrast, for neo-liberalism, the rational principle for regulating and limiting governmental activity must be determined by reference to *artificially* arranged or contrived forms of the free, *entrepreneurial* and *competitive* conduct of economic-rational individuals. Here again the rationality of government must be pegged to a form of the rational self-conduct of the governed themselves, but a form that is not so much a given of human nature as a consciously contrived style of conduct.

In neither case are we dealing with the simple application of a technical know-how of domination to individuals *qua* bodies with certain capacities, forces and aptitudes. In both cases the principle of government requires of the governed that they freely conduct themselves in a certain rational way, whether in the form of a "natural liberty", as Adam Smith puts it (Smith 1976), or as a freedom that is an "artefact", as Hayek puts it (Hayek 1979). In any case, it is a principle that requires the proper use of liberty. Individual freedom, in appropriate forms, is here a technical condition of rational government rather than the organizing value of a Utopian dream.

I must now expand on the very partial stories given in these two examples. For early liberalism, and here I am thinking especially of Anglo-Scottish early liberal thought, the individual to be governed is not only a rational, interest-motivated economic ego. He (and here the male pronoun is, for the most part, appropriate) is also, and equally naturally, a member of society and part of a biological population. Economic exchanges – private, individual, atomistic, egoistic – are seen as arising within a natural and historical milieu comprising a tissue of proximate, passional ties, associations, affiliations, antagonisms, enmities and friendships, communitarian bonds and so on, which characterize *civil society* (or society, or the nation). Within this milieu a historical dynamic is identified that arises from, on the one hand, the fissiparous tendency of economic egoism that leads exchanging individuals to engage in an abstract form of activity involving relations with others that are indifferent to their membership of any particular society or nation and, on the other hand, the complex interplay of particular localized patterns of sociability, of allegiances and antagonisms. It is on the basis of this natural and historical dynamic society that there evolve spontaneous relationships of power, authority and subordination or, in other words, forms of the "self-government" of civil society.

It is in relation to this dynamic, historico-natural, both economic and non-economic domain that government as the exercise of nationally unified political sovereignty comes to define its tasks. Liberal governmental reason does not so much set out what in any particular case government policy should be, as define the essential problem-space of government, and define it in such a way as to make a definite art of government both thinkable and practicable. Early liberalism determines the questions of *how* to govern in relation to an object-domain which is a kind of quasi-nature with its own specific self-regulating principles and dynamic. This natural domain is both what has to be governed and what government must produce or, at least, maintain in the optimum condition of what naturally it is. Civil society becomes at the same time both object and end of government.

Early liberalism, then, describes a problem-space of government. This problem-space is an open-ended space of real politico-technical invention, of a governmental constructivism. Liberalism sets limits to what government can know or do *vis-à-vis* a civil society that must none the less be governed even if, as in the most radical proposals, it is sometimes maintained that civil society or the nation is entirely capable of governing itself and does not require a State. Liberalism fixes the terms of the problem of *how* political sovereignty must be exercised: what relationship must political sovereignty establish with this quasi-natural reality over which it presides but with which it cannot do just what it likes? What is within and what outside of its competence? What techniques, what procedures, what regulations and laws enable this reality to function in accordance with its nature and to optimum effect in the production of wealth and the promotion of wellbeing? This general liberal problematic makes intelligible, as techniques of a liberal art of government, early liberal governmental experimentation, such as the legal instrumentalization and enframing by the State of diverse relations of authority–subordination that are considered to be naturally and spontaneously evolved forms of the self-government of civil society. It enables us to make sense of the construction of that characteristically hybrid domain the public and the private, of the utilization of private forms of power – the power of employers over the workplace and the conditions for efficient and well-ordered economic activity – for public ends – the good of society as a whole. It also helps us to make sense of the often privately conducted public campaigns aimed at the moralization and normalization of the population through practical systems situated at the interface of society and the State, private and public (medical, psychiatric, educational, philanthropic, social . . .).

Clearly, the assembled techniques that give shape to a distinctive liberal art of government are not reducible to the disciplines, although these may well be incorporated into the armoury of governmental techniques. In so far as these varied techniques are viewed from the point of view of a general liberal problematic, we can also see how they might interweave and link up with each other in mutually reinforcing series. In particular, they frequently require and integrate within them ways in which individuals conduct themselves. That is to say, they involve governed individuals adopting particular practical relations to themselves in the exercise of their freedom in appropriate ways: the promotion in the governed population of specific techniques of the self around such questions as, for example, saving and providentialism, the acquisition of ways of performing roles like father or mother, the development of habits of cleanliness, sobriety, fidelity, self-improvement, responsibility and so on.

However, liberal government is far from being the perfect realization of an idea or doctrine called liberalism. The invention and assembly of particular techniques into an art of government might answer to the liberal definition of the problem of how to govern, but it takes place through particular attempts to resolve diverse local problems and difficulties, through the need to address unforeseen consequences or the effects of the "failure" of previous actions and under always uncertain conditions. It takes place in relation to problems the invented solutions to which may result in challenges to the liberal problematic itself. To that extent there is no necessarily adequate or perfect fit between the *form* of problematization characteristic of early liberalism, and the assemblage of governmental techniques and practices that construct the shape eventually taken by a *real* liberal art of government.

This lack of fit may take many forms. One seems frequently to recur and concerns the claim to superior competence made by real liberal governments. Liberal government is pre-eminently economic government in the dual sense of cheap government and government geared to securing the conditions for optimum economic performance. There is a sense in which the liberal rationality of government is necessarily pegged to the optimum performance of the economy at minimum economic *and socio-political* cost. And yet there are no universally agreed criteria for judging the success of government in this respect. This can give rise to what might seem to be a paradoxical situation where the conduct of government is rationalized and justified in terms of liberal principles of economic government, but where it is quite possible to argue that it is failing completely and causing poor economic performance at high socio-political cost. The paradox lies in the fact that this situation may not of itself result in a public rejection or disqualification of this style or art of government. It would seem that the relationship between governmental activities and the self-conduct of the governed takes hold within a space in which there can be considerable latitude *vis-à-vis* criteria for judging whether government has met the criteria advanced by itself for its capacity to govern.

Neo-liberalism similarly defines a general problematic or problem-space of governmental invention and experiment. Just as early liberalism did not mean that regulatory, legislative and creative governmental activity was rejected or abandoned, so too modern forms of neo-liberalism define positive tasks for a governmental activism. Here it becomes a question of constructing the legal, institutional and cultural conditions that will enable an artificial competitive game of entrepreneurial conduct to be played to best effect. For the Chicago economic liberals it is a question of extending a model of rational-economic conduct beyond the economy itself, of generalizing it as a principle for both limiting and rationalizing government activity. Government must work for the game of market competition and as a kind of enterprise itself, and new quasi-entrepreneurial and market models of action or practical systems must be invented for the conduct of individuals, groups and institutions within those areas of life hitherto seen as being either outside of or even antagonistic to the economic.

On the one hand, neo-liberalism argues that what we call society is the product of governmental intervention and has been given its modern shape by the system of social insurance, unemployment and welfare benefits, social work, State education and the whole panoply of "social" measures associated with the Welfare State. "Society", then, is an invention of government and, in the famous phrase, does not really exist. It further argues that this governmental apparatus has become an economically and socially costly obstacle to the economic performance upon which it depends and leads inexorably to an uncontrollable growth of the State. There is a clear sense in which neo-liberalism is anti-society just as it is opposed to excessive government. But, on the other hand, there is another sense in which one could describe neo-liberalism as promoting what might be called an *autonomization* of society through the invention and proliferation of new quasi-economic models of action for the independent conduct of its activities (Donzelot 1984, 1991a).

An example might clarify what I mean here. While the Conservative government in the UK is often presented as being engaged in a project of "rolling back the State", or as returning to a Victorian morality, it has none the less been very inventive in the models of action that it has constructed in different areas of social life, models of action that are based upon an idea of the (economic) "enterprise". In the area of education, for example, individual schools and other educational establishments are increasingly required to operate according to a kind of competitive "market" logic within an invented system of institutional forms and practices. On the one hand, they function within a framework set by central government that involves, for example, the direct funding of schools by the State according to a national formula, a compulsory National Curriculum with the periodic testing of pupils, government approval of the system and conduct of school management that must conform to a complex body of legislation and ministerial orders, the compulsory publication of individual schools' examination results, and so forth. However, on the other hand, individual schools are required to function more and more as independently managed quasi-enterprises in competition with other schools. They are encouraged to strive to acquire a specific status or value within the "market" for school services. They have to promote themselves so as to attract more pupils of the right kind so that they can achieve better examination results so that they will continue to attract the right pupils from "parent-consumers" and so that they will obtain increased funding from the State and other private sources.

Now for a long time individual schools have had considerable autonomy in the UK system, but what we are seeing here is a new and different kind of autonomization according to a kind of economic or enterprise model of action that pursues a competitive logic. But this is still a technology of government. Here, as in other recent innovations in government, we can see again the formation of a shared problem-space in which different practical systems of government interconnect and link up with each other with a certain degree of consistency. One way in which this consistency might be described is, as I have suggested, the autonomization of society. Casual references to civil society are common today, often evoking a misplaced nostalgia. We should, I think, follow Foucault here and be a bit more nominalistic about terms like society or civil society or nation or community. Civil society was for early liberalism a kind of critical concept, an instrument of critique. It outlined the correlate or schema for a possible liberal art of government. During the course of the nineteenth century, and throughout the present century, it was fundamentally recast into what some call the social, or just society, by all those governmental techniques we associate with the Welfare State. Today, under the influence of what we are calling neo-liberalism, we are witnessing attempts to transform it again and to give it, if you like, the capacity to function autonomously by reshaping its characteristic model of action.

The neo-liberal problem-space describes a fertile but inherently uncertain and open-ended domain of politico-technical invention with different possible outcomes. One might want to say that the generalization of an "enterprise form" to *all* forms of conduct – to the conduct of organizations hitherto seen as being non-economic, to the conduct of government and to the conduct of individuals themselves – constitutes the essential characteristic of this style of government: the promotion of an enterprise culture. But the concrete ways in which it is given a definite shape, both in and through governmental techniques, are extremely varied and uncertain as to their consequences and the forms of action they make possible on the part of both government and the governed. The forms of action constructed for schools, hospitals, general practitioners, housing estates, prisons and other social forms are new, invented, and clearly not a simple extension or reproduction of already existing economic forms of action. None the less, it does seem possible to detect a general consistency in these invented forms and in the style of government that has constructed them. Corresponding to this, it also seems to be the case that these forms encourage the governed to adopt a certain entrepreneurial form of practical relationship to themselves as a condition of their effectiveness and of the effectiveness of this form of government. A characteristic form of relationship that has developed throughout these new practical systems is what Jacques Donzelot (1991b) has called procedures of "contractual implication". This involves "offering" individuals and collectivities active involvement in action to resolve the kind of issues hitherto held to be the responsibility of authorized governmental agencies. However, the price of this involvement is that they must assume active responsibility for these activities, both for carrying them out and, of course, for their outcomes, and in so doing they are required to conduct themselves in accordance with the appropriate (or approved) model of action. This might be described as a new form of "responsibilization" corresponding to the new forms in which the governed are encouraged, freely and rationally, to conduct themselves.

As in the case of early liberalism, neo-liberalism seeks in its own ways the integration of the self-conduct of the governed into the practices of their government and the promotion of correspondingly appropriate forms of techniques of the self. Likewise, individuals may alter their relationship to themselves in their new relationships with government, without it being clear that the outcomes that are supposed to justify this rationality of government are in fact being achieved. And equally, they may not. Liberalism, particularly its modern versions, constructs a relationship between government and the governed that increasingly depends upon ways in which individuals are required to assume the status of being the subjects of their lives, upon the ways in which they fashion themselves as certain kinds of subjects, upon the ways in which they practise their freedom. Government increasingly impinges upon individuals in their very individuality, in their practical relationships to themselves in the conduct of their lives; it *concerns them at the very heart of themselves by making its rationality the condition of their active freedom*. And to the extent that practices of the self are what give concrete shape to the exercise of freedom, that is to say, are what give a concrete form to *ethics*, there opens up a new, uncertain, often critical and unstable domain of relationships between politics and ethics, between the government of others and practices of the self.

The ethics of intellectual work

I want now to suggest another type of continuity within Foucault's work that concerns the relationship between this kind of analysis and the ethics of intellectual work as a practice of self. There often appears to be a *motivating experience* for adopting the kind of approach that Foucault called the "history the present" that seems to me to involve the experience of not being a citizen of the community or republic of thought and action in which one nevertheless is unavoidably implicated or involved. It is an experience of being in a goldfish bowl in which one is obliged to live but in which it seems impossible to live, that is to think and act. An experience, then, in which what one is oneself is, precisely, in doubt. The experience is not at all just a matter of holding a different opinion from everyone else, but of finding oneself not knowing what or how to think. And this experience is one that involves, quite directly, the relations it is possible to enter into or maintain with others. And, of course, it involves the relations one has with practices of government.

This experience, I suggest, seems to call for a certain kind of criticism that, following Paul Veyne, might be called a *historico-transcendental criticism* (Veyne 1988). It calls, that is to say, for a kind of criticism by which our view from the inside of our goldfish bowl is made to appear as no more than the historically contingent effect of a kind of selective determination by a particular "outside" of practices. Foucault's work provides us with a number of splendid examples of "ways out" in relation to certain features of our goldfish bowl. His genealogies work in this way by revealing to us the (often quite recent) inventedness of our world. His descriptions enable us to discern the broken lines of the irregular contours of our goldfish bowl, of our present, taking shape in all their necessarily contingent exteriority. We are witness through his works to a kind of operation of an "exteriorization" of the present "in" which we live, to a kind of operation that turns the present inside out. And afterwards we have to ask ourselves: where are we? who are we?

To understand this operation-experience, the notion of *problematization* might guide us. This notion refers to the historically conditioned emergence of new fields of experience. These new fields of experience involve new truth games, new ways of objectifying and speaking the truth about ourselves, and new ways in which we are able to be and required to be subjects in relation to new practices of government (Foucault 1988a, 1988b). But this notion also designates the activity of the historian of the present. The historian of the present *reproblematizes*, that is to say engages in an activity that dismantles the co-ordinates of his or her starting point and indicates the possibility of a different experience, of a change in his or her way of being a subject or in his or her relation to self – and so also, of a change of others' selves. This experience dictates that each particular work is an experiment the outcome of which cannot be known in advance, that it is an experience in which one risks oneself in the sense that one emerges from it transformed not only in what and how one thinks, but thereby in how one is or might possibly be.

What I am trying to suggest is that there is a continuity between the genealogical approach as a kind of historico-transcendental criticism of actuality and the ethic of intellectual work as a kind of *askesis*. Both involve a distinctive posture towards the present that I would characterize as *non-identitarian* and in which there is both an initial distance from ready-made identities or positions, and a subsequent effect of the undoing of these constituted standpoints. What I mean by this might be made clearer by consideration of two essentially connected aspects of the work of the historian of the present: a *concern for truth* and a *concern for existence*.

The concern for truth

Notwithstanding some commentators' hasty conclusions drawn from Foucault's remark that his works are "fictions", it is safe to say that the historian of the present has too much concern for truth to endorse some kind of irrationalism or a sort of lazy peddling of alternative "narratives". Our rationality may well be associated with a number of intolerable and catastrophic realities, but this does not license a transfer of rights to irrationality. Precisely because nothing is more historical than truth, the historian of the present must have a concern for it, must be attentive to its different forms, must be curious about its real and possible transformations, must be meticulous in describing the shapes it assumes, must be accurate in the accounts he or she gives of it and must be willing to be disturbed or even changed by it.

One way of approaching this concern for truth might be by way of the old question of value freedom. This theme implies that research must not be subservient to already-constituted value positions concerning what is good or bad. Previously held positions cannot dictate either the conclusions to be arrived at or the procedures of investigation adopted to determine what was or is the case. Of course, this does not mean that the genealogist does not have any values, nor that an ethical experience may not influence what is studied and the questions or problems addressed. But this ethical experience is determining to the extent that its *what* and its *how* are, precisely, problematic. Nor does value freedom mean that present ethical concerns do not influence the historian's themes (say, the historical forms of truth and subjectivity), perspectives (say, the point of view of *how* questions at the level of government and practices of the self), analytical procedures (say, the archaeology of forms of problematization and the genealogy of the practices that are the basis for problematizations) or domains of investigation (say, madness, health, criminality, sexuality, etc.).

Secondly, value freedom means, quite simply, respect for the usual demand of truthfulness, and conformity to the procedures and criteria for doing evidential adequacy, conceptual and argumentative coherence, descriptive accuracy, appropriateness of method to material and problem, consideration of the testimony and criticism of others, and so on. *But* this does not mean historians of the present are not free to invent or contrive new ways of saying the truth, to determine new kinds of evidence, to identify new relations between facts, to formulate new problems . . . in short, to introduce a new experience in relation to the truth. Indeed, recognition of the historicity of truth, of the historical contingency and arbitrariness of the ways in which we have spoken the truth about ourselves, would seem to oblige the historian of the present to formulate new problems, in new ways, with new methods, and in relation to new material.

The historian of the present's work disturbs existing ways of thinking and is relevant for contemporary concerns in a way that is *conditional upon its truth*. That is to say, its effect is an experience that involves an essential relation to truth. It produces – or invites – a modification of the historian's and others' relationship to truth through the problematization of what is given to us as necessary to think and do. It is at this level that it produces both its critical effect (making it more difficult for us to think and act in accustomed ways) and its positive effect (clearing a space for the possibility of thinking and being otherwise, for a consideration of the conditions for a real transformation of what we are).

It is by modifying their own and others' relation to the present through a modification of their relation to truth that historians of the present "play their part", reshaping the space of public debate, for example, by introducing a different way of asking questions and by inventing new rules for the game of truth in relation to which we conduct ourselves individually and collectively. This makes possible the introduction of new players into the game, the elaboration of new rules of the game, existing players finding new parts to play, new relationships between the players, and new stakes of the game. If democracy be thought of not as an essence but as an always modifiable practice of individual and collective self-constitution (as a practice of freedom as way of life), then the ethic here might be described as a democratic one.

The concern for existence

Corresponding to the concern for truth there is also, I think, a concern for existence. As a historian of *truth*, the historian of the present knows that what at any given moment we are enjoined to think it is necessary to think, do and be, does not exhaust all the possibilities of existence or fix once and for all the limits of thought. Moreover, it is not a matter of indifference that, at any given moment, this, rather than some other form of existence prevails. After all, the historian's starting point is the non-necessity of what passes for necessary in our present. Historians of the present therefore have a concern for the *selectivity* of what exists as a covering over of what might exist. This gives genealogical analyses a kind of diagnostic value in the sense that, by plotting the historically contingent limits of present thought and action, attention is drawn to what might be called the costs of these limits: *what does it cost existence for its truth to be produced and affirmed in this way?* What is imposed on existence when our goldfish bowl is given this shape? What sorts of relationships with ourselves, others and the world does this way of speaking the truth presuppose, make possible and exclude? What other possibilities of existence are necessarily excluded, condemned, constrained, etc.?

Genealogical analyses do not enable us to fix a tariff of the costs of different modes of existence. But they do enable us to pose specific, concrete questions of evaluation. They make possible the elaboration of an ethics without any grounding in transcendent values. For example, at what cost is the truth of individuals spoken when, say, its condition and effect is their efficient disciplinary subjection? Foucault's analysis of the disciplines shows how a way of speaking the truth of individuals was conditional upon practices that contributed to a significant increase in their real capacity to transform and produce things, acquire skills, develop forms of conduct or ways of acting, and so on. But it also shows how this was at the same time at the cost of an intensified and more efficient hold of power on their bodies and actions, of an intensification of relations of domination at the level of their individual existence. We do not need a tariff to ask whether an increase in our capabilities must necessarily be purchased at the price of our intensified subjection. Foucault's analysis enables us to ask questions about the necessity of the relation between capabilities and domination, and about the possibility of modifying this relation or of disengaging one from the other. And his analysis shows the complexity of the stakes involved in this question at the level of the reciprocal relations between truth, subjectivity, techniques of domination and techniques of the self.

I have said that this concern for truth and existence, along with the diagnostic notion of costs it makes possible, does not involve any final tariff. However, the questions raised here do have a normative orientation or mark out an ethical space. It seems to me that this kind of analysis does point in a certain direction: given that what exists does not exhaust the possibilities of existence, might not the cost of what exists be seen as a function of an assessment of the possibilities for individuals, either singly or collectively, to transform their goldfish bowls without falling back into another in which those possibilities are more narrowly and strictly constrained? Is not this, at least in part, what Foucault meant when he spoke of a permanent *agonism:* the endless task of finding different ways of establishing the play between regulation and openness, between constraint and possible transformation? Might not this concern for truth and existence be also a concern for freedom as requiring an endless exploration of the possibilities for the always-to-be-re-invented activity of individual and collective self-creation?

In conclusion, I would like to make just two remarks. First, it is obvious that histories of the present are not an adequate response to the challenges set to how we live by the development of a neo-liberal style in politics. Beyond an evaluation of the possible costs of neo-liberal government in the terms I have suggested, there is also the need to invent other possible practicable alternative forms of governing others and ourselves, the need for an equal effort of experimentation. Secondly, an interesting thing about some of the neo-liberal innovations in governmental methods is that they are not all unambiguously "bad". Or, at least, it is by no means obvious that in every case they are clearly either better or worse than the methods they have replaced. We have not really begun to consider the complexity of the questions involved in the political evaluation of governmental techniques.

Notes

1. This chapter combines material drawn from lectures given at the University of Technology Sydney, the University of Melbourne and Griffith University, Brisbane, and from an interview conducted by David Burchell (no relation) for *Australian Left Review*, while I was Visiting Scholar in the Faculty of Humanities at Griffith University from July to September 1992. The lecture and interview material has not been revised to any great extent. This accounts for the paucity of notes and detailed references. I would like to express my thanks to the Faculty of Humanities at Griffith, and in particular to Jeffrey Minson and Ian Hunter for providing such a welcoming and stimulating environment in which to work. I would also like to thank David McCallum, Paul Patton and Mitchell Dean for invaluable conversations and discussions and for insights and comments that would have improved the chapter if I had been able to incorporate them.
2. Much of the discussion in this chapter follows the lectures given by Foucault at the Collège de France in 1978 and 1979. Transcripts of the lectures have not yet been published, but cassette recordings can be consulted at the Bibliothèque du Saulchoir, Paris. Foucault's own course summaries have been published (Foucault 1989). A more detailed treatment of many of this chapter's themes can be found in Burchell (1991), Foucault (1991) and Gordon (1991).
3. I am not convinced that Foucault is always strictly consistent in his use of the words government and governmentality. Just as the introduction of the theme of government seems to produce a reconfiguring of the analysis of power, so too the introduction of the theme of techniques of the self seems to have a similar effect on the notion of government. Needless to say, it is not a question of the later analyses disqualifying the earlier but, as it were, of casting them in a new light.
4. Nikolas Rose (1993) is among the first to begin exploration of the domain of government and freedom in terms similar to those put forward here. My own thoughts are indebted to the stimulus given to them by his inaugural lecture at Goldsmiths College.

References

Burchell, G. 1991. Peculiar interests: civil society and governing "the system of natural liberty". See Burchell et al. (1991), 119–50.

Burchell, G., C. Gordon, P. Miller (eds) 1991. *The Foucault effect*. Hemel Hempstead, England: Harvester Wheatsheaf.

Donzelot, J. 1984. *L'invention du social*. Paris: Fayard.

Donzelot, J. 1991a. Le social du troisième type. See Donzelot (1991b).

Donzelot, J. 1991b. *Face à l'exclusion*. Paris: Ed. Esprit.

Dreyfus, H. L. & P. Rabinow 1982. *Michel Foucault, beyond structuralism and hermeneutics*. Chicago: University of Chicago Press.

Foucault, M. 1977. *Discipline and punish: the birth of the prison*. London: Penguin.

Foucault, M. 1980. Truth and subjectivity. The Howison Lecture, Berkeley, mimeo.

Foucault, M. 1982. The subject and power. See Dreyfus & Rabinow (1982), 208–26.

Foucault, M. 1985. *The uses of pleasure*. London: Viking.

Foucault, M. 1986. *The care of the self*. New York: Pantheon.

Foucault, M. [Maurice Florence] 1988a. (Auto)biography: "Michel Foucault, 1926–1984". *History of the Present* **4**(Spring).

Foucault, M. 1988b. On problematization. *History of the Present* **4**(Spring).

Foucault, M. 1989. *Résumé des cours 1970–1982*. Paris: Juillard.

Foucault, M. 1991. Governmentality. See Burchell et al. (1991), 87–104.

Gordon, C. (1991. Governmental rationality: an introduction. See Burchell et al. (1991), 1–52.

Hayek, F. A. 1979. *Law, legislation and liberty*, vol. III. London: Routledge & Kegan Paul.

Rose, N. 1993. Towards a critical sociology of freedom. Inaugural Lecture delivered 5 May 1992, London: Goldsmiths College.

Smith, A. 1976. *An inquiry into the nature and causes of the wealth of nations*. Oxford: Oxford University Press.

Veyne, P. 1988. *Did the Greeks believe in their myths?* Chicago: University of Chicago Press.

Chapter 2
Governing "advanced" liberal democracies

Nikolas Rose

When feminists began to campaign under the slogan "the personal is the political", they drew attention to fundamental flaws in modern political reason.[1] Politics had become identified, on the one hand, with the party and the programme and, on the other, with the question of who possesses power in the State, rather than the dynamics of power relations within the encounters that make up the everyday experience of individuals. One of the virtues of the analyses carried out by Michel Foucault and his co-workers has been to further problematize the forms of political reason that constituted this orthodoxy, to demonstrate the debility of the language that has captivated political philosophy and sociology for over a century, with its constitutive oppositions of State/civil society, domination/emancipation, public/private and the like. In the name of public *and* private security, life has been accorded a "social" dimension through a hybrid array of devices for the management of insecurity. In the name of national *and* individual prosperity, an "economic machine" has taken shape, which may have as its object an economy made up of enterprises competing in a market, but structures that domain through implanting modes of economic calculation, setting fiscal regimes and mandating techniques of financial regulation and accounting. In the name of public citizenship *and* private welfare, the family has been configured as a matrix for organizing domestic, conjugal and child-rearing arrangements and instrumentalizing wage labour and consumption. In the name of social *and* personal wellbeing, a complex apparatus of health and therapeutics has been assembled, concerned with the management of the individual and social body as a vital national resource, and the management of "problems of living", made up of techniques of advice and guidance, medics, clinics, guides and counsellors.

The strategies of regulation that have made up our modern experience of "power" are thus assembled into complexes that connect up forces and institutions deemed "political" with apparatuses that shape and manage individual and collective conduct in relation to norms and objectives but yet are constituted as "non-political". Each complex is an assemblage of diverse components – persons, forms of knowledge, technical procedures and modes of judgement and sanction – a machine for government only in the sense in which Foucault compared the French legal system to one of those machines constructed by Tinguely – more Heath Robinson than Audi, full of parts that come from elsewhere, strange couplings, chance relations, cogs and levers that don't work – and yet which "work" in the sense that they produce effects that have meaning and consequences for us (cited in Gordon 1980). The lines between public and private, compulsory and voluntary, law and norm operate as *internal* elements within each of these assemblages, as each links the regulation of public conduct with the subjective emotional and intellectual capacities and techniques of individuals, and the ethical regimes through which they govern their lives.

The term "politics" can no longer be utilized as if its meaning was self-evident; it must itself be the object of analysis. Indeed, at stake within our own unsettled political reason is the very meaning, legitimacy and limit of politics itself. The idea of the State was, and is, certainly one of the most powerful ways of seeking to codify, manage and articulate – or alternatively contest, overturn and re-articulate – the proliferation of practices of authoritative rule throughout our "modern" experience. But the dream or nightmare of a society programmed, colonized or dominated by "the cold monster" of the State is profoundly limiting as a way of rendering intelligible the way we are governed today. One needs to ask how, and in what ways, and to what extent the rationales, devices and authorities for the government of conduct in the multitude of bedrooms, factories, shopping malls, children's homes, kitchens, cinemas, operating theatres, classrooms and so forth have become linked up to a "political" apparatus? How did the obligations of political authorities come to extend to the health, happiness and wellbeing of the population and those families and individuals who comprised it? How did different political forces seek to programme these new domains? To what extent were they successful in establishing centres of calculation and action such that events in distant places – hospitals, social security offices, workplaces, homes, schools – could be known and regulated by political decisions? What new authorities in the conduct of conduct – notably bureaucrats, managers and experts – were born or transformed in the process? And what, if anything, has been specific about attempts to govern in ways that term themselves liberal and democratic?

Three propositions on liberal rule

What is liberalism if we consider it neither as a political philosophy nor as a type of society but from the perspective of governmentality? Let me put forward three hypotheses.

1. Nineteenth-century liberalism, if it is considered as a *rationality of rule* and not simply as a set of philosophical and normative reflections *upon* rule, produced a series of problems about the governability of individuals, families, markets and populations. These arose out of the insistence upon the necessary limits of political authority, notably in relation to economic and industrial life, public freedoms of debate and the expression of thought, religious practice, and familial authority. Expertise – authority arising out of a claim to knowledge, to neutrality and to efficacy – came to provide a number of solutions to this apparent opposition between the need to govern in the interests of morality and order, and the need to restrict government in the interests of liberty and economy. Liberal rule was thus rendered operable, not merely by the politico-philosophical pronouncement of the sanctity of the opposition of public and private, politics and market, state and civil society, but through the capacity of various knowledgeable persons to render this formula operable. The philanthropist may be seen as one of the first of these personae, exercising a new form of moral and technical authority. But over the second half of the nineteenth century philanthropy was supplemented and displaced by the truths produced and disseminated by the positive sciences of economics, statistics, sociology, medicine, biology, psychiatry and psychology. One sees also the rise of the expert figures of the scientist, the engineer, the civil servant and the bureaucrat: new techniques for the ethical formation and capacitation of persons who would exercise authority and the deployment of a range of scientific and technical knowledges that allowed the possibility of exercising rule over time and space (Osborne 1994, Barry, this volume).

2. Over the late nineteenth and early twentieth centuries this formula of government was perceived, from a variety of political, moral and philosophical perspectives, as failing to produce the necessary economic, social and ethical consequences. One sees the rise of a new formula for the exercise of rule, which one can call "social". The authority of expertise becomes inextricably linked to the formal political apparatus of rule, as rulers are urged to accept the obligation to tame and govern the undesirable consequences of industrial life,

wage labour and urban existence in the name of society: social solidarity, social security, social peace, social prosperity. The theories, explanations, modalities of information and specialist techniques offered by experts were, through different struggles and strategies, connected into complex devices of rule that sought to re-establish the integration of individuals in a social form. This was not so much a process in which a central State extended its tentacles throughout society, but the invention of various "rules for rule" that sought to transform the State *into* a centre that *could* programme – shape, guide, channel, direct, control – events and persons distant from it. Persons and activities were to be governed *through society*, that is to say, through acting upon them in relation to a *social* norm, and constituting their experiences and evaluations in a *social* form. In the face of the threat of a socialism conceived as the swallowing up of society by the State, these formulae for a state of welfare sought to maintain a certain extra-political sphere at the same time as developing a proliferating set of techniques for acting upon it. The truth claims of expertise were highly significant here: through the powers of truth, distant events and persons could be governed "at arms length": political rule would not itself set out the norms of individual conduct, but would install and empower a variety of "professionals", investing them with authority to act as experts in the devices of social rule. And the subject of rule was reconceptualized: where the subject invented in the nineteenth century was subject to a kind of individualizing moral normativity, the subject of welfare was a subject of needs, attitudes and relationships, a subject who was to be embraced within, and governed through, a nexus of collective solidarities and dependencies.

3. The strategies of rule generated under this formula of "the state of welfare" have changed fundamentally over the last 50 years. These changes have arisen, on the one hand, though an array of different critiques that problematized welfare from the point of view of its alleged failings and its deleterious consequences for public finances, individual rights and private morals. On the other hand, strategic mutations have been made possible through the proliferation of new devices for governing conduct that have their roots, in part at least, in the "success" of welfare in authorizing expertise in relation to a range of social objectives, and in implanting in citizens the aspiration to pursue their own civility, wellbeing and advancement. In the multiple encounters between these two lines of force, a new formula of rule is taking shape, one that we can perhaps best term "advanced liberal".

Advanced liberal rule depends upon expertise in a different way, and connects experts differently into the technologies of rule. It seeks to degovernmentalize the State and to de-statize practices of government, to detach the substantive authority of expertise from the apparatuses of political rule, relocating experts within a market governed by the rationalities of competition, accountability and consumer demand. It does not seek to govern through "society", but through the regulated choices of individual citizens, now construed as subjects of choices and aspirations to self-actualization and self-fulfilment. Individuals are to be governed through their freedom, but neither as isolated atoms of classical political economy, nor as citizens of society, but as members of heterogeneous communities of allegiance, as "community" emerges as a new way of conceptualizing and administering moral relations amongst persons.

Government

Colin Gordon has pointed out that Foucault utilized the concept of government in two senses (Gordon 1991, cf. Foucault 1981, Gordon 1986). First, to draw attention to a dimension of our experience – not itself specifically modern – constituted by all those ways of reflecting and acting that have aimed to shape, guide, manage or regulate the conduct of persons – not only other persons but also oneself – in the light of certain principles or goals. What made these forms of reflection *governmental*, rather than theoretical, philosophical or moral, is their wish to make themselves practical, to connect themselves up with various procedures and apparatuses that would seek to give them effect – whether these be the practice of diary writing in order to govern conscience, practices of child rearing in order to govern children, practices of security and subsistence in order to govern pauperism, or techniques of financial inscription and calculation in order to govern economic activity. No doubt throughout the ages humans have reflected upon the conduct of themselves and others, but such thought becomes governmental to the extent that it seeks to render itself technical, to insert itself into the world by "realizing" itself as a *practice*.

Foucault uses the term government in a second, and more circumscribed manner, one that helps us to repose our analyses of the problematics of rule as they have taken shape in the West over the last three centuries. By problematics of rule, I mean the ways in which those who would exercise rule have posed themselves the question of the reasons, justifications, means and ends of rule, and the problems, goals or ambitions that should animate it. Here the notion of government addresses itself specifically to the domain of the political, not as a domain of State or a set of institutions and actors but in terms of the varieties of political reason. Govern*mentality* both extends the concerns of rulers to the ordering of the multitudinous affairs of a territory and its population in order to ensure its wellbeing, and simultaneously establishes divisions between the proper spheres of action of different types of authority.

As *political rationality*, governmentalities are to be analyzed as practices for the "formulation and justification of idealized schemata for representing reality, analyzing it and rectifying it" – as a kind of intellectual machinery or apparatus for rendering reality thinkable in such a way that it is amenable to political programming (Rose & Miller 1992: 179, cf. Miller & Rose 1990). Despite the undoubted salience of all the petty deals and corruptions of political activity, political rationalities have a *moral* form, in so far as they concern such issues as the proper distribution of tasks between different authorities and the ideals or principles to which government should be addressed. Further, political rationalities have an *epistemological* character, in that they embody particular conceptions of the objects to be governed – nation, population, economy, society, community – and the subjects to be governed – citizens, subjects, individuals. And they deploy a certain *style of reasoning*: language here understood as itself a set of "intellectual techniques" for rendering reality thinkable and practicable, and constituting domains that are amenable – or not amenable – to reformatory intervention.

As an array of *technologies of government*, governmentality is to be analyzed in terms of the strategies, techniques and procedures through which different authorities seek to enact programmes of government in relation to the materials and forces to hand and the resistances and oppositions anticipated or encountered. Hence, this is not a matter of the implementation of idealized schema in the real by an act of will, but of the complex assemblage of diverse forces (legal, architectural, professional, administrative, financial, judgmental), techniques (notation, computation, calculation, examination, evaluation), devices (surveys and charts, systems of training, building forms) that promise to regulate decisions and actions of individuals, groups, organizations in relation to authoritative criteria (cf. Rose & Miller 1992: 183).

The technologies and devices that are assembled into the apparatus of a State have neither the unity nor the functionality often ascribed to them. The "power of the State" is a resultant, not a cause, an outcome of the composition and assembling of actors, flows, buildings, relations of authority into relatively durable associations mobilized, to a greater or lesser extent, towards the achievement of particular objectives by common means. This is not a matter of the domination of a "network" by "the State" but rather a matter of *translation*. The translation of political programmes articulated in rather general terms – national efficiency, democracy, equality, enterprise – into ways of seeking to exercise authority over persons, places and activities in specific locales and practices. The translation of thought and action from a "centre of calculation" into a diversity of locales dispersed across a territory – translation in the sense of a movement from one place to another. Through a multitude of such mobile relays, relations are established between those who are spatially and temporally separated, and between events and decisions in spheres that none the less retain their formal autonomy. The composition of such networks is the condition of possibility for "action at a distance": it is only to the extent that such alignments of diverse forces can be established that calculated action upon conduct across space and time can occur at all (cf. Latour 1986). However, the strategies of government that I term "advanced liberal" explicitly seek to utilize and instrumentalize such possibilities: they are rationalities animated by the desire to "govern at a distance".

Liberalism

Eighteenth-century European science of police dreamed of a time in which a territory and its inhabitants would be transparent to knowledge – all was to be known, noted, enumerated and documented (Foucault 1989, 1991, cf. Pasquino 1991). The conduct of persons in all domains of life was to be specified and scrutinized in minute particulars, through detailed regulations of habitation, dress, manners and the like – warding off disorder through a fixed ordering of persons and activities (cf. Oestreich 1982). Liberalism, as a mentality of rule, abandons this megalomaniac and obsessive fantasy of a totally administered society. Government now confronts itself with realities – market, civil society, citizens – that have their own internal logics and densities, their own intrinsic mechanisms of self-regulation. As Graham Burchell has pointed out, liberalism thus repudiates *raison d'état* as a rationality of rule in which a sovereign exercises his totalizing will across a national space (Burchell 1991, and cf. Burchell, this volume). Rulers are confronted, on the one hand, with subjects equipped with rights and interests that *should not* be interdicted by politics. On the other hand, rulers are faced with a realm of processes that they *cannot* govern by the exercise of sovereign will because they lack the requisite knowledge and capacities. The objects, instruments and tasks of rule must be reformulated with reference to these domains of market, civil society and citizenship, with the aim of ensuring that they function to the benefit of the nation as a whole.

The two, apparently illiberal, poles of "power over life" that Foucault identifies – the disciplines of the body and the bio-politics of the population – thus find their place within liberal mentalities of rule, as rule becomes dependent upon ways of rendering intelligible and practicable these vital conditions for the production and government of a polity of free citizens (Foucault 1977, 1979). Those mechanisms and devices operating according to a disciplinary logic, from the school to the prison, seek to produce the subjective conditions, the forms of self-mastery, self-regulation and self-control, necessary to govern a nation now made up of free and "civilized" citizens. At the same time, bio-political strategies – statistical enquiries, censuses, programmes for enhancement or curtailment of rates of reproduction or the minimization of illness and the promotion of health – seek to render intelligible the domains whose laws liberal government must know and respect: legitimate government will not be arbitrary government, but will be based upon intelligence concerning those whose wellbeing it is mandated to enhance (Foucault 1980a). From this moment onwards, rule must be exercised in the light of a knowledge of that which is to be ruled – a child, a family, an economy, a community – a knowledge both of its general laws of functioning (supply and demand, social solidarity) of its particular state at any one time (rate of productivity, rate of suicide), and of the ways in which it can be shaped and guided in order to produce desirable objectives while at the same time respecting its autonomy.

We can draw out four significant features of liberalism from the perspective of government.

1. *A new relation between government and knowledge.* Although all formulae of government are dependent upon a knowledge of that which is to be governed, and indeed themselves constitute a certain form of knowledge of the arts of government, liberal strategies tie government to the positive knowledges of human conduct developed within the social and human sciences. The activity of government becomes connected up to all manner of facts (the avalanche of printed

numbers and other information examined by Ian Hacking (1991)), theories (philosophies of progress, conceptualizations of epidemic disease . . .), diagrams (sanitary reform, child guidance . . .), techniques (double-entry book keeping, compulsory medical inspection of school children), knowledgeable persons who can speak "in the name of society" (sociologists, statisticians, epidemiologists, social workers). Knowledge here flows around a diversity of apparatuses for the production, circulation, accumulation, authorization and realization of truth: in the academy, in government bureaux, in reports of commissions, public enquiries and pressure groups; it is the "know-how" that promises to render docile the unruly domains over which government is to be exercised, to make government possible and to make government better.

2. *A novel specification of the subjects of rule as active in their own government.* Liberal mentalities of rule are characterized by the hopes that they invest in the subjects of government. The claim, in politics, law, morality and so forth, that subjects are individuals whose freedom, liberty and rights are to be respected by drawing certain limits to the legitimate scope of political or legal regulation goes hand in hand with the emergence of a range of novel practices which seek to shape and regulate individuality in particular ways. Liberal strategies of government thus becomes dependent upon devices (schooling, the domesticated family, the lunatic asylum, the reformatory prison) that promise to create individuals who do not need to be governed by others, but will govern themselves, master themselves, care for themselves. And although the abstract subject of rights may be specified in universalistic form, novel technologies of rule throughout the nineteenth century produce new demands and possibilities for positive knowledges of particular subjects. This is the moment of the disciplines, which simultaneously specify subjects in terms of certain norms of civilization, and effect a division between the civilized member of society and those lacking the capacities to exercise their citizenship responsibly: the infanticidal woman or the monomaniacal regicide in the court of law, the delinquent boys and girls to be reformed in industrial or reformatory establishments, the prostitute or fallen women, the men and women thought mad. One sees the beginning of a painful and resisted migration of rights to truth over humans from theology or jurisprudence to the disciplines that owe their very conditions of disciplinization to these new technologies of government. From this time forth, liberal governmentalities will

dream that the national objective for the good subject of rule will fuse with the voluntarily assumed obligations of free individuals to make the most of their own existence by conducting their life responsibly. At the same time, subjects themselves will have to make their decisions about their self-conduct surrounded by a web of vocabularies, injunctions, promises, dire warnings and threats of intervention, organized increasingly around a proliferation of norms and normativities.

3. *An intrinsic relation to the authority of expertise.* Liberal arts of rule from the middle of the nineteenth century sought to modulate events, decisions and actions in the economy, the family, the private firm, and the conduct of the individual person while maintaining and promoting their autonomy and self-responsibility. These modes of intervention did not answer to a single logic or form part of a coherent programme of "State intervention" (cf. Foucault 1980a). Rather, largely through the proselytizing of independent reformers, a number of frictions and disturbances – epidemics and disease, theft and criminality, pauperism and indigence, insanity and imbecility, the breakdown of marital relations – were recoded as "social" problems that had consequences for national wellbeing and thus called for new forms of remedial authoritative attention. The relations that were brought into being between political authorities, legal measures and independent authorities differed according to whether one was seeking to regulate economic exchanges through contract, to mitigate the effects of factory labour upon health, to reduce the social dangers of epidemics through sanitary reform, to moralize the children of the labouring classes through industrial schools and so forth. In each case, experts, in demanding that economic, familial and social arrangements are governed according to their own programmes, attempt to mobilize political resources such as legislation, funding or organizational capacity for their own ends. Political forces seek to give effect to their strategies, not only through the utilization of laws, bureaucracies, funding regimes and authoritative State agencies and agents, but through utilizing and instrumentalizing forms of authority other than those of "the State" in order to govern – spatially and constitutionally – "at a distance". Authority is accorded to formally autonomous expert authorities and simultaneously the exercise of that autonomy is shaped through various forms of licensure, through professionalization and through bureaucratization. From this time forth, the domain of "politics" will be distinguished from other

spheres of authoritative rule, yet inextricably bound to the authority of expertise.

4. *A continual questioning of the activity of rule.* Sociologies of our post-modern condition have stressed the "reflexivity" that they consider to be characteristic of our age (Giddens 1990, Lash & Urry 1994). But the "reflexivity" that imbues all attempts to exercise rule in our present is not distinctive to some terminal stage of modernity; it characterized liberal political rationalities from their inception. Liberalism confronts *itself* with the question "Why rule?" – a question that leads to the demand that a constant critical scrutiny be exercised over the activities of those who rule – by others and by authorities themselves. For if the objects of rule are governed by their own laws, "the laws of the natural", under what conditions can one legitimately subject them to "the laws of the political"? Further, liberalism confronts itself with the question "Who can rule?" Under what conditions is it possible for one to exercise authority over another, what founds the *legitimacy* of authority? This question of the authority of authority must be answered, not transcendentally or in relation to the charismatic *persona* of the leader, but through various technical means – of which democracy and expertise prove to be two rather durable solutions. Liberalism inaugurates a continual dissatisfaction with government, a perpetual questioning of whether the desired effects are being produced, of the mistakes of thought or policy that hamper the efficacy of government, a recurrent diagnosis of failure coupled with a recurrent demand to govern better.

Governing the state of welfare

The real history of liberalism, over the late nineteenth and twentieth centuries, is bound up with a series of transformations in the problematics of rule. What Foucault refers to as the governmentalization of the State is here bound up with the emergence of a problem in which the governability of democracy – to use Jaques Donzelot's term – seems to raise a number of difficulties to which the "socialization of society" seemed to be the solution (Donzelot 1991, see also Rabinow 1989: Chs 4–6 and Ewald 1991). From a variety of perspectives it was argued that the projects of nineteenth-century liberalism had failed, and the philanthropic and disciplinary projects for avoiding demoralization and maintaining moral order in urban labouring classes were proving powerless in the face of the forces of social fragmentation and individualization of modern society, evidenced by rates of suicide, crime and social disaffection. Further, economic affairs – in particular the uncertainties of employment and the harsh conditions of factory work – had profound social consequences that had not been alleviated by the vestigial constraint of factory legislation and the like – they damaged health, produced danger through the irregularity of employment and encouraged the growth of militant labour. "Welfare" was one formula for recoding, along a number of different dimensions, the relations between the political field and the management of economic and social affairs, in which the authority of experts as those who can speak and enact truth about human beings in their individual and collective lives, was to be accorded a new role. Within this new formula of welfare, political authorities, through their utilization of the financial, technical and juridical possibilities of the State, were to become the guarantor of both the freedom of the individual and the freedom of the capitalist enterprise. The State was to take responsibility for generating an array of technologies of government that would "social-ize" both individual citizenship and economic life in the name of collective security. This was a formula of rule somewhere between classical liberalism and nascent socialism. Perhaps its most contested plane of action was the economic domain itself, where interventions would weaken the privacy of the market and the enterprise while retaining their formal autonomy. But the security of economy was also to be assured by acting upon the social milieux within which production and exchange occurred: by governing society itself (cf. Procacci 1989).

Social insurance and social work can exemplify two axes of this new formula of government – one inclusive and solidaristic, one individualizing and responsibilizing. Social insurance is an inclusive technology of government (O'Malley 1992 and this volume, Rose 1993). It incarnates social solidarity in collectivizing the management of the individual and collective dangers posed by the economic riskiness of a capricious system of wage labour, and the corporeal riskiness of a body subject to sickness and injury, under the stewardship of a "social" State. And it enjoins solidarity in that the security of the individual across the vicissitudes of a life history is guaranteed by a mechanism that operates on the basis of what individuals and their families are thought to share by virtue of their common sociality. Social insurance thus establishes new connections and association between "public" norms and procedures and the fate of individuals in their "private" economic and personal conduct. It was only one of an assortment of ways in which, at the start of the twentieth century, the "privacy" of the private spheres of family and factory was attenuated. Together with other regulatory devices such as public housing schemes, health and safety legislation and laws on child-care, the autonomy of both economic and familial spaces was weakened, and new vectors of responsibility and obligation took shape between State and parent, child or employee.

Social work, correlatively, operates within a strategy in which security is to be secured by enjoining the responsibilities of citizenship upon individuals incapable or aberrant members of society (Donzelot 1979, Rose 1985, Parton 1991). It acts on specific problematic *cases*, radiating out to them from locales of individualized judgement on particular conducts judged as pathological in relation to social norms. The juvenile court, the school, the child guidance clinic operate as centres of adjudication and co-ordination of these strategies, targeted not so much at the isolated individual citizen, but at individuals associated within the matrix of the family. The everyday activities of living, the hygienic care of household members, the previously trivial features of interactions between adults and children, were to be anatomized by experts, rendered calculable in terms of norms and deviations, judged in terms of their social costs and consequences and subject to regimes of education or reformation. The family, then, was to be instrumentalized as a *social machine* – both *made* social and utilized to *create* sociality – implanting the techniques of responsible citizenship under the tutelage of experts and in relation to a variety of sanctions and rewards. Complex assemblages would constitute the possibility of State departments, government offices and so forth acting as centres, by enabling their deliberations to be relayed into a whole variety of micro-locales within which the conduct of the citizen could be problematized and acted upon in terms of norms that calibrated personal normality in a way that was inextricably linked to its social consequences. The individual and the family were to be "simultaneously assigned their social duties, accorded their rights, assured of their natural capacities, and educated in the fact that they need to be educated by experts in order to responsibly assume their freedom" (Rose 1993: 13).

The political subject was thus to be reconceptualized as a citizen, with rights to social protection and social education in return for duties of social obligation and social responsibility, both refiguring and retaining the liberal character of "freedom" and "privacy" (Rose 1987). Security would be combined with responsibility in a way that was conducive both to democracy and to liberty. When counterposed to the moralistic, philanthropic and disciplinary projects of nineteenth-century liberalism, social government extends the boundaries of the sphere of politics through proliferating networks through which the state could seek to extend its rule over distant events, places and persons. Expertise acquires powerful capacities, not only in linking deliberations in one place with actions in another, but also in promising to align the self-governing capacities of subjects with the objectives of political authorities by means of persuasion, education and seduction rather than coercion. These new technologies of expert social government appear to depoliticize and technicize a whole swathe of questions by promising that technical calculations will overrule existing logics of contestation between opposing interests. Judgements and deliberations of experts as to rates of benefit or patterns of child-care are accorded capacities for action that were previously unthinkable. But in becoming so integral to the exercise of political authority, experts gain the capacity to generate "enclosures", relatively bounded locales or fields of judgement within which their authority is concentrated, intensified and rendered difficult to countermand.

Advanced liberalism

The conditions that stripped the self-evidence away from social government were heterogeneous. In the immediate aftermath of the Second World War, at the very same time as some were learning the lesson that it was feasible for the whole of the productive and social organization of a nation to be governed, in some way or other, by a central State, a number of European intellectuals drew exactly the opposite conclusion. Most notable, perhaps, was Friedrich von Hayek's suggestion that the logics of the interventionist State, as they had been manifested in the wartime organization of social and economic life, were not only inefficient and self-defeating, but set nations on the very path towards the total State that had been manifested in Nazi Germany and could be seen in Stalin's Soviet Union – they were subversive of the very freedoms, democracies and liberties they sought to enhance (Hayek 1944, cf. Gordon 1987, 1991, the following discussion draws on Rose 1994). The arguments set out in *The road to serfdom* (Hayek 1944) were to be elaborated in a series of subsequent texts: the principle of individual freedom was both the origin of our progress and the guarantor of future growth of civilization; although we must shed the hubristic illusion that we can, by decisions and calculations of authority, deliberately create "the future of mankind", we must also recognize that freedom itself is an artefact of civilization, that "the discipline of civilization . . . is at the same time the discipline of free-dom" (Hayek 1979: 163).

Only some three decades later were such critiques of the social State to be assembled into a politically salient assault on the rationalities, pro-grammes and technologies of welfare in Britain, Europe and the United States. An economic thesis articulated in different forms by Left and Right had a particular significance here – the argument that the increas-ing levels of taxation and public expenditure required to sustain social, health and welfare services, education and the like were damaging to the health of capitalism as they required penal rates of tax on private profit. This contradiction was formulated from the Left in terms of the "fiscal crisis of the state" and from the Right in terms of the contradiction between the growth of an "unproductive" welfare sector – that created no wealth – at the expense of the "productive" private sector in which all national wealth was actually produced (O'Connor 1972, Bacon & Eltis 1976). The very socialization of capitalist private enterprise and market relations that had been seen as its salvation in the face of the twin threats of socialism and moral and social disintegration now appeared to be anti-thetical to the very survival of a society based upon a capitalist economy.

This economic argument chimed with a range of other criticisms of social government: of the arrogance of government overreach; of the dangers of imminent government overload; the absurdity of politicians trying to second-guess the market by picking winners; claims that Keynesian demand management stimulated inflationary expectations and led to the debasement of the currency. Others claimed that measures intended to decrease poverty had actually increased inequality; that attempts to assist the disadvantaged had actually worsened their disad-vantage; that controls on minimum wages hurt the worse paid because they destroy jobs. Further, welfare bureaucracies themselves, together with their associated specialisms of welfare and social expertise, came under attack from all parts of the political spectrum – from classical liber-als and libertarians, from left-wing critics of the social control of deviance, from social democratic activists concerned about the lack of effectiveness of social government in alleviating inequality and disadvantage. It appeared that behind their impassioned demands for more funding for their services lay a covert strategy of empire-building and the advance-ment of sectional interests; that it was actually the middle classes, rather than the poor, who benefited both from the employment opportunities and from the services of the Welfare State; and that welfare services actu-ally destroyed other forms of social support such as church, community and family; that they did not produce social responsibility and citizenship but dependency and a client mentality (Murray 1980, Adler & Asquith 1981, Friedman 1982, cf. for an earlier version Reich 1964 and for a discussion of all these "rhetorics of reaction" see Hirschman 1991).

Simultaneously, the empire of social expertise was itself fracturing into rivalry between different specialisms: experts on the child, the elderly, the disabled, the alcoholic, the drug abuser, the single mother, psychiatric nurses, community workers, occupational therapists and many more. Each of these "specialisms" sought to organize on professional lines, to demand its own rights and field of discretion: the world of welfare fragmented through an ever-finer division of labour and through divergent conceptual and practical allegiances. Equally, clients of expertise came to understand and relate to themselves and their "welfare" in new ways. In a whole range of sectors, individuals came to reconceptualize themselves in terms of their own will to be healthy, to enjoy a maximized normality. Surrounded by images of health and happiness in the mass media and in the marketing strategies deployed in commodity advertising and consumption regimes, narrativizing their dissatisfactions in the potent language of rights, they organized themselves into their own associations, contesting the powers of expertise, protesting against relations that now appeared patronizing and demeaning of their autonomy, demanding increased resources for their particular conditions and claiming a say in the decisions that affected their lives. In the face of the simultaneous proliferation, fragmentation, contestation and de-legitimization of the place of experts in the devices of social government, a new formula for the relation between government, expertise and subjectivity would take shape.

A number of strategies were developed. Civil libertarians sought to surround experts with a paraphernalia of legal restraints, tribunals and rights that would modulate their decisions: these techniques were cumbersome, slow and expensive and merely redistributed social powers to new experts; in the UK they achieved only a limited foothold on reality (Reich 1964, Adler & Asquith 1981). Critics of the Left largely contented themselves with denouncing expert powers as covert social control by the state, with seeking to distinguish the use of knowledge from its abuse, or to separate emancipatory true knowledge from ideology that disguised and legitimated the exercise of power in "ideological State apparatuses". One radical politics of expertise, with its own version of the Maoist slogan "better Red than expert", sought to do away with all expertise (as in antipsychiatry and some forms of feminism): the "counter-expertise" it generated rapidly professionalized itself, with its own organizations, pedagogies and so forth. Another left-wing politics of expertise operated under the rubric of "the generalization of competencies" as in certain movements for workers' co-operatives to replace hierarchically owned and managed workplaces (e.g. Cooley 1980). In the economic field, in Britain at least, this ran into difficulties not only from bosses but also from the traditional representatives of labour concerned about the erosion of their own powers and the co-optation of opposing interests into some new corporatism. An analogous fate lay in store for attempts to democratize expertise in other domains such as psychiatry and law.

It would be misleading to suggest that the neo-conservative political regimes that were elected in Britain and the United States in the late 1970s were underpinned by a coherent and elaborated political rationality that they then sought to implement, still less one that identified bureaucratic and professional power as a key problem. Initially, no doubt, these regimes merely sought to engage with a multitude of different problems of welfare, to reduce cost, to undercut the power of professional lobbies, etc. But gradually, these diverse skirmishes were rationalized within a relatively coherent mentality of government that came to be termed neo-liberalism. Neo-liberalism managed to re-activate the sceptical vigilance over political government basic to classical liberalism, by linking different elements of the "rhetoric of reaction" with a series of techniques – none of them in itself particularly new or remarkable – that could render these criticisms governmental. Indeed one thing that is perhaps paradoxical about neo-liberalism is that, despite posing itself as a critique of political government, it retains the programmatic *a priori*, the presupposition that the real is programmable by authorities: the objects of government are rendered thinkable in such a way that their difficulties appear amenable to diagnosis, prescription and cure (cf. Rose & Miller 1992: 183). Neo-liberalism does not abandon the "will to govern": it maintains the view that failure of government to achieve its objectives is to be overcome by inventing new strategies of government that will succeed.

What is it "to govern in an advanced liberal way"? The breathless celebrations or condemnations of Thatcherism have proved to be overblown. But it is none the less possible to identify a more modest yet more durable transformation in rationalities and technologies of government. "Advanced liberal" strategies can be observed in national contexts from Finland to Australia, advocated by political regimes from left and right, and in relation to problem domains from crime control to health. They seek techniques of government that create a distance between the decisions of formal political institutions and other social actors, conceive of these actors in new ways as subjects of responsibility, autonomy and choice, and seek to act upon them through shaping and utilizing their freedom. Let me rapidly sketch out three characteristic shifts.

1. *A new relation between expertise and politics.* Welfare might be considered a "substantive" rationality of rule: expert conceptions of health, income levels, types of economic activity and the like, were to be more or less directly transcribed into the machinery and objectives of political government. Simultaneously, the very powers that the technologies of welfare accorded to experts enabled them to establish enclosures within which their authority could not be challenged, effectively insulating experts from external political attempts to govern them and their decisions and actions. In contrast, advanced liberal modes of rule have a certain "formal" character. The powers once accorded to positive knowledges of human conduct are to be transferred to the calculative regimes of accounting and financial management. And the enclosures of expertise are to be penetrated through a range of new techniques for exercising critical scrutiny over authority – budget disciplines, accountancy and audit being three of the most salient. These certainly rely upon a claim to truth, but it is one that has a different character from that of the social and human sciences: these "grey sciences", these know-hows of enumeration, calculation, monitoring, evaluation, manage to be simultaneously modest and omniscient, limited yet apparently limitless in their application to problems as diverse as the appropriateness of a medical procedure and the viability of a university department.

Marketization, for example, seeks various forms of distance between the political and the expert machines: an apparent devolution of regulatory powers from "above" – planning and compulsion – to "below" – the decisions of consumers. In its ideal form, this imagines a "free market" where the relations between citizens and experts are not organized and regulated through compulsion but through acts of choice. It addresses the pluralization of expertise, not by seeking to adjudicate between the rival claims of different groups of experts, but by turning welfare agencies – social service departments, housing departments, health authorities – into "purchasers" who can choose to "buy" services from the range of options available. Whether it be in the "purchaser–provider" split in the health services, in "case management" techniques in social services, in the autonomization of schools from control by local educational authorities so that they may compete in a market for pupils, one sees a reconfiguration of the political salience of expertise, a new way of "responsibilizing" experts in relation to claims upon them other than those of their own criteria of truth and competence, their assembling into new relations of power.

Similarly, monetarization plays a key role in breaching welfare enclosures within the networks of social government. Transforming activities – operating on a patient, educating a student, providing a social work interview for a client – into cash terms establishes new relations of power. Making people write things down, prescribing what must be written down and how, is itself a kind of government of individual conduct, making it thinkable according to particular norms. Budgetary discipline transforms the activity of the budget holder, increasing choices at the same time as regulating them and providing new ways of ensuring the responsibility and fidelity of agents who remain formal autonomous. Not merely in the setting of the budget, but in the very "budgetization" of the activity, the terms of calculation and decision are displaced and new diagrams of force and freedom are assembled.

Within these new strategies of government, audit becomes one of the key mechanisms for responding to the plurality of expertise and the inherent controversy and undecidability of its truth claims. Michael Power has suggested that audit, in a range of different forms, has come to replace the trust that formulae of government once accorded to professional credentials (Power 1992, 1994). As Power points out, audit responds to "failure" and insecurity by the "remanagerialisation of risk". Risk is to be rendered manageable by new distantiated relations of control between political centres of decision and the "non-political" procedures, devices and apparatuses – such as schools, hospitals or firms – upon which the responsibility for health, wealth and happiness is to be devolved. In this process, the entities to be audited are transformed: they have to be "made auditable", producing a new grid of visibilities for the conduct of organizations and those who inhabit them. Audit may make heavy demands, but it travels well across space and time, is capable of being propagated in a multitude of locales, channelling and organizing activities and linking centres of calculation to sites of implementation according to new vectors. Despite the fact that its "epistemological profile" is, if anything, even lower than the knowledges that it displaces, and that there is nothing novel in the techniques of audit themselves, the mode of its operation – in terms of procedures rather

than substantives, in terms of apparently stable and yet endlessly flexible criteria such as efficiency, appropriateness, effectiveness –
renders it a versatile and highly transferable technology for governing at a distance.

2. *A new pluralization of "social" technologies.* Strategies of pluralization and
autonomization, which characterize many contemporary pro-
grammes for reconfiguring social technologies from various parts of
the political spectrum, embody a wish for a kind of "de-governmentalization of the State" and a "de-statization of government" – a phenomenon that is linked to a mutation in the notion of "the social",
that invention of the late nineteenth century that both sociology and
welfare government constituted as their object and target. The relation between the responsible individual and their self-governing
community comes to substitute for that between social citizen and
their common society (cf. Rose 1996b). In the course of this mutation, one sees a detaching of the centre from the various regulatory
technologies that, over the twentieth century, it sought to assemble
into a single functioning network, and the adoption instead of a form
of government through shaping the powers and wills of autonomous
entities: enterprises, organizations, communities, professionals, individuals. This has entailed the implantation of particular modes of
calculation into agents, the supplanting of certain norms, such as
those of service and dedication, by others, such as those of competition, quality and customer demand. It has entailed the establishment
of different networks of accountability and reconfigured flows of
accountability and responsibility in fundamental ways.

Perhaps most significant has been the disassembling of a variety of
governmental activities previously assembled within the political
apparatus: the phenomenon referred to, in Britain, as the "quango-
ization" of the state. Quasi-autonomous non-governmental organizations have proliferated, taking on regulatory functions, such as the
regulation of securities and investments in the financial sector, planning functions as in the rise of new entities for the government and
regeneration of urban locales, educative functions as in the rise of
organizations responsible for the provision of training to school
leavers, responsibilities for the provision of previously "public" utili-
ties such as water, gas, electricity, the "privatization" of the civil service, prisons and police. This has been linked to the invention and
deployment of a raft of other measures for the government of these
entities, measures whose emphasis upon the apparent objectivity and

neutrality of numbers underpins a claim that they now operate according to an apolitical agenda (cf. Hood 1991). Contracts, targets, indicators, performance measures, monitoring and evaluation are used to govern their conduct while according them a certain autonomy of decisional power and responsibility for their actions. One sees the displacement of electoral mechanisms as the way of ensuring democratic control via the intermediary of local councils by novel techniques of accountability, such as representation of "partners" from different "communities" – business, local residents, voluntary organizations, local councils – on the boards. The reconfiguration of political power involved here cannot usefully be understood in terms of the opposition of State and market: shaped and programmed by political authorities, new mechanisms are utilized to link the calculations and actions of a heterogeneous array of organizations into political objectives, governing them "at a distance" through the instrumentalization of a regulated autonomy.

3. *A new specification of the subject of government.* The enhancement of the powers of the client as customer – consumer of health services, of education, of training, of transport – specifies the subjects of rule in a new way: as active individuals seeking to "enterprise themselves", to maximize their quality of life through acts of choice, according their life a meaning and value to the extent that it can be rationalized as the outcome of choices made or choices to be made (Rose 1992, 1996a). Political reason must now justify and organize itself by arguing over the arrangements that are adequate to the existence of persons as, in their essence, creatures of freedom, liberty and autonomy. Within this new regime of the actively responsible self, individuals are to fulfil their national obligations not through their relations of dependency and obligation to one another, but through seeking to *fulfil themselves* within a variety of micro-moral domains or "communities" – families, workplaces, schools, leisure associations, neighbourhoods. Hence the problem is to find means by which individuals may be made responsible through their individual choices for themselves and those to whom they owe allegiance, through the shaping of a lifestyle according to grammars of living that are widely disseminated, yet do not depend upon political calculations and strategies for their rationales or for their techniques (Rose 1996b).

It has become possible to actualize this notion of the actively responsible individual because of the development of new apparatuses that integrate subjects into a moral nexus of identifications and allegiances in the very processes in which they appear to act out their most personal choices. Contemporary political rationalities rely upon and utilize a range of technologies that install and support the civilizing project by shaping and governing the capacities, competencies and wills of subjects, yet are outside the formal control of the "public powers". To such basic nation-forming devices as a common language, skills of literacy and transportation networks, our century has added the mass media of communication, with their pedagogies through documentary and soap opera; opinion polls and other devices that provide reciprocal links between authorities and subjects; the regulation of lifestyles through advertising, marketing and the world of goods; *and* the experts of subjectivity (Rose 1990). These technologies do not have their origin or principle of intelligibility in "the State", but none the less have made it possible to govern in an "advanced liberal" way. They have provided a plethora of indirect mechanisms that can translate the goals of political, social and economic authorities into the choices and commitments of individuals, locating them into actual or virtual networks of identification through which they may be governed.

The reconfiguring of the subject of government confers obligations and duties at the same time as it opens new spaces of decision and action. Each of the two dimensions of social government that I discussed earlier undergoes a mutation. Thus social insurance, as a principle of social solidarity, gives way to a kind of privatization of risk management. In this new prudentialism, insurance against the future possibilities of unemployment, ill health, old age and the like becomes a private obligation. Not merely in relation to previously socialized forms of risk management, but also in a whole range of other decisions, the citizen is enjoined to bring the future into the present, and is educated in the ways of calculating the future consequences of actions as diverse as those of diet to those of home security. The active citizen thus is to add to his or her obligations the need to adopt a calculative prudent personal relation to fate now conceived in terms of calculable dangers and avertable risks (O'Malley 1992 and this volume). And social work, as a means of civilization under tutelage, gives way to the private counsellor, the self-help manual and the telephone helpline, as practices whereby each individual binds themselves to expert advice as a matter of their own freedom (Rose 1990). The regulation of conduct becomes a matter of each individual's desire to govern their own conduct freely in the service of the maximization of a version of their happiness and fulfilment that they take to be their own, but such lifestyle maximization entails a relation to authority in the very moment as it pronounces itself the outcome of free choice.

Here we can witness the "reversibility" of relations of authority – what starts off as a norm to be implanted into citizens can be repossessed as a demand which citizens can make of authorities. Individuals are to become "experts of themselves", to adopt an educated and knowledgeable relation of self-care in respect of their bodies, their minds, their forms of conduct and that of the members of their own families. Of course, this new configuration has its own complexities, its own logics of incorporation and exclusion. However, the "power effects" certainly do not answer to a simple logic of domination, and nor are they amenable to a "zero sum" conception of power. Consider, for example, the proliferation of the new psychological techniques and languages of empowerment in relation to those subject now coded as "marginalized" or "excluded". It is true that neo-liberal political regimes enacted an array of measures to reduce benefits for those out of work, to discipline delinquents and lawbreakers and impose personal responsibility upon them, to dismantle the archipelago of institutions within which welfare government had isolated and managed their social problems. One would not wish to minimize the intensification of misery and impoverishment that these changed specifications of the responsibilities of individuals for their own fate have brought about. It is difficult, for example, to contemplate the terminological change in which the unemployed person has come to be designated a "jobseeker" and the homeless person a "rough sleeper" without cynicism and repugnance. But these neo-liberal programmes that respond to the sufferer as if they were the author of their own misfortune share something with strategies articulated from other political perspectives. From a variety of directions, the disadvantaged individual has come to be seen as potentially and ideally an active agent in the fabrication of their own existence. Those "excluded" from the benefits of a life of choice and self-fulfilment are no longer merely the passive support of a set of social determinations: they are people whose self-responsibility and self-fulfilling aspirations have been deformed by the dependency culture, whose efforts at self-advancement have been frustrated for so long that they suffer from "learned helplessness", whose self-esteem has been destroyed. And, it thus follows, that they are to be assisted not through the ministrations of solicitous experts proffering support and benefit cheques, but through their engagement in a whole array of programmes for their ethical reconstruction as active citizens – training to equip them with the skills of self-promotion, counselling to restore their sense of self-worth and self-esteem, programmes of empowerment to enable them to assume their rightful place as the self-actualizing and demanding subjects of an "advanced" liberal democracy (cf. Cruikshank, this volume).

This is not to suggest that the "making up" of the modern citizen as an active agent in his or her government is in some ways an "invention" of recent political regimes: the conditions for this shift in our "relation to ourselves" are complex, and have no single origin or cause (Rose 1995a, 1995b, cf. Hacking 1986). None the less, the ethical *a priori* of the active citizenship in an active society, this respecification of the ethics of personhood, is perhaps the most fundamental, and most generalizable, characteristic of these new rationalities of government, and one that justifies the assertion that what we are seeing here is not merely the vicissitudes of a single political ideology – that of neo-liberal conservatism – but something with a more general salience, which underpins mentalities of government from all parts of the political spectrum, and which justifies the designation of all these new attempts to "re-invent government" as "advanced liberal".

The power of the governmentalities of the Right over the past two decades lies in the fact that it is the Right, rather than the Left, that has managed to articulate a rationality of government consonant with this new regime of the self, to develop programmes that translate this ethic into strategies for the regulation of precise problems and difficulties such as those in the housing market, or in relation to health, and to invent the technical forms that promise to give effect to it. It is the Right, rather than the Left, that has made the running in relation to a "politics of human technologies", one that does not merely question the relations of power between experts and their subjects but which seeks to give this questioning a technological form. For all the Left critiques of State and social control of the powers of experts and the ills of professional and bureaucratic discretion, it does not yet seem to have been able to propose alternative models for regulating these citizen-shaping devices that answer to the needs of plurality. Is it possible for the Left to provide an alternative rationality for articulating these plural technologies and autonomizing ethics without losing the gains that they represent, yet at the same time providing security for those that they expose? This would require the Left to articulate an alternative ethics and pedagogy of subjectivity that is as compelling as that inherent in the rationality of the market and the "valorization" of choice.

Conclusions

The formulae of liberal government that I have termed "advanced" are much more significant than the brief flowering of neo-liberal political rhetorics may indicate. Although strategies of welfare sought to govern *through society*, "advanced" liberal strategies of rule ask whether it is possible to govern without governing *society*, that is to say, to govern through the regulated and accountable choices of autonomous agents – citizens, consumers, parents, employees, managers, investors – and to govern through intensifying and acting upon their allegiance to particular "communities". As an autonomizing and pluralizing formula of rule, it is dependent upon the proliferation of little regulatory instances across a territory and their multiplication, at a "molecular" level, through the interstices of our present experience. It is dependent, too, upon a particular relation between political subjects and expertise, in which the injunctions of the experts merge with our own projects for self-mastery and the enhancement of our lives.

My aim in this chapter has not been to make a judgement of these new programmes, strategies or relations, but rather to disturb those political logics of Left and Right within which judgement is easy, within which it appears easy and self-evident to be "for" or "against" the present. The "freedom" programmed by recent reconfigurations of power and expertise is certainly no simple liberation of subjects from their dreary confinement by the shackles of political power into the sunny uplands of liberty and community. But neither is it merely an ideological fiction or a rhetorical flourish. I have tried to show that the freedom upon which liberal strategies of government depend, and which they instrumentalize in so many diverse ways, is no "natural" property of political subjects, awaiting only the removal of constraints for it to flower forth in forms that will ensure the maximization of economic and social wellbeing. The practices of modern freedom have been constructed out of an arduous, haphazard and contingent concatenation of problematizations, strategies of government and techniques of regulation. This is not to say that our freedom is a sham. It is to say that the agonistic relation between liberty and government is an intrinsic part of what we have come to know as freedom. And thus, I suggest, a key task for intellectual engagement with contemporary relations of power is the critical analysis of these practices of freedom.

Note

1. In this chapter I have drawn upon three earlier papers written with Peter Miller: Miller & Rose (1989, 1990), Rose & Miller (1992).

References

Adler, M. & S. Asquith (eds) 1981. *Discretion and welfare*. London: Heinemann.

Bacon, R. & S. Eltis 1976. *Britain's economic problems: too few producers?* London: Macmillan.

Burchell, G. 1991. Peculiar interests: civil society and governing "the system of natural liberty". See Burchell et al. (1991), 119–50.

Burchell, G., C. Gordon, P. Miller (eds) 1991. *The Foucault effect: studies in governmentality*. Hemel Hempstead, England: Harvester Wheatsheaf.

Cooley, M. 1980. *Architect or bee: the human/technology relationship*. Slough, England: Langley Technical Services.

Donzelot, J. 1979. *The policing of families* [with a foreword by G. Deleuze]. London: Hutchinson.

Donzelot, J. 1991. The mobilization of society. See Burchell et al. (1991), 169–80.

Ewald, F. 1991. Insurance and risk. See Burchell et al. (1991), 197–210.

Foucault, M. 1977. *Discipline and punish: the birth of the prison*. London: Penguin.

Foucault, M. 1979. *The history of sexuality*, vol. I: *An introduction*. London: Penguin.

Foucault, M. 1980a. The politics of health in the eighteenth century. In *Power/knowledge*, C. Gordon (ed.), 166–82. Brighton: Harvester.

Foucault, M. 1980b. Two lectures. In *Power/knowledge*, C. Gordon (ed.), 78–108. Brighton: Harvester.

Foucault, M. 1981. Omnes et singulatim: towards a criticism of "political reason". In *The Tanner Lectures on human values II*, S. McMurrin (ed.), 223–54. Salt Lake City: University of Utah Press.

Foucault, M. 1989. *Résumés des cours*. Collège de France, Paris.

Foucault, M. 1991. Governmentality. See Burchell et al. (1991), 87–104.

Friedman, M. 1982. *Capitalism and freedom*. Chicago: University of Chicago Press.

Giddens, A. 1990. *Consequences of modernity*. Cambridge: Polity.

Gordon, C. 1980. Afterword. In *Michel Foucault: Power/knowledge*, C. Gordon (ed.), 229–60. Brighton: Harvester.

Gordon, C. 1986. Question, ethos, event: Foucault on Kant and Enlightenment. *Economy and Society* **15**(1), 71–87.

Gordon, C. 1987. The soul of the citizen: Max Weber and Michel Foucault on rationality and government. In *Max Weber, rationality and modernity*, S. Lash & S. Whimster (eds), 293–316. London: Allen & Unwin.

Gordon, C. 1991. Governmental rationality: an introduction. See Burchell et al. (1991),1–52.

Hacking, I. 1986. Making up people. In *Reconstructing individualism*, T. C. Heller et al. (eds), 222–36. Palo Alto, California: Stanford University Press.

Hacking, I. 1991. *The taming of chance*. Cambridge: Cambridge University Press.

Hayek, F. A. 1944. *The road to serfdom*. London: Routledge & Kegan Paul.

Hayek, F. A. 1979. *The constitution of liberty*. London: Routledge & Kegan Paul.

Hirschman, A. 1991. *The rhetoric of reaction*. Cambridge, Mass.: Belknap Harvard.

Hood, C. 1991. A public management for all seasons. *Public Administration* **69**(1), 3–19.

Lash, S. & J. Urry 1994. *Economies of signs and spaces*. Cambridge: Polity.

Latour, B. 1986. The powers of association. In *Power, action and belief*, J. Law (ed.). London: Routledge & Kegan Paul.

Miller, P. & N. Rose 1989. Political rationalities and technologies of government. In *Texts, contexts, concepts*, S. Hanninen & K. Palonen (eds), 171–83. Helsinki: Finnish Political Science Association.

Miller, P. & N. Rose 1990. Governing economic life. *Economy and Society* **19**(1), 1–31.

Murray, C. 1980. *Losing ground: American social policy 1950–1980*. New York: Basic Books.

O'Connor, J. 1972. *The fiscal crisis of the state*. New York: St. Martin's Press.

Oestreich, G. 1982. *Neostoicism and the modern state*. Cambridge: Cambridge University Press.

O'Malley, P. 1992. Risk, power and crime prevention. *Economy and Society* **21**(3), 283–99.

Osborne, T. 1994. Bureaucracy as a vocation: governmentality and administration in nineteenth century Britain. *Journal of Historical Sociology* **7**(3), 289–313.

Parton, N. 1991. *Governing the family: child care, child protection and the State*. London: Macmillan.

Pasquino, P. 1991. "Theatrum Politicum": the genealogy of capital – police and the state of prosperity. See Burchell et al. (1991), 105–18.

Power, M. 1992. The audit society. Paper delivered to London History of the Present Research Network, 4 November 1992.

Power, M. 1994. *The audit society*. London: Demos.

Procacci, G. 1989. Sociology and its poor. *Politics and Society* **17**, 163–87.

Rabinow, P. 1989. *French modern: norms and forms of the social environment*. Cambridge, Mass.: MIT Press.

Reich, C. 1964. Individual rights and social welfare. *Yale Law Journal* **74**, 1245.

Rose, N. 1985. *The psychological complex: psychology, politics and society in England, 1869–1939.* London: Routledge & Kegan Paul.

Rose, N. 1987. Beyond the public/private division: law, power and the family. *Journal of Law and Society* **14**(1), 61–76.

Rose, N. 1990. *Governing the soul: the shaping of the private self.* London: Routledge.

Rose, N. 1992. Governing the enterprising self. In *The values of the enterprise culture: the moral debate*, P. Heelas & P. Morris (eds), 141–64. London: Routledge.

Rose, N. 1993. *Towards a critical sociology of freedom.* Inaugural Lecture delivered on 5 May 1992 at Goldsmiths College, University of London: Goldsmiths College Occasional Paper.

Rose, N. 1994. Eriarvoisuus ja valta hyvinvointivaltion jalkeen (Finnish translation of Disadvantage and power "after the Welfare State"). *Janus* (Journal of the Finnish Society for Social Policy) **1**, 44–68.

Rose, N. 1995a. Authority and the genealogy of subjectivity. In *De-traditionalization: authority and self in an age of cultural change*, P. Heelas, P. Morris, S. Lash (eds). Oxford: Basil Blackwell.

Rose, N. 1995b. Identity, genealogy, history. In *Questions of cultural identity*, S. Hall & P. du Gay (eds). London: Sage.

Rose, N. 1996a. *Inventing our selves: psychology, power and personhood.* Cambridge: Cambridge University Press.

Rose, N. 1996b. The death of the social? Refiguring the territory of government. *Economy and Society*, in press.

Rose, N. & P. Miller 1992. Political power beyond the state: problematics of government. *British Journal of Sociology* **43**(2), 172–205.

Chapter 3
Liberalism, socialism and democracy: variations on a governmental theme

Barry Hindess

> there is nothing more thoroughly harmful to freedom than liberal
> institutions . . . they are the levelling of mountain and valley exalted
> to a moral principle, they make small, cowardly, and smug.
> (Nietzsche 1968: 92)

I

Liberalism is commonly understood as a political doctrine or ideology
concerned with the maximization of individual liberty and, in particular,
with the defence of that liberty against the State.[1] However, following
Foucault's work on governmentality, a number of authors have suggested
a rather different usage based on the idea of a liberal mode of government.[2] This usage suggests first, that the sphere of individual liberty
should be seen, not so much as reflecting the natural liberty of the individual, but rather as a governmental product – that is, as the effect of a
multiplicity of interventions concerned with the promotion of a specific
"form of life" (Dean 1991: 13). It suggests, secondly, that the form of life
in question is centred on the regulative ideal of personal autonomy – a
composite notion including, on the one hand, ideas of personal independence, rationality and responsibility, and on the other, a persistent slippage
between the idea of the person as adult individual and the idea of the person as (male) head of household. Personal autonomy, then, is often understood as involving responsibility for oneself and also for the care and the
behaviour of a few select others – who are accordingly regarded as less
than fully autonomous. The liberal mode of government fosters the form
of life appropriate to a community of such autonomous individuals.

There is clearly an important difference between accounts of liberalism
as, on the one hand, treating government as an evil to be minimized and,

on the other, using government to promote a specific form of life. Nevertheless, there is a sense in which these usages can be seen as relating to aspects of the same phenomena, and I will suggest that the differences between them derive from a fundamental ambiguity in the liberal project. The invocation of figures that are regarded both as natural or historically given realities and as artefacts that may not be fully realized is a ubiquitous feature of political life: consider the status of the "nation" or the "people" in nationalist discourse or of the "working class" in Marxist and many other socialisms. In the discourse of liberal politics in particular, the figure of a community of autonomous individuals appears on the one hand as given reality, serving to identify the character and the limits of legitimate government. On the other hand, it appears as yet to be realized positivity, serving to define the objective for a variety of governmental projects.

One of the central figures of liberal discourse, in other words, has a distinctly ambiguous ontological status. This chapter examines the implications of that ambiguity for the understanding first of liberalism as doctrine and secondly of its relationship to other contemporary doctrines – democracy, socialism and neo-liberalism in particular. Since the figure of the community of autonomous persons considered as given reality tends to dominate standard characterizations of liberalism as doctrine of government, it also plays an important part in the contrasting characterizations of democracy and socialism. We should expect the view of such a community as artefact to produce a rather different picture.

II

Consider, in this section of the chapter, the standard characterizations of liberalism and other political doctrines or ideologies. We may begin with democracy and liberalism since both can be regarded as elaborations on the issue of how a community of autonomous individuals should govern itself – although they work with rather different understandings of autonomy. They are most commonly distinguished by reference to the priority accorded to popular government in the one case and to limited government in the other.

Democracy is a doctrine of government for the people (the *demos*) and usually, if not always, by them.[3] It therefore supposes that the relevant *demos* can be identified and distinguished from other groups and collectivities. A democratic community is usually supposed to be a republic –

in which members of the *demos* are citizens who collectively govern their lives together. The citizens, in other words, exercise what Dahl calls final control over the agenda of government (Dahl 1989: especially Ch. 8) – meaning that the community or agencies that are accountable to the community must be able to decide what matters should be subject to the will of the community and what may safely be left to others. However, to say that members of the *demos* are citizens is also to say that they participate in the affairs of their community as independent persons. There is an obvious tension between these two aspects of the idea of democratic government (Hindess 1991a). The one suggests that there can be no limits to the ends that government might choose to pursue, while the other suggests a case for regarding the independence of citizens as setting limits to the actions of government – on the grounds that otherwise the community of citizens would risk becoming a community of a very different kind.

While in most accounts of liberalism the stress is placed on its character as a doctrine of *limited* government, it is nevertheless a doctrine of *government*. It is also a doctrine of government for the members of the community – if not for "the people" in the manner of democratic thought – since both the activities of government and the limits to those activities are generally thought to promote their interests, and to promote their liberty in particular. The importance of limits is usually argued on one or both of two grounds. One is the claim that the primary task of government is to secure the liberty of its subjects – that requires, of course, that governments be powerful enough both to defend the community against external attack and to defend the liberty of each of its citizens against the actions of others. Many of the distinctive concerns of liberal political thought can then be seen as arising from the fact that a government regarded as powerful enough to secure these aims could also be seen as posing a threat to the liberty of its subjects. The liberal problem then is to build internal restraints into the system of government itself.

The other argument for limited government is based on a perception of the political community as also constituting an entity with a life of its own – an "economy" or a "society" for example – operating according to its own laws and functional requirements. These laws and functional requirements would then be regarded as setting limits to the objectives that governments might realistically set for themselves.

Like democracy, then, liberalism is a doctrine concerned with the government of well-defined political communities of persons who are regarded as being in some sense autonomous. Where the one regards citizens as officers of the community whose civic duties require that they possess a significant degree of autonomy, the other regards autonomy as a natural condition. Where the one understands government primarily as implementing the will of the community, the other understands it essentially as a matter of collective self-control.

Given these characterizations of liberalism and democracy, liberal or representative democracy, as the former name suggests, can then be seen as an uneasy compromise in which the institutions of representative government are supposed to play a major part in satisfying the demands of both positions. On the one hand, in terms of liberalism, representative government and the rule of law might be described as containing the influence of the people within strict limits. Against the tyranny of majority or minority factions, they could be said to secure defences of a kind once associated with estates and the separation of powers. On the other hand, in terms of democracy, representative government could be thought to allow government by the people to be extended to large, geographically dispersed and relatively differentiated populations.

How does socialism as doctrine fit in to this account? Socialism has appeared in many different forms, and what all of these have in common is not much more than a desire to bring economic activity, and therefore property, within the remit of community control – that again requires that the relevant community can be distinguished from others. Socialists have not been much impressed by the liberal vision of the economy as a benignly self-regulating realm of social activity – preferring rather to see it as a field of potentially disruptive forces that must always be carefully controlled. In aiming to subject a significant area of social life to the will of the community, socialism is not unlike democracy. However, socialism has not always identified the relevant community as a community of citizens – that is, as consisting of autonomous persons whose capacity for independent action should be secured.

In fact, the two most influential socialisms of the twentieth century can be distinguished by the position they take on just this issue. On the one hand, social democracy has attempted to manage economic activity while retaining both the commitment to representative democracy and the constitutional restraints of liberal democracy. Communism, on the other hand, has proposed bringing economic activity under popular control while dismissing what it regarded as essentially bourgeois arguments in favour of governmental restraint. The result has been a doctrinal legitimation of political regimes that not only failed to secure the social conditions of autonomous action on the part of their subjects but actively sought to prevent them.

No doubt these distinctions will seem terribly familiar. What should be noted at this point is the role of a particular understanding of liberty or autonomy in distinguishing liberalism as political doctrine from either democracy or socialism. Many self-confessed liberals and earlier political thinkers who have come to be regarded as part of the liberal tradition have presented autonomy both as a natural feature of the human condition – or at least of the condition of the normal adult male – and as a feature that the political community should aim to preserve to the highest degree possible. This view of natural autonomy as political ideal corresponds to an understanding of government as able to operate legitimately only on the basis of the agreement of those autonomous persons who are subject to its power. Legitimate government, in other words, operates primarily by means of injunctions that call on autonomous persons to perform the obligations they have incurred as a result of their (real or implicit) agreement to what amounts to a social contract – that is, it operates through the making of laws and through a variety of more specific commands. A government that failed to act only in this way would then be seen as violating the autonomy of at least some of its subjects. What Foucault calls the juridico-discursive conception of power is implicated in any attempt to reconcile the government of others with the idea of the person as naturally autonomous.[4]

If we take the view of the person that this implies as the key to liberal thought then, the differences between liberalism on the one hand and democracy and socialism on the other appear to take a particularly clear form: where the one acknowledges the natural liberty of the person and aims to defend it against external obstacles, the others threaten to undermine that liberty in the name of what they describe as collective interests and priorities.

III

Unfortunately, there is an obvious difficulty with this elegant account of the differences between liberalism on the one hand and democratic and socialist political thought on the other: what is normally constructed as the tradition of liberal political thought in fact makes considerable use of the idea of the person as a product of social conditions. This is obviously a very different – and potentially contradictory – view of the person from that normally associated with liberalism as outlined above. Furthermore, it involves a rather different understanding of the notion of individual autonomy.

I noted earlier that one of the standard liberal arguments in favour of limited government was based on a perception of the political community as constituting an entity with a life – and therefore with functional exigencies – of its own: an "economy" or a "society". This perspective suggests that failure of government to act within the constraints of those exigencies is likely to produce damaging consequences.[5] Political economy and its successor, economics, have been particularly successful exponents of one major variant of this perspective. Smith's critique of mercantilism in *The wealth of nations* provides a model for a style of argument that has since become familiar. While not disputing the goal of national economic improvement, it maintains that direct governmental action in pursuit of that goal will often prove counter-productive. A proper understanding of the nature of economic activity suggests, in Smith's view, that governments should more appropriately direct their regulation of the economy to securing the conditions under which individuals are free to pursue their own concerns without improper interference. Here the nature of "economic activity" itself is thought to limit the kinds of economic policy that might reasonably be placed on the agenda of government.

A second major variant of this perspective on the political community concerns itself with the moral and other standards that are often thought to regulate the life of the community and are themselves said to be sustained by the interactions that take place within it. Locke's account of the workings of the Law of Opinion and Reputation in *An essay concerning human understanding* is a well-known early elaboration of this type of position. More recent examples include the sociological notion of "society", considered as a realm of social interaction governed by its own distinctive "culture", and Hayek's use of the Humean treatment of language, law and custom as spontaneous social orders serving, like markets, to co-ordinate activities "without deliberate organisation by a commanding intelligence" (Hayek 1960: 159).

The nature of "society" or of these "spontaneous social orders" is regarded as setting limits to government in two rather different ways. First, paralleling liberal accounts of "the economy" as outlined above, there is the view that government interference in the functioning of an order that requires no commanding intelligence carries the risk of damaging social consequences – for example, by undermining the integrity of the moral and other standards on which orderly social interaction normally depends. Secondly, there is the view that governments should themselves be governed by, and held accountable to, the standards of public morality that emerge from the life of what is often now called civil society.[6]

The important point to note here is that this perception of the political community as constituting an entity with a life of its own suggests that the intellectual and moral character of the person is substantially formed in the course of interaction with others – through experience of the gains and losses of economic exchange, of approval and disapproval in the life of civil society, and so on. Locke's *Essay* provides an excellent case in point. Here human individuals are depicted as acting and thinking largely in accordance with acquired habits. These habits are themselves said to be formed in response to repeated experiences of pleasure and pain, the most important of which are occasioned by individuals' interactions with others. This suggests that habits of thought and understandings of what is true and false should be seen as products of social conditioning, rather than as expressions of an intrinsic human rationality. In other words, the human individual is seen as being in large part a creature of social conditions – and to that extent as lacking an essential autonomy.

In fact, many examples of liberal thought do not require the assumption of a natural human autonomy. Rather than establish this point by reference to the original sources, allow me, for reasons of space, to refer first to Larmore's sympathetic account of liberalism as based on a powerful commitment to the virtue of compromise (Larmore 1987) – that is to say, that liberalism entails a certain respect for the integrity of competing standpoints and a corresponding governmental reluctance to impose on them. In effect, it is to accord the advocates of those standpoints a considerable degree of autonomy from direct governmental control. It is only a short step from such a characterization to Schmitt's hostile account of liberalism as a doctrine of government by interminable discussion – i.e. as advocating a mode of decision-making subject to the constraint that the views of minorities should not be overridden by governmental fiat (Schmitt 1985). In these accounts it is not necessary that the promotion of "autonomy" be seen as reflecting an essential feature of the human condition: rather, it need be regarded as little more than a consequence of governmental reluctance to allow certain kinds of dispute to be settled by force.

A similar point may be made with respect to the perception that, while all individuals may have a right to their natural freedom, they are nevertheless born "ignorant and without the use of Reason" (Locke 1988: 305). Locke articulates this claim in the course of a limited defence of parental power, but its force need hardly be restricted to that context. The supposed "natural autonomy" of individuals is all too easily seen as something that may be imperfectly realized in practice: prevented from developing by obstacles located in the character of the individuals themselves or by a variety of external factors such as debilitating illness or economic insecurity, and relations of enforced dependence on others (dependence on government in particular).

In fact, Locke's account of the formation of the moral and other standards by which we regulate our behaviour in *An essay concerning human understanding* can also be seen as suggesting ways in which some of the internal obstacles to autonomy might be overcome – and this is made explicit in his discussions of education and his proposal for reform of the Poor Law.[7] This connection between theoretical discussion and practical advice that we find in parts of Locke's work can also be identified in the more recent discourses of political economy, economics and the human sciences. While these discourses represent the person as heteronomous creature of social conditions, they also suggest conditions likely to promote patterns of rationality, self-control and personal responsibility in particular individuals and collectivities. In short, they suggest ways of turning people into "autonomous" and calculable members of society, able to be left for the most part to regulate their own behaviour.

It would not be difficult to present a history of the great nineteenth- and twentieth-century experiments in social policy in exactly these terms. Indeed, this is precisely what Marshall does in his well-known depiction of modern British social policy as a matter of the rights involved in what he saw as the full realization of citizenship (Marshall 1950). Social rights, in this account, complete the citizenship package by securing both the internal conditions (through the knowledge and character formation provided by the system of compulsory education) and the external conditions (through policies on housing, welfare and income support) under which all adult members can participate in the life of the community as independent persons. On this view, the fundamental purpose of social policy is to ensure that the legal and political community is also a community of citizens.

Together with a whole tradition of British social policy analysis, Marshall offers a participatory, welfarist gloss to the practices of what the authors noted at the beginning of this chapter have called a liberal mode of government – a mode of government that aims to work through, and must therefore work to realize, a community of independent persons. In this type of analysis, autonomy comes to be seen not simply as a presupposition of full community membership, and therefore of the liberal mode of governance, but also as a practical accomplishment of that governance.

IV

Liberalism, then, presents us with at least two distinct images of the relationship between a community of autonomous persons and its government. In the first, autonomy is regarded as a matter both of personal freedom and of rationality, and it appears as a natural feature of the human condition. Reference to a community of autonomous persons thus serves to define both the character of legitimate government and its principal mode of action. In other words, it gives us what Foucault calls the juridico-discursive conception of power.

In the second image – precisely because the person is regarded as one whose habits of thought and patterns of behaviour are formed and regulated in the course of interaction with others – the figure of a community of autonomous persons can appear as the (realized or projected) artefact of a variety of governmental practices. The form of government appropriate to an existing community would then be seen as one that acts on its subjects from a distance in so far as they could reasonably be regarded as already autonomous, and acts on them more directly in so far as their autonomy is seen as something that has yet to be realized. Reference to personal autonomy then plays a part, first, in the definition of behavioural norms, both for the subject population and for government agencies, and, secondly, in the construction of programmes for the normalization of those in the subject population whose behaviour fails to conform.

The figure of the community of autonomous persons, in other words, appears ambiguously in liberal discourse as a reality that is the basis of government in some contexts and as artefact of government practices in others. In fact this ambiguity in liberal attitudes towards government has often been noted: it can be seen, for example, in the distinction noted at the beginning of this chapter between liberalism as doctrine and liberalism as mode of government.

The more important point to recognize is that recourse to figures of such ambiguous ontological status is in no way peculiar to liberalism.[8] It is clear, for example, that the figure of the community of autonomous persons plays a remarkably similar role in democratic (and social democratic) discourse. In fact, some of the most powerful political projects in the modern period have been articulated in terms of collectivities that are treated in some contexts as if they were natural or historically given realities and in other contexts as if they were artefacts that had yet to be fully realized – "nations", "peoples", "the working class" and "women" are familiar examples. In the relevant discourses they appear at times as objective realities producing effects in the present and possessing interests that can or should be represented by some party or movement. At other times they appear as collectivities that do not (or do no longer) properly exist. In the one case practical decisions may be taken on the basis of what are thought to be the "natural" or essential features of such entities and their current situation, while in the other case the practical issue is how to create or re-create these collectivities.

The ambiguous ontological status of one of its central figures, then, should not itself be regarded as a distinctive feature of liberal discourse. What is distinctive is the fact that the ambiguity in this case turns on the notion of autonomy. There are several points to notice here. First, whether understood as given reality or as presently unrealized, the liberal figure of the community of autonomous individuals is readily, and indeed normally, assimilated to other representations of the political community in question – for example, as a "people" or a "nation" with its own distinctive "culture". This means, of course, that many government programmes that might be represented in liberal terms as promoting the formation of a community of autonomous persons could also be represented as promoting the formation of a distinctive national community.

A related point is that there is no necessary connection between support for the promotion of particular kinds of autonomous behaviour and commitment to a notion of natural human autonomy. This too reflects a common feature of political life: objectives or even principles that achieve a broad range of political support are usually open to a variety of interpretations that make it possible for them to be supported for a number of different reasons (Hindess 1991b). I noted earlier that democratic thought usually involves some notion of the citizen as an autonomous agent – without necessarily regarding that autonomy as a natural feature of the (male) human condition. While governmental programmes promoting certain kinds of autonomy as artefact may be seen by liberals as removing internal or external obstacles to natural human autonomy, they may also be supported by civic republicans, democrats or socialists, each for reasons of their own.

Notice finally that the ambiguous representation of autonomy both as natural and as artefact produces a characteristic tension of its own. To see what is at issue here consider first the closely related treatment of autonomy in Nietzsche's fiercely anti-liberal writings. I began this chapter with an extract from one of his polemics describing liberalism as a matter of institutions that have the effect of levelling and normalization, which he sees as resulting in "reduction to the herd animal".[9] In other parts of his work such conditions are presented as if they were necessary for the emergence of a capacity for self-control – and therefore for the appearance of the autonomous individual:

> The task of breeding an animal with the right to make promises presupposes as a preparatory task that one first *makes* men to a certain degree necessary, uniform, like among like, regular, and consequently calculable. (Nietzsche 1967: essay 2, s.2)

If individuals are to be able to commit their future action, they must first of all be able to experience their own behaviour as calculable and predictable. Nietzsche's point is that condition should not be taken for granted. It is possible only as the outcome of a long history of discipline and regimentation.

The liberal institutions that Nietzsche condemns from one perspective as the antithesis of freedom can therefore be seen from another perspective as if they secured precisely the conditions from which it may be possible for the sovereign individual to emerge. Nietzsche's sovereign individual is the "ripest fruit" of pervasive conditions of subordination and control. Nietzsche also takes the view that very few individuals will take advantage of the opportunity to liberate themselves. You can bring a horse to water, but you cannot make it drink.

The tension so clearly represented in Nietzsche's work in fact appears wherever "autonomy" is represented both as essentially human and as artefactual. Once autonomy can be represented in this second way, as the product of particular conditions, then it can also be seen as heteronomy, as a state in which individuals' decisions and actions are subject to determinations that lie beyond their control – that is, as a negation of real autonomy. The result is that conditions that could be seen as promoting autonomy in one sense can also be seen as undermining it in another: programmes of welfare provision that could be defended on Marshallian grounds as securing conditions in which all adults can participate as independent persons in the life of the community are notoriously vulnerable to the claim that they promote a culture of dependency; aspects of schooling designed to promote discipline and self-control might also be seen as inhibiting the capacity for free expression (and conversely, the promotion of free expression at one stage can be seen as frustrating the habits of self-discipline needed for the development of more complex capacities at a later stage), and so on.

75

The difference is a function of the ambiguity of the notion of autonomy itself – that is, of the central defining trope of the liberal project. In one case the focus is on the "natural" status of human autonomy, and therefore on behaviour that is subject to no involuntary constraint. In the other case the focus is on the "artefactual" status of autonomy, and therefore on the conditions under which it may be created.

V

These points suggest that the difference between the two accounts of liberalism noted at the beginning of this chapter should be seen as arising out of a fundamental ambiguity in the notion of individual autonomy – considered on the one hand as a natural or historical given and on the other as an artefact that may not be fully realized.

Where does this leave the distinctions between liberalism and other positions as set out in the initial sections of this chapter? If, as Foucault suggests, there is no distinctively socialist technology of government, then the conclusion must be that there is also a sense in which the same could be said of liberalism. Most if not all of the governmental devices that might be seen as falling under the heading of the liberal mode of government could be and were supported by those who had no particular commitment to liberalism as doctrine.

I noted earlier that the two most influential of twentieth-century socialisms could be distinguished in part by their attitudes towards individual autonomy. On the one side, communism deliberately set out to prevent autonomous action in certain respects – while also of course actively promoting it in others. Much the same is true of National Socialism. The extent to which the Nazi policy of extermination was able to work through the active and rational co-operation of the Jewish community is an object lesson in the governmental use and promotion of "autonomy" as artefact for decidedly non-liberal purposes.[10]

On the other side, social democracy aimed to work through and therefore to promote a community of autonomous persons – although without always taking autonomy to be the single most important political value. It is interesting to note in this context that liberalism and social democracy have been able to present themselves as competing rationalities of government in the second half of the twentieth century, since both have taken the view that government for the most part has to work in and through a community of autonomous persons, and both, again for the most part, have been able to take the existence of a suitably calculable population of citizens more or less for granted. Both, in other words, have depended on the more or less successful workings of what has been called the "liberal mode of government" in producing such a population. This fact serves to distinguish liberalism and social democracy from rationalities of government that make other assumptions about the subject population and also, of course, to define the limits to their applicability – i.e. to populations already rendered to some considerable degree (in Nietzsche's words) "uniform, . . . regular, and consequently calculable".

In this respect, the account of liberalism as acknowledging the natural autonomy of the individual and therefore insisting on a corresponding view of the limited role of government gives rise to a misleadingly sharp set of demarcations between liberalism on the one hand and democracy and social democratic versions of socialism on the other. Precisely because it represents the autonomy of members of the subject population as given, this view of the individual takes no account of the pervasive workings of the artefactual mechanisms that produce and sustain whatever habits and forms of autonomy members of the population actually enjoy – except perhaps to criticize the workings of these mechanisms in particular cases. The clear implication of the present argument is that on the contrary, what these rationalities of government take for granted, and therefore what they have in common, may be more significant than the more obvious doctrinal points on which they differ.

Finally, what of the more recent rise of neo-liberalism? It would be tempting to interpret this simply as a counterpoint to the decline of the Left. In that respect it would be a product of the same conditions that have generated a widespread loss of support for, and an equally widespread loss of faith in, political programmes that seemed to rely on the effectiveness of a broadly Keynesian programme of economic management to provide the foundation for mildly egalitarian and welfarist social policies.

Such an interpretation would not be unreasonable, but it would certainly be incomplete. The neo-liberal insistence on market mechanisms entails a repudiation of social programmes that many liberals of an earlier generation – along with social democrats and others – worked to promote. In this respect, neo-liberalism appears to involve a shift of focus within liberalism itself. It is more than just the resurgence of an earlier liberalism following a period of left-öf-centre ascendancy. An important part of the difference, I suggest, relates to the tension noted earlier that is generated by the representation of autonomy both as given reality and as artefact. Against the background of conditions in which the great nineteenth- and twentieth century social policy regimes were set in place, many governmental programmes now repudiated by neo-liberalism could plausibly be represented as promoting autonomy. Against a very different contemporary background in which, at least in the more advanced Western societies, the existence of a suitably calculable population is easily taken for granted, these same programmes can be seen as undermining autonomy. Neo-liberalism is a liberal response to the achievements of the liberal mode of government.

Notes

1. I am grateful to Doug McEachern, Nikolas Rose and the anonymous referees of *Economy and Society* for their comments on an earlier version of this chapter, and especially to Christine Helliwell for her efforts to clarify and to improve the argument of this published version.
2. See papers by Burchell and Gordon in Burchell, Gordon and Miller (1991), Dean (1991), Rose & Miller (1992), Minson (1985).
3. Pericles' funeral oration is a celebration of Athens as a democracy, which he presents as a society governed *for* its people but clearly not *by* them.
4. See my *Discourses of power: Hobbes to Foucault* (Hindess 1995).
5. Where liberalism tends to regard the "economy" and other supposedly self-regulating aspects of the life of the community as naturally existing in a relationship of mutual accommodation – and therefore as both supporting its arguments for limited government – the contrary view is by no means uncommon. Conservatives and socialists, for example, have insisted that an unconstrained "economy" presents a serious threat to the existing order, and perhaps even to the life, of "society". Polanyi (1957), provides one of the clearest examples of this perspective. For a more recent case consider Habermas's (1984, 1987) treatment of the "mediatization" of the life-world.
6. See the discussion of the emergence of this perception of government in Koselleck (1988).
7. Locke 1969 [1876]. See also the discussion in Ivison (1993) and Tully (1989). Many of the writings of J. S. Mill address the internal and external obstacles to liberty from a later, and rather different, liberal perspective.
8. Nor, of course, is it restricted to political discourses. The ambiguity noted in this chapter is one element in a larger set of confusions in Western thought concerning distinctions between features of social life that are thought to be natural and those that are thought to be social or historical. See the careful discussion of these issues in Helliwell (1995).

9. See the commentary in Ansell-Pearson (1991).
10. The evidence is extensively surveyed, from a somewhat different perspective, in Bauman (1991).

References

Ansell-Pearson, K. 1991. Nietzsche on autonomy and morality. *Political Studies* **34**, 270–87.

Bauman, Z. 1991. *Modernity and the Holocaust*. Cambridge: Polity.

Burchell, G., C. Gordon, P. Miller (eds) 1991. *The Foucault effect: studies in governmentality*. Chicago: University of Chicago Press.

Dahl, R. A. 1989. *Democracy and its critics*. New Haven, Connecticut: Yale University Press.

Dean, M. 1991. *The constitution of poverty. Toward a genealogy of liberal governance*. London: Routledge.

Habermas, J. 1984, 1987. *The theory of communicative action*. [2 volumes]. Boston: Beacon Press.

Hayek, F. A. 1960. *The constitution of liberty*. London: Routledge & Kegan Paul.

Helliwell, C. J. 1995. Autonomy as natural equality: inequality in "egalitarian" societies. *Journal of the Royal Anthropological Institute* **1**(2), 359–76.

Hindess, B. 1991a. Imaginary presuppositions of democracy. *Economy and Society* **20**, 173–95.

Hindess, B. 1991b. Taking socialism seriously. *Economy and Society* **20**, 363–79.

Hindess, B. 1995. *Discourses of power: Hobbes to Foucault*. Oxford: Basil Blackwell.

Ivison, D. 1993. Liberal conduct. *History of the Human Sciences* **6**, 25–59.

Koselleck, R. 1988. *Critique and crisis. Enlightenment and the pathogenesis of modern society*. Oxford: Berg.

Larmore, C. E. 1987. *Patterns of moral complexity*. Cambridge: Cambridge University Press.

Locke, J. 1969 [1876]. A Report of the Board of Trade to the Lords Justices Respecting the Relief and Employment of the Poor (1697). In *The life and times of John Locke*, H. R. Fox-Bourne. Darmstadt [London]: Scientia Verlag Aalen.

Locke, J. 1988. *Two treatises of government*. Cambridge: Cambridge University Press.

Marshall, T. 1950. *Citizenship and social class*. Cambridge: Cambridge University Press.

Minson, J. 1985. *Genealogies of morals. Nietzsche, Foucault, Donzelot and the eccentricity of ethics*. London: Macmillan.

Nietzsche, F. 1967. *On the genealogy of morals*. New York: Random House.

Nietzsche, F. 1968. *Twilight of the idols*. London: Penguin.

Polanyi, K. 1957. *The great transformation*. Boston: Beacon Press.

Rose, N. & P. Miller. 1992. Political power beyond the State: problematics of government. *British Journal of Sociology* **43**(2), 173–205.

Schmitt, C. 1985. *The crisis of parliamentary democracy.* Cambridge, Mass.: MIT Press.

Tully, J. 1989. Governing conduct. In *Conscience and casuistry in early modern Europe*, E. Leites (ed.), 12–71. Cambridge: Cambridge University Press.

Chapter 4
The promise of liberalism and the performance of freedom

Vikki Bell[1]

... between the original "I will", "I shall do this" and the actual dis-
charge of the will, its *act*, a world of strange new things, circumstances, even acts of will may be interposed without breaking this
long chain of will. But how many things this presupposes! To
ordain the future in advance in this way, man must first have
learned to distinguish necessary events from chance ones, to think
causally, to see and anticipate distant eventualities as if they
belonged to the present, to decide with certainty what is the goal
and what the means to it, and in general be able to calculate and
compute. Man himself must first of all have become calculable,
regular, necessary, even in his own image of himself, if he is to be
able to stand security for his own future, which is what one who
promises does! (Nietzsche 1967 [1887]: 58)

I

An undelivered promise is not failed but unkept: a lie. The flame of liberal
politics – heat both necessary and dangerous for such an order – is kin-
dled at this point. More than its rivals, liberalism is grounded upon man's
capacity to promise, for liberal democracy advocates a world in which
social order rests crucially upon the citizenry's faith in the good con-
sciences of those who govern. That liberalism rests upon this capacity to
promise, and on the related notion of a conscience, is the locus between
liberalism's present and its future – its vision – creating its sense of causality and temporality. More broadly, this vision entails a general promise, a
promise of happiness to the citizen who partakes in his own freedom.
According to Adorno & Horkheimer, liberalism's promise of happiness
to those without power cheated and mocked the masses; the repeated
suppression of their longing encrypts a destructive lust for a civilization

as yet unachieved, a lust in danger of becoming fascistic (Adorno & Horkheimer 1979 [1944]: 172). Liberalism is fuelled, then, both by its general promise and by the specific promises of those entrusted with power. It requires a sense of calculability about the world and its inhabitants that enables such promises to be made and believed. Any moment of disbelief, any lack of faith in another's promise, is a moment that liberalism can contain – indeed, that it invites – but it is also the most fearful moment for the liberal machinery, the moment at which the general vision is doubted and alternative paths left and right are dreamt and drawn. Thus liberalism contains a necessary but potentially destabilizing point at which the ability to make promises joins the ability to hesitate and, by the tracing of lines of causality, to imagine the future differently. The possibility of beginning anew, the possible moment at which promises are exchanged and plans laid down, is a profoundly political moment, one that Hannah Arendt valued as having the potential to enable political communication and community – the move from the "I will" to the "we can" (Arendt 1963, see also Miller 1979). But truly beginning anew – the true performance of freedom – is arguably incompatible with the notion of calculable man upon which the ability to promise rests, and clashes with the supposition of a clarity of thought and will that is represented by the "many-headed one" (the phrase is Arendt's in 1963: 72) of liberalism constituted by, or standing in for, individual wills. The freedom offered and defended by liberal rhetoric is a freedom that is entwined with these images of a subject whose integrity is an impossible perfection, a subject who can be calculated and predicted into the future at the same time as he or she has a clarity of thought and will that directs these very promises and predictions.

Foucault's distance from liberalism takes a cue from Nietzsche, in the sense that the two share the suspicion of the liberal citizen as a package for freedom. Foucault takes that suspicion as the impetus for the interrogation of the calculation to which Nietzsche refers and which surrounds the liberal citizen as variously conceived. Once one refuses this notion of predictability, once one positions it as "merely" a way of speaking and acting towards the subject, part of a certain way of practising liberal citizenry, then the notion of freedom within such an order becomes a contested one. The notion that liberalism's most triumphantly held trophy – that it allows its citizens to participate on the basis of opposition and discontent – might be freedom enough, is anathema to Foucault's purpose. Such a picture trusts the machinery of representation as the guarantor of freedom, while simultaneously it presents a notion of true freedom somewhere in the future. Instead, Foucault writes in an attempt to move away from the notion that freedom can be given a grounding in the subject who thinks, protests and awaits. The encrypted longing that such a view suggests is a version of the repressive hypothesis against which Foucault set so much of his later work.

Those who seek a more overtly political inflection to Foucault's work might mistake his project for a contribution versioned around the dialectical tradition that proceeds by the schema of recognize, rally and reconstruct. The calls for a strategy or escape route from the networks of bio-political techniques, from disciplinary modes of normalization and judgement or from individualization, tend to be coded in the very terms from which Foucault flees. And such debates have not taken us far, with alignments taking place around an axis formed predictably enough between Foucault and Habermas. Yet it would be churlish to deny that the debates revolve around a nagging issue in Foucault's work. For there is a persistence of the question of freedom in Foucault, a question that he turns to without sustained attention, but frequently.

There is, seemingly, a paradox in Foucault's thought around the concept of freedom, which has meant that the commentary that has flowed in his wake has tended to tell two differing stories. On the one hand, Foucault has been cast as a pessimist, because he suggested that narratives of escaping strategies of power are themselves entangled in power/knowledge networks, as in, for example, his retelling of psychoanalysis in *The history of sexuality*, vol. I. Or because, having detailed the micro-physics of power, such as the analyses in *Discipline and punish*, Foucault refused to present strategies for escape. On the other, however, Foucault's point was to show us that we are "freer than we think we are"; that radical political and psychoanalytic thought has led us to conceptualize our freedom as curtailed or repressed, such that true freedom becomes figured as the totalized breaking out of a current state of repression or oppression, and as an absence of any determinacy. But such a zero sum conception of power is one that has limited our political visions, directing them away from the possibilities in the present and on to the hope of some future radical change. If political theorizing follows such a notion, the all-consuming image of power misses the opportunity to understand the glimmers of hope that open up as one moves amongst and between the techniques by which power relations attempt but never truly succeed in "holding" their pattern. This more optimistic telling of Foucault's arguments attends genealogically to the present in order to see the contingency of power, its points of weakness and the possibilities of change. The articulation of this second position clings to those moments at which Foucault seemed to represent his work with respect to future possibilities, such as the moment in *The history of sexuality*, vol. I, where he speaks of bodies and pleasures as somehow grounds of resistance, and of life always escaping bio-power. Or the interviews in which he suggested that one can experiment in going "beyond" by adopting "an attitude, an ethos, a philosophical life in which what we are is at one and the same time the historical analysis of the limits that are imposed upon us and an experiment in going beyond them" (Foucault, in Rabinow 1984: 50). Mostly, however, this version of Foucault has attended to his later works where, it is argued, he begins to detail a practice of freedom that is a mode of liberation involving the related concepts of an aesthetics of existence and techniques of the self.

This debate can be refigured as one concerned with what might be termed the temporality of freedom. As I have suggested elsewhere, Foucault became interested in the relationship that has been established between "the modern subject" and his/her present (Bell 1994). Although that relationship, posed in terms of a present self-interrogation – "Who are we now?" – has been accompanied by a question of the future and of freedom – Kant's further question "What may I hope for?" – Foucault attempted to remain with the initial question. He did so not in order to provide a more accurate answer than has hitherto been available, but in order to trace how such an enquiry has become *the* way of understanding our being in the world, and in order to ask what that way of posing the question has meant in terms of the modes of politics and conceptions of the subject it deploys (see his essay on Kant's "What is Enlightenment?": Foucault 1984). For Foucault was interested in the ways in which we conceptualize our political strategies, and the ways in which we turn ourselves into subjects located within time (Foucault 1982). Agamben has put the distinction between a historical materialist perspective and that of Foucault's succinctly: "man is not a historical being because he falls into time, but precisely the opposite; it is only because he is a historical being that he can fall into time, temporalizing himself" (Agamben 1993: 99).

Those modes of thinking that pose freedom as the other side of a future and totalized break mobilize a form of (modern) discourse that understands its present as tending towards some event or events, be that apocalyptic, revolutionary or monotony, that can be effected, avoided or brought about by action in the present. Foucault's position would suggest that such a mode of thought is a mode of temporalizing oneself with respect to the present and the future. Peter Osborne has suggested that the characteristically modern attitude is one that speaks of the "new" in modernity not simply as recent or chronologically new but *historically* new, something qualitatively different about the present. This is why modernity is so interlinked with theories of progress, even as it is also always haunted by the idea of decline (Osborne 1994; the title is a quotation from Adorno). Modernity is not a category of history but is an infinite task, a way of attempting to come to terms with the present in its presentness. Moreover, the task of "being modern" is linked up with questions of validation and justification; it is epistemological and political, entwined with the questions "How do you know?" and "What are the consequences of acting in this way?" Rather than extending this enquiry, Foucault's interrogations were concerned with the investigation of the spaces – discursive and non-discursive – that sustain such an anxious ethos. Why is it, he asked, that we attempt to understand our worlds through the schema that rests upon these particular assumptions about the operations of power, the nature of history and our capacity to act?

Thus Foucault's work became in part an exploration of the problem of freedom outside the view of subjectivity and the concept of will so central to liberal philosophy and institutionalized practice. Once the ability to promise and to predict into the future is doubted, one is left in the sea of the present, and with the adoption of a more sceptical attitude towards political designs on the future, the condemnation to be free in this present is in effect, and necessarily, about a mode of remaining somehow without complacency. Arguably, Foucault's concern in his later work was to investigate this state through the notion of practising one's liberty, and through that exploration, to argue that there is in a sense a *political* space that arises in the relation of self to self. Without rehearsing the argument here, it can be said that, according to Foucault, in antiquity the search for an ethics of existence was mainly an attempt to affirm one's liberty and to give one's own life a certain form in which "one could recognize oneself and which could be recognized by others"; it was "essentially a practice, a style of liberty"(Foucault 1988b: 49). This elaboration of one's own life "as a personal work of art", even though it related to the common prescriptive texts, was to be, with Christianity, increasingly replaced with an idea of morality in the form of a code of rules (ibid.: 49). However,

> for a whole series of reasons, the idea of a morality as obedience to a code of rules is now disappearing, has already disappeared. And to this absence of morality corresponds, must correspond, the search for an aesthetics of existence. (ibid.: 49)

Foucault's interest in antiquity was therefore premised on a contemporary reflection about the changing nature of morality. The idea of an aesthetics of existence in Foucault's later work (1986, 1988a) is not a solution to the analyses of power of which he had previously written (1977, 1981). It is, however, concerned with how one lives a freedom in one's present. In *The use of pleasures*, Foucault describes the reflection on sexual behaviour of that time as "a means of developing – from the smallest minority of the population made up of free, adult males – an aesthetics of existence, the *purposeful art of a freedom* perceived as a power game" (Foucault 1986: 252–3, emphasis added). As such, "aesthetics of existence" is related to what he referred to as his "distrust" of the theme of liberation:

> I do not mean to say that liberation or such and such a form of liberation does not exist. When a colonial people tries to free itself of its colonizer, that is truly an act of liberation, in the strict sense of the word. But we also know that . . . this act of liberation is not suffi-cient to establish the *practices of liberty* that later on will be necessary for this people, this society and this individual to decide upon receivable and acceptable forms of their existence or political society. (Foucault 1988b: 2–3, emphasis added)

The aesthetics of existence is a mode of practising liberty that takes the performance of freedom as the opportunity to open up the political. It is purposeful, but not – or not only – the expression of a will. The space between self and self is politicized as freedom, is *presented* both in the sense of tying freedom to the present and in the sense of performing or gifting freedom; that performance or show of freedom is what makes the practice of liberty aesthetic. Foucault uses these texts to suggest the possibility of thinking politics outside the model, in which the citizen's thought is re-presented on a separate stage, as it were, disembodied and located at an analytically higher plane. Where the notion of will is replaced by a performance, the issue of representation carries different corollaries. Aesthetically speaking, the representation of many bodies by one is an impossibility. Temporally speaking, the representation of a practice can-not be carried over in the way that opinion can; it needs the space of time.

However, the practice of liberty is not a set of activities that could ever be exhausted by the notion of an aesthetics of self. In the very interview that Foucault speaks of the aesthetics of existence, he also suggested participation in the present political machinery was also a form of the practice of liberty. We can demand, he says, "the *parrhesia* (free speech) of the governed, who can and must question those who govern them, in the name of knowledge, the experience they have, by virtue of being citizens, of what those who govern do, of the meaning of their action, of the decisions they have taken" (Foucault 1988b: 51–2). Having said this, I would not wish to dilute Foucault's attempt to move away from a concept of freedom as based on the expression of will. In order to further investigate this impulse within Foucault's work, I want to set his thought alongside that of Hannah Arendt, another political theorist who also took a cue from Nietzsche, who has the same Heideggerian backdrop, and whose arguments touched on similar issues, although, I shall argue, with different theoretical consequences for the notion of freedom and of politics.

II

Perhaps the easiest place to begin a discussion of Arendt is with her dismissive attitude towards Rousseau, which is, partially, due to the fact that his vision of liberal democracy presumes an individual whose opinion is formed independently of other citizens. There should be no communication between citizens if the process of general will is to operate as Rousseau described, that is, if the general will is to be a faithful abstraction that arises upward, and only ever upward, from the wills of individual citizens. Communication cannot operate sideways. As such, the general promise of freedom presented by Rousseau entails an individualism that conceives of political power as a translation of individual will-power into the generalized, non-individualistic (because without a body *per se*) but still sovereign power; in effect, another form of will-power (Arendt 1961: 163). In "The social contract" Rousseau wrote,

> In reality, if it is not impossible for a particular will to agree on some point with the general will, it is at least impossible for the agreement to be lasting and constant; for the particular will tends, by its very nature, to partiality, while the general will tends toward equality. It is even more impossible to have any guarantee of this agreement; for even if it should always exist, it would be the effect not of art, but of chance. The Sovereign may indeed say: "I will actually what this man wills, or at least what he says he wills"; but it cannot say: "What he wills tomorrow, I too shall will" because it is absurd for the will to bind itself for the future, nor is it incumbent on any will to consent to anything that is not for the good of the being who

wills. If then the people promises to obey, by that very act it dissolves itself and loses what makes it a people; the moment a master exists, there is no longer a Sovereign, and from that moment the body politic has ceased to exist. (Rousseau 1973 [1762]: 200)

Sovereignty, then, rests not with any particular individual nor even with a group of individuals, but with the general will, with the body politic as a whole. That will only ever properly exists in the present; it is "*absurd* for the will to bind itself for the future". The body politic, in other words, is placed in a position in which it has to agree to temporary obedience, to trust in the promises that are issued it. The hope of the body politic is future-orientated and its obedience provisional; the articulation of the general will has therefore to maintain its credibility by offering not simply reflection but promises. Any one specific promise may not be the echo of any one individual's will – this is Rousseau's point – but the general promise of liberalism is that participation delivers a freedom more profound than the satisfaction of a personal or specific aim achieved.

Arendt's objection to classic liberalism turns on the sense in which participation and the Rousseaunian achievement of freedom involve an individualistic project based on an untenable concept of will-power. Her concept of freedom, by contrast, places interaction and concerted performance centre stage. In her essay "What is freedom?" Arendt begins with the paradox by which citizens of liberal orders orientate themselves to the world as if they had the capacity to act responsibly, to be free, although at the same time there is a sense that such an actor is never a credible figure, since everyday life is an experience of causation. Especially in political matters, the freedom of the citizen is evoked, and it is "on this axiomatic assumption that laws are laid down in human communities, that decisions are taken, that judgements passed" (Arendt 1961: 143). In scientific and theoretical endeavour, however, the no less self-evident truth is constantly underscored that

even "our own lives are, in the last analysis, subject to causation" and that if there should be an ultimately free ego in ourselves, it certainly never makes its unequivocal appearance in the phenomenal world, and therefore can never become the subject of theoretical ascertainment. (Arendt 1961: 143–4)

The Kantian solution to this non-appearance was the institution of a division between "pure" or theoretical reason, which can never be known or seen in the phenomenal world, and a "practical reason" that is based upon free will. However, argues Arendt, not only does such a formulation result in the strange position that the faculty of the will – "whose essential activity consists in dictate and command" – becomes the harbourer of freedom, but such a solution also does little to tackle the sense in which "thought itself . . . makes freedom disappear" (1961: 145), because reflection upon the world cannot but make acts appear causal.

Moreover, Arendt insists, attempts to revise a philosophical tradition that has posited freedom as essentially an inner domain identified as a person's capacity to do what s/he *wills*, via a notion of an inner *sense* of freedom, become politically speaking irrelevant. Such a sense is a retreat from the world, an inwardness that finds absolute freedom within one's own self. Historically, Arendt suggests, this sense of freedom was one propounded by those who had no place or property in the world, the prerequisites for freedom (1961: 146–7). It is a conception of freedom that values an inner dialogue, an isolated, solitary contemplation. For Arendt, any retreat to an inner sense of freedom is not a solution but merely a response to a lack of freedom in intercourse with others. Freedom "is actually the reason that men live together at all. Without it, political life would be meaningless. The *raison d'etre* of politics is freedom, and its field of experience is action" (1961: 146).

This is the point at which Arendt indicates her commitment to a concept of public space, a space within which men meet in order to speak and act freely as a body politic:

> Without a politically guaranteed public realm, freedom lacks the worldly space to make its appearance. To be sure it may dwell in men's hearts as desire or will or hope or yearning; but the human heart, as we all know, is a very dark place, and whatever goes on in its obscurity can hardly be called a demonstrable fact. Freedom as a demonstrable fact and politics coincide and are related to each other like two sides of the same coin. (Arendt 1961: 149)

Arendt argues this position against one that would regard freedom as the opposite of politics, as defined by an *absence* of politics. The modern age has attempted to divorce freedom from politics, she argues, placing freedom outside or beyond the sphere of the political, and regarding people's engagement in politics as the result of a mistrust of those with power, rather than the result of a love of freedom (1961: 150).

Engagement within the public sphere enables freedom to become manifest. For freedom is not, according to Arendt, about the ability to choose between two given things, but is about the ability to "call something into being which did not exist before, which was not given, not even as an object of cognition or imagination" (1961: 151). Action "insofar as it is free, is neither under the guidance of the intellect nor under the dictate of the will – although it needs both for the execution of any particular goal" (1961: 152). Arendt prefers to place centre stage the concept of principle. Principles differ from motives because they do not issue from within, but rather from outside the self in a generalized manner. They are, therefore, unlike any specific political aim. The inspiring principle becomes fully manifest only in the performance, losing none of its strength in that performance (as will and judgement do); the principle is universal and inexhaustible. Arendt gives as her examples, honour, glory, love of equality, distinction, excellence, but also "fear or distrust or hatred" (1961: 152). Freedom is manifest only in its act – "men are free – as distinguished from possessing the gift of freedom – as long as they act, neither before nor after; for to be free and to act are the same" (1961: 153).

This performance of freedom, its virtuosity, needs to *appear*, to be witnessed, in order for it to be political. Moreover, "everything that occurs in that space of appearances is political by definition, even when it is not a direct product of action" (1961: 155). This public realm of political action is one that is not about necessity and the safeguarding of life processes. It differs from the private realm in this respect where security "of family and home" is paramount. The public realm "cannot afford to give primary concern to individual lives and the interests connected with them"; here we have arrived in a realm where the concern for life has lost its validity. One needs courage, because it liberates men "from the worry about life for freedom of the world. Courage is indispensable because in politics not life but the world is at stake" (1961: 156).

Arendt expresses the import of the public realm by describing it as the "guarantee against the futility of individual life, the space protected against this futility and reserved for the relative permanence, if not immortality, of mortals" (1958: 56). Questions of necessity – bodily, "life" issues – can therefore never be questions of freedom. When Arendt praises the story of the American Revolution over the French, it is partly because the social question was absent from the colonists' demands for an American constitution (Wolin 1990: 297–8). Further, the American Declaration of Independence is a performative utterance. The new regime's authority arose from the performative "we hold" and not from the constitutive reference to self-evident truths; this results in a new political community that constitutes itself as a "we" (Honig 1992: 217). This new political community is one that is about the capacity to promise and to begin anew. It is about the acting out of a principle, a practice of freedom through mutual co-operation.

> The principle which came to light during those fateful years when the foundations were laid – not by one architect but by the combined power of the many – was the interconnected principle of mutual promise and common deliberation. (Arendt 1963: 215)

The survival of the American Declaration, argues Arendt, is testament to the importance of the *act* of foundation that was this revolution, an act that carried authority in and of itself and not by "belief in an immortal Legislator, of the promises of reward and the threats of punishment in a 'future state' or even the doubtful self evidence of the truths enumerated in the preamble to the Declaration of Independence" (Arendt 1963: 200).

III

The replacement of will with performance or action attempts to disturb the philosophical tradition within which the former has been elevated such that freedom becomes a form of tyranny, or, at least, of sovereignty, making freedom individual and independent of others. As a corollary, freedom is purchased only at the expense of the freedom of others. Both Foucault and Arendt strove towards a notion of freedom that centres on action and not on will or sovereignty. Further, they share the rejection of contentment in a solitary freedom that elevates a feeling of freedom; both stress, instead, performance as integral to freedom. For Foucault the practice of liberty is an exercise in making the self appear; it is not a cognitive act of will, but it is purposeful. Such freedom does not rest on a subject who designs and desires a particular future, but one who is engaged in the present because s/he is open to the future as unknown. Similarly, for Arendt, the possibility of action is the possibility of establishing a new reality, and where action interrupts the automatism of life it is unexpected, a "miracle", an improbability that constitutes the "texture" of reality.

> The chances that tomorrow will be like today are always over-whelming . . . The decisive difference between the "infinite improb-abilities" on which the reality of our earthly life rests and the

miraculous character in those events which establish historical reality is that, in the realm of human affairs, we know the author of the "miracles". It is men who perform them – men who because they have received the twofold gift of freedom and action can establish a reality of their own. (Arendt 1961: 170–71)

While Arendt is close to Foucault in some of these arguments, they part ways when one comes to the issue of the space of this performance, and, relatedly, the possibility of freedom as an individual practice. For Arendt, to have freedom is to have "the faculty of beginning", and this beginning has to be in collaboration with others. Where this capacity to begin anew is articulated, political action occurs and appears: "[freedom] develops fully only when action has created its own worldly space where it can come out of hiding, as it were, and make its appearance" (Arendt 1961: 169).

True freedom is practised, then, via the couplet of beginning and concerted accomplishment. By contrast, Foucault implies that concerted action is not a requirement for the performance of freedom that concerns instead the relationship of self to self, a challenge through the display of certain techniques of self.

Although Arendt, like Nietzsche, thought brilliant individuals should be able to appear, she was clear that political action cannot take place in isolation – "real political action takes place as a group act. And you join that group or you don't. And whatever you do on your own you are not really an actor – you are an anarchist" (Arendt, in Hill 1979: 310). Arendt's argument appears to revert, ultimately, to the machinery of institutionalized politics as the site of the concerted action of beginning anew. Her focus was on clarifying that space, and improving it as the stage of freedom. Arendt bemoaned the sense in which "the political" has been invaded by "social" questions, and regarded the solution as the removal of those social issues – the "life" questions – from the sphere of the political. "Greatness" will be prevented from appearing where politics becomes concerned with the administration of things; the uniqueness of man, of "ek-sistenz", has been denied in the passivity of a twentieth century shocked by its experiences of totalitarianism and attempting to respond through a system of liberal representation that Arendt, at her most Nietzschean, saw as paving the way for mediocrity.

By contrast, Foucault's arguments look like a form of "anarchy" because his practices of liberty seem to be concerned within a non-spatial space, that between the self and self. That politics has become concerned with the administration of life is, he suggested, a condition of modern man, who has taken his existence as the target of political life such that politics is bio-political, attempting to govern people as populations to be known, measured or monitored. Foucault did not hold a distinction comparable to Arendt's attempt to distinguish social from political questions, but he did on occasion suggest that there is a limit to the governability of the populations constituted through bio-political government; in *The history of sexuality*, vol. I, Foucault (1981) argues that life escapes bio-politics. Without forcing the coherence of Foucault, one might ruminate upon whether it is at that moment of "escape" where the possibility of practising one's liberty, of presenting one's self, differently, opens up. And yet, implicitly, the performance takes place in order to be looked upon; that is, there is an aesthetic at work that implies the returning importance of communication. Arendt's position would refuse to call an aesthetics of existence political unless it could communicate something publicly and something beyond a personal existence. If, in politics "not life but the world" is at issue, how can techniques of the self as practices of liberty engage politically? This is the point at which commentators have suggested that an aesthetics of existence requires a conception of public space (cf. Fraser 1989 and McNay 1992).

Lois McNay has written: "ultimately [Foucault's] ethics privileges a notion of the self establishing a relation with the self, rather than understanding the self as embedded in and formed through types of social interaction" (1992: 164). This leads, she suggests to an isolated and inadequate strategy against the processes of normalization that Foucault has elaborated. This means that Foucault cannot provide an account of how the radical nature of that relationship of self to self is communicated in a progressive way. A politics of solidarity that one finds in the Habermasian vision, however depleted his image of the embodied self, is in some ways a move away from a politics of introversion (McNay 1992: 191) that Foucault's ethics of the self slides towards. Such a critique has a tonality of realism about it, and is an attractive "solution" to the question of political Foucault. However, one might argue that there is a notion of public space in Foucault's philosophy; it is not, however, the public space of politics of which Arendt writes, nor what the Frankfurt tradition upholds, but rather, one might consider it a discursive space. Such a space can be challenged individually, through a relation of self to self, and even outside one's own space and time – that is, even after one's death (witness Barbin's diaries (Foucault 1980), or Foucault's interest in Pierre Rivière (Foucault 1975)) – for "discourse is not life – it's time is not yours" (Foucault, quoted in Butler 1993: 223). That moment of challenge is not one, then, that could be a function of the will – its purpose cannot be formulated in, let alone before, its articulation.

The importance of thought in this scenario is governed by the condition that its time is always within the human life span. Arendt argues that the "thought-event", man's desire to strike out alone, cannot be sketched above or below the line of battle between the force of the past (a tradition that pushes one on) and the future, because such a region, outside time, is exactly the impossible dream of metaphysics – a "timeless, spaceless, suprasensuous realm" of thought. Thinking is not outside human time, and it is for this reason that Arendt suggests that the clash between past and future be figured not as a head-on collision along a line but as two forces meeting at an angle. Thought is, metaphorically speaking, the resultant of the two forces; it has its origin in the present, in the clash between forces of past and future, but has no terminal point – it extends towards infinity.

> This diagonal force, whose origin is known, whose direction is determined by past and future, but whose eventual end lies in infinity is the perfect metaphor for the activity of thought. If Kafka's "he" were able to exert his forces along this diagonal line, as it were, forward and backward, with the slow, ordered movements that are the proper motion for trains of thought, he would not have jumped out of the fighting line . . . for this diagonal . . . remains bound to and is rooted in the present; but he would have discovered . . . the enormous ever changing time-space which is created and limited by the forces of past and future. (Arendt 1961: 12)

The walking of the diagonal (thought) is a tiring activity, and exhaustion is more likely; "he" is liable to "die of exhaustion" from this constant battling, and, having forgotten his initial aims, "he" becomes "aware only of the existence of this gap in time which, as long as he lives, is the ground on which he must stand, though it seems to be a battleground and not a home" (Arendt 1961: 13). Acting according to principles, therefore, similar to acting according to an ethics of existence, is a way of conceptualizing political action that remains in the present but that is not bound by the finite nature of any one particular political goal.

For Jean-Luc Nancy " thinking, undoubtedly, is for us what is most free. But freedom is this fact which less than any other can be reduced to thinking" (Nancy 1988: 172). A groundless subjectivity, one that Foucault, and later philosophers such as Nancy, attempt to insert into the philosophical

tradition, can never be a foundation. Foucault and Arendt are both irrec-
oncilable with any naïvely conceived form of identity politics. For Arendt,
"facts" of one's private identity offer nothing for a political engagement;
nothing follows from identity (see Honig's 1992 discussion of Arendt's
Jewishness and her exchange with Gershom Scholem). For Foucault, to
participate politically according to one's identity is to tie oneself to a
subjectification that itself needs to be exposed. Honig (1992) brings her
discussion of Arendt and feminism to a place that sounds remarkably
Foucauldian. If Arendt's purpose is to give up the willing self for an acting
self, for a concept of action that can be self-surprising, an action that
cannot be decided in advance, that "comes to us" and "involves us in
ways that is not deliberate, wilful or intended" (Honig 1992: 223),

> the strategy, then, is to unmask identities that aspire to constatation,
> to deauthorize and redescribe them as performative productions by
> identifying spaces that escape or resist administration, regulation,
> and expression. These are spaces of politics, spaces (potentially) of
> performative freedom. (Honig 1992: 226)

One is left, it seems, with an attempt to challenge what Nancy terms the
"positivity of wickedness" that attempts to ground and thereby to erase
existence, but to do so without the delusion of a positivity of the "good".
Such an anti-foundationalism cannot ground identity, freedom or political engagement. With their different emphases, both Arendt and Foucault
pause before the comfort of a liberal order that invites a dissenting subject
to articulate its freedom within a system of representation. That freedom
returns as a promise that arrests the subject – individual or "community"
– in its performance, that attempts to hear, to understand and to "know"
it. The comfort is one that stills the present performance with a promise
of an assured future mastery. But awaiting the total mastery of freedom is
no longer an option, for "today the threat of a devastation of existence
alone has any positivity" (Nancy 1988: 147). However, one must not
abandon thought, once thinking does not necessarily involve a grounding
of politics; one must not adopt an existentialism that turns away from
thought in its elevation of action, but struggle to stay, however wearily, on
the vector that extends towards infinity, and "to ploddingly pave it anew"
(Arendt 1961: 13). The openness to the future, the "coming up" of action
and the beginning anew of performance are not found in thought *per se*,
but "the hope of thinking signifies that we would not even think if existence were not the surprise of being" (Nancy 1988: 147).

Note

1. For Justin and for Michael, with thanks for your generosity while I was writing this chapter.

References

Adorno, T. & M. Horkheimer 1979 [1944]. *The dialectic of enlightenment*. London: Verso.

Agamben, G. 1993. *Infancy and history*. London: Verso.

Arendt, H. 1958. *The human condition*. Chicago: University of Chicago Press.

Arendt, H. 1961. *Between past and future: six exercises in political thought*. London: Faber & Faber.

Arendt, H. 1963. *On revolution*. London: Faber & Faber.

Bell, V. 1994. Dreaming and time in Foucault's philosophy. *Theory, Culture and Society* **11**, 151–63.

Butler, J. 1993. *Bodies that matter*. London: Routledge.

Foucault, M. (ed.) 1975. *I, Pierre Rivière, having slaughtered my mother, my sister, and my brother . . . : a case of patricide in the 19th century*. New York: Pantheon Books.

Foucault, M. 1977. *Discipline and punish: the birth of prison*. London: Penguin.

Foucault, M. 1980. *Herculine Barbin: being the recently discovered memoirs of a nineteenth century French hermaphrodite*. Brighton: Harvester.

Foucault, M. 1981. *The history of sexuality*, vol. I: *An introduction*. London: Penguin.

Foucault, M. 1982. The subject and power. Afterword. In *Michel Foucault: beyond structuralism and hermeneutics*, P. Dreyfus & H. Rabinow. Brighton: Harvester.

Foucault, M. 1984. On Kant's What is Enlightenment? In *The Foucault reader*, P. Rabinow (ed.). London: Penguin.

Foucault, M. 1986. *The use of pleasures: the history of sexuality*, vol. II. London: Viking.

Foucault, M. 1988a. *The care of the self: the history of sexuality*, vol. III. New York: Vintage.

Foucault, M. 1988b. *Politics, philosophy, culture*. L. Kritzman (ed.). London: Routledge.

Fraser, N. 1989. *Unruly practices: power, discourse and gender in contemporary social theory*. Cambridge: Polity.

Hill, M. 1979. *Hannah Arendt: the recovery of the public world*. New York: St. Martin's Press.

Honig, B. 1992. Toward an agonistic feminism: Hannah Arendt and the politics of identity. In *Feminists theorize the political*, J. Butler & J. Scott (eds). London: Routledge.

McNay, L. 1992. *Foucault and feminism*. Cambridge: Polity.

Miller, J. 1979. The pathos of novelty: Hannah Arendt's image of freedom in the modern world. In *Hannah Arendt: the recovery of the public world*, M. Hill (ed.). New York: St. Martin's Press.

Nancy, J.-L. 1988. *The experience of freedom*. Palo Alto, California: Stanford University Press.

Nietzsche, F. 1967 [1887]. *On the genealogy of morals*. New York: Vintage.

Osborne, P. 1994. Modernity is a qualitative, not a chronological category. *New Left Review* **192**, 65–84.

Rabinow, P. (ed.) 1984. *The Foucault reader*. London: Penguin.

Rousseau, J.-J. 1973 [1762]. The social contract. In *The social contract and discourses*. London: Everyman.

Wolin, S. 1990. Hannah Arendt: democracy and the political. In *Hannah Arendt: critical essays*, L. & S. Hinchman (eds). New York: SUNY.

.

Chapter 5

Security and vitality: drains, liberalism and power in the nineteenth century[1]

Thomas Osborne

The vital and the political

How might medical regulation be analyzed under the rubric of political technologies and rationalities of government? What new forms of intelligibility, if any, does this vocabulary allow us? One of its merits may be as an aid in distancing ourselves from some reductionist ways of thinking about medical power in our societies. We need, first of all, to replace the negative language of "medical monopoly", "medicalization" or "medicine as an instrument of social control" with a more positive form of explanation that would be concerned, not with a critique of medical power, but with specification of the varied fields of application and modes of objectivation characteristic of particular medical programmes, and with the ways that such programmes are tied or seek to tie themselves to wider rationalities of government (cf. *inter alia*, Illich 1976, Conrad & Schneider 1980, Navarro 1986, Zola 1986). Secondly, we need to hold in suspension some of our present-day certainties concerning the nature of medicine itself. Accounts of medicalization and so forth tend to assume a particular given identity for medical endeavour; above all, they presuppose that there exists an antinomical relation between the medical and the social spheres, often with the former "colonizing" the latter.

In place of such emphases, it might be preferable to work with different terms of reference; to posit as the axis of our analyses, not the relations between the medical and the social, but more generally between the *vital* and the *political* spheres. For on the one hand, the social is not some kind of transcendental domain colonized by that of the medical; rather, in some part medical knowledge and technology have been constitutive of what we have come to mean by the "social" (Rose 1994, cf. Osborne 1993). Yet, on the other hand, to speak of medicine at all in this context may be misleading. Medicine is not the only player upon the stage of what

Michel Foucault called "bio-politics". There is a sphere beyond the merely medical which is the sphere more generally of vital regulation, the domain of health, welfare, security and longevity, and this domain has been as much the province of statisticians, engineers, bureaucrats, and architects as it has been of doctors.

Bio-politics, police, liberalism

Foucault wrote of a kind of "great transformation" that occurred in the modern period with regard to the relation between the domain of politics and the sphere of human vitality. The emergence of bio-power as a key pole of modernity signalled, for him, something like a reversal in previous relations between life and that which threatens life. Historians have demonstrated the extent to which matters of biology and disease have been determinants in the history of mankind (McNeill 1976, Nikiforuk 1991). With the coming of modernity, Foucault says, we see something of a reversal in the form of this determination, "the entry of life into history"; through an anatomo-politics of the human body and through "regulatory controls", or "a bio-politics of the population" (Foucault 1979: 139).

Perhaps invocations of bio-politics or such like can seem to have rather a sinister ring to them; we conjure up visions of eugenics or the Nazi politics of life. And it is true that bio-politics can take a more or less, if not necessarily sinister, than totalizing form. The prototype here might be the eighteenth-century science of "police" in the German states. Police was a science of populations; the purpose was to maximize the numbers of people, since people were seen as being both the source and main instance of a nation's wealth. The heterogeneity of the concerns of police only testifies to the totalizing aspirations of the general project (Small 1909). Everything was to be administered: roads, canals, morals, health, commodities. Foucault instances the chapter headings in Delamare's *Traité de la police* (1705); these raise the issue of religion, morals, health, supplies, roads, highways, town buildings, public safety, liberal arts, trade, factories, manservants and factory workers, the poor. Nothing was to be impervious to the gaze of knowledge; the exercise of government demanded a thoroughgoing instrumental command of the domain to be governed.

One can make a heuristic comparison – without suggesting a concrete periodization – of a totalizing political rationality such as police science with a non-totalizing one such as liberalism. Clearly, by liberalism here is not meant the doctrines of Mill or Rawls; liberalism designates in this context not the subject matter of a certain political philosophy but the general idea of a critique of State reason, coupled with an attention to the technological means for bringing about forms of government detached from totalizing forms of sovereignty (Gordon 1991, cf. Kneymeyer 1980: esp. 189). Whereas police represented a political technology that was happy to intervene as much as possible in the interests of happiness, liberalism invokes a kind of habitual suspicion relating to the means and ends of government. A central problem, and paradox, of liberal governmentality is the perception that one is always in danger, so to speak, of *over*-governing, in so far as the very activity of government can act to contort and frustrate its own ends (Gordon 1991: 15–22, Osborne 1994). Since the domain to be governed is not conceived as being transparent, actually or politically, to those who govern, the role of knowledge and expertise is also transformed under liberalism; knowledge loses the direct link to governmental intervention that it possesses in police science. With liberalism, knowledge confronts a domain with its own normativity; liberalism is receptive to the idea that society has natural laws and norms proper to itself (Burchell 1991, Gordon 1991, cf. e.g. Collini 1980: 204, Foucault 1989). The purpose of knowledge is to inform government as to the norms proper to this domain, rather than to provide the direct rationale for government itself.

What, then, might a non-totalizing bio-politics look like? In particular, can there be a specifically liberal art of regulating the vital sphere? Police is instrumental and interventionist; it seeks to direct the domain of life, labour and population on the basis of a totalizing knowledge. One would expect a liberal public health in contrast to be rather the consequence of the acceptability, even the desirability, of a space of indetermination, and of possible conflict, between the aims and desires of government and the norms of the domain to be governed (Minson 1985: 104–8, Gordon 1991: 15–16). Here, life is not merely subjected directly to the forces of government since a space opens up between what can be known and what can be done. In liberal political discourse, according to Foucault, public debate is itself viewed as a principle of the delimitation of State power; indeed, one might expect there to be a public agonism over the regulation of life (Foucault 1989: 116). In short, the *politics* of bio-politics is important in liberalism. But, above all, one might expect a public health to be integral to the establishment of mechanisms of *security* within a liberal order. The concern with technologies of security – as opposed to those centring upon discipline or the sovereignty of a territory – is a distinctive feature of liberal political rationalities. The focus of liberal security is not the territory or the body, but the "ensemble of a population"; and the function of such mechanisms of security will be to assure the integrity of "natural phenomena, economic processes of population" while affirming the vulnerability of such natural processes and the need for a well-modulated intervention in relation to them (Foucault 1989, Gordon 1991: 19–20).

A liberal public health?

But where might one look for empirical evidence of such a liberal format in the regulation of life? There are good grounds for seeing the British nineteenth-century revolution in public health and urban sanitation in just such terms; that is, as something of the order of an "event" within the development of liberal technologies of government. This is not to say that nineteenth-century public health was a straightforward expression of liberal rationalities of government. Rather, I shall argue that public health and sanitary discourse exemplify the points of tension existing between a liberal order and the mechanisms of security by which it seeks to guarantee its existence.

From the 1830s there was a concern to map the dynamics and characteristics of populations; "we are looking at a society that suddenly knew a great deal more about itself" (Goldman 1991: 420). The trigger for this had been the reform of the Poor Law in the early 1830s, and a whole series of investigations and inquiries that followed in its wake. The circumstances of the nation became a giant archive; not just for the attentions of Royal Commissions and Select Committees (Clokie & Robinson 1937: 97–114) but for the famous Inspectorates concerned with factories, prisons, schools, railways and the mines (Young 1936: 57). Medical and sanitary discourse became a key part of this revolution. Chadwick published his famous *Report into the sanitary condition of the labouring population of Great Britain* in 1842 (P.P. 1842); this was preceded by the ground-breaking medical reports of Arnott, Kay and Southwood Smith on fever in parts of the metropolis, and followed by the work of the Health of Towns Commission with its batteries of expert evidence from engineers, commissioners of sewers, parish registrars, doctors and others (P.P. 1837–8, P.P. 1844).

From here followed a plethora of inquiries and investigations into the medical and sanitary condition of the populace, reaching their culmination with Farr's work at the office of the Registrar General, John Simon's medical reports of the 1860s and the Royal Sanitary Commission of

1869–71. There was public agitation too; notably dating from the foundation of the Health of Towns Association in the 1840s, and also opposition, focusing upon accusations of centralization; and finally, of course, legislation. There were major Public Health Acts in 1848, 1866 and 1875, mostly concerned with facilitating the local provision of water and sewerage systems and regulations, and a host of other acts relating to matters from the control of nuisances to the burial of the dead. Even if these items of legislation did not lead to the realization of the full expectations of the original reformers, it is nevertheless beyond question that this period signals something of a revolution in styles of political – if not perhaps epistemological – reasoning concerning the health and vital well-being of the populace (Hutchins 1909, Simon 1897, Brockington 1965, Lambert 1963, Lewis 1952, Rosen 1958, Pelling 1978).

Clearly these measures cannot be described as being liberal in the sense of political philosophy. The Victorian reform legislation has long been troubling to historians precisely because of its apparent contravention of the supposed Victorian shibboleth of *laissez-faire*. Yet this verdict is really to adopt the perspective of the opponents of the legislation such as Toulmin Smith, seeing policies of centralization everywhere (Redlich & Hirst 1958 [1903]: 150–52). Liberalism is not simply the absence of government. The position of the proponents of reform and intervention was certainly more subtle than an emphasis on centralization or contravention of *laissez-faire* principles can suggest; as can be seen immediately by juxtaposing the "sanitary empiricism" of Chadwick or Simon with proponents of a truly totalizing "state medicine" such as Henry Wyldbore Rumsey who campaigned tirelessly for the imposition of a complete sanitary code supervised by a state-sanctioned medical profession in what he termed an "anglicization" of medical police (Rumsey 1856: 47–9, 61, cf. Hutchins 1909: 126–33).

But Rumseys's ambitions were not to be fulfilled, and we cannot speak of a medicalization of society under the auspices of the State in this period. It was not medicine but statistics – albeit a statistics based largely on a medical problematic, seeing disease as the "iron index of misery" – that was the technical embodiment of public health, that expressed most the vital conscience of the early Victorians (Goldman 1991, Szreter 1991). In the eighteenth century, statistics had been, so to speak, a secret affair, concerned with a kind of State espionage; the gathering of facts was linked to a more or less direct imperative of control (Hacking 1990: Ch. 3). By the second quarter of the nineteenth century, statistics had gone public; hence, the emphasis upon what has been called the avalanche of *printed* numbers (Hacking 1982: 281). Public statistics were also part of a project of delimiting the range of government; whereby "what had been a scientific prospectus for the exercise of state power became a programme for reversing the growth of government" (Buck 1982: 28). This is something like "modernity" in statistics; embodying much less of a totalizing aspiration than its previous forms, and coming to concern not subjects so much as citizens. For whereas police tended to equalize subjects, modern statistics began to differentiate; it became a technology of individuation; and statistics became, in effect, an instrument, not simply for the policing of a territory, but for the determination of individual difference and the regulation of citizenship (cf. Porter 1986, Rose 1991).

Statistics was the political economy of the Victorian vital conscience. This is not to say that statistics was just the expression of a liberal interest but that liberalism conditioned the "mode of existence" of statistics (cf. Eyler 1979: 23–36). The exercise of statistical reason seemed to point to a natural domain resistant to *coups d'authorité*, a domain with its own inertia, an autonomous dimension of existence, and one to be investigated not just by State bureaucrats but, at its leading edge by amateurs separated from the direct exercise of government. With the coming of modern statistics "Population was no longer pliable, to be manipulated by enlightened leaders, but the product of recalcitrant customs and natural laws that stood outside the domain of mere politics. Government could not dominate society, for it was itself constrained by society" (Porter 1986: 26). This is no doubt what made it possible for a notion of statistical "law" to appear around the beginning of the nineteenth century; a concept that was unavailable to the police-minded Germans (Hacking 1990: 35–7).

Economy and medicalization

It was this natural, vital domain of the population, with its own regularities, that was to be seized upon by public health and sanitary science and to become its proper object. But rather than being expressions of a centralizing impulse, contrary to Victorian principles of non-intervention, these disciplines were also intrinsically concerned with *economy*. They were conceived as measures of security, forms of government that saved on interventions and costs in other sectors of the social order. The very impetus behind Chadwick's original report was that of finding a means of preventing disease in order to save on outlay on the Poor Law. Disease was wastage; Morpeth calculated that it cost the Poor Law Authorities

£15 million a year, besides which, a diseased population was not likely to be a productive population but a surplus extravagance (Briggs 1985a: 137–8). Chadwick himself – the (contemporary) idea of him as some kind of "Prussian minister" is surely misleading – was concerned with implementing sanitary regulation along principles of economy. This concern, almost an obsession, took a technological form in his insistence that the sewerage and drainage systems should be linked into a single network – an "arterial-venous" system – with water moving continuously through narrow pipes at high pressure, and that a principle of exchange should govern sanitary regulation, with sewage from the cities being used, through a network of "sewage farms", to fertilize the agriculture that in turn fed the cities. But Chadwick's concerns also ran to an economy in terms of legislation; and the principles he advocated certainly belie the image of him as an interventionist simply for interventionism's sake. John Simon was impressed by the technical and financial innovations introduced by Chadwick and his colleagues at the General Board of Health (1848–54) in setting up a limited system of trade monopolies in funeral, water and sanitary improvement works in the metropolis so that "there should be competition *for* the field of service, instead of competition *within* the field of service", and so that an improvement in efficiency might go along with "improvement or cheapening of certain trade-services to the public" (Simon 1897: 224). Even security must be conducted so far as possible upon liberal principles of economy and exchange.

But what was the role specifically of medicine within this bio-politics of security? Pasquale Pasquino emphasizes continuity between a totalizing police science and later developments within the regulation of health, arguing that the birth of the police disciplines of population lead directly to the great social interventions of the nineteenth century: "Population is wealth, health is a value. A century later, a great campaign of medicalization was launched across Europe" (Pasquino 1991: 116). A more or less straightforward historical fact can be used to disturb this continuist view. We can point to the fact that the great public health campaigns of the nineteenth century had their apotheosis in mid-nineteenth-century Britain, a country without a tradition of police, but with a strong tradition of liberalism. George Rosen long ago counselled against seeing too much of a continuity here between police science and later developments within public health (Rosen 1953: 42, Rosen 1957, Jordanova 1980). Moreover, police science actually had rather a limited medical component until quite late in the day; the idea of a specifically "*medical* police" dates from the work of Rau in the mid-1760s, and the discipline flourished from the

1770s (Rosen 1953: 38, Risse 1992: 173). Perhaps the emergence of a more or less autonomous medical police served effectively to undermine the totalizing aspirations implied in the project of a general police science. Perhaps one can speculate that medicine was responsible for, or at least an index of, what one might call the "de-totalization" of police.

In any case, the public health reforms of the mid-nineteenth century were not the product of a strategy of medicalization. Something of their specificity can be isolated through a positive comparison, not this time with continental police but with the indigenous tradition of British eighteenth-century discourses on the health of populations (Keith-Lucas 1953–4, cf. Simon 1897: 107–27, Hennock 1957–8, Riley 1987). This entails not so much the establishment of a coherent genealogy for these ideas, but the location of something like an epistemological tradition in Britain, a kind of internally "normed" logic of development, that is, certainly at some remove from the imperatives of continental police. This tradition, in turn, was at some remove from sanitary science as it emerged in the mid-nineteenth century; but one might say that it posed the right problems, and erected the right obstacles, such as to make the emergence of sanitary discourse in Britain a coherent possibility.

Public security

Nineteenth-century public health was, precisely, *public* health in so far as it went beyond a mere concern of specialized expertise but "could not be separated from politics" (Briggs 1985a: 149–50). The theorists of police did not operate within a "public" domain in this sense. Their role was to regulate the population; here, there could be no concept of a public health as such since the population was conceived not so much as a natural order but as the consequence and target of political technique and governmental artifice. Nineteenth-century public health points to a domain that is not simply that of the maximization of a population by a State, but the regulation of something positive in its own right – "public health" – via infrastructural techniques that were designed to monitor it as a kind of dependent variable. Disease was a public issue in so far as it affected public finances, particularly with regard to the running of the Poor Law; but also because of the recognition that sectors of towns infected by disease and squalor could have effects on more salubrious areas. Moreover, by the early Victorian period there had emerged a public domain amenable to the reception of blue books, reports and debates on the general question of the public health. The concept of public health, then, has to be understood within the context of other valorizations of the notion of the public (public opinion, public interest, public powers, etc.) in this period; those that we now sum up under the rubric of the public sphere.

At least in the context of the arts of preserving health, the eighteenth century operated with a different concept – the word itself is barely found – of the public. How did the question of disease confront the public gaze? One was by way of a localized and temporary mobilization of disciplinary-style tactics. But such tactics were not at all an intended application of the principles of continental police. From Richard Mead's treatise on the plague – the first programme for an official machinery of public health – through to the debates of 1815–25, the activities of the Cholera Board in 1831 and the General Board in 1848, an argument simmered concerning the merits and demerits of systems of quarantine (Mead 1720, cf. Smith 1825, Brockington 1965, Pelling 1978: 65). In Britain there had long been a strain of resistance to the principle of quarantine. There was obviously an economic argument against it; quarantine impedes the circulation of goods. But there was also a long-standing political resistance; quarantine represented an infringement upon liberty. Mead himself warned against the effects of drawing hard and fast lines across populations; these could be self-defeating not least because they only encouraged people to conceal having the disease (Mead 1720: esp. 165, Jones 1931: 16). One may witness too the disapproval with which the Privy Council greeted the recommendations of the Cholera Board (dominated by the elite of the medical profession), which in 1831 proposed strict police-style powers based upon a rigorous quarantine; "it may be necessary to draw troops or a strong body of police around infected places", and to apply "a set of regulations approaching nearly the martial law" (Brockington 1965: 23, 15).

Clearly, quarantine represented an anti-liberal form of discourse, a secretive drawing of lines across spaces (Armstrong 1993). And obviously, it enhanced one's libertarian credentials to be against quarantine. In quarantine, all is secrecy; lines are to be drawn up but, although the public is to be made aware of the coming of the disease, the forms of regulation are to be conducted according to a logic of secrecy. Moreover, quarantine is an exceptional measure; it deals with the particular moment, the extreme threat; with the epidemic irruption rather than with the slow sedimentation of endemic diseases. It is interesting that the eighteenth century was, in contrast to the concerns of the early Victorian period, not particularly preoccupied at the discursive level with endemic disease; or, at least, not as a general problem for *government*. It is true that there was much attention given to "sore-throat"; to "marsh ague" or intermittent fever; and to the question of yellow fever in the tropics. Creighton also singles out measles (Creighton 1965 [1894]: vii). And then of course there was smallpox, a particularly interesting example. There occurred a famous culmination of institutional innovations in relation to smallpox from about the 1770s; Haygarth in Chester, for example, proposed plans for the inoculation of the poor after the epidemics of 1774 and 1777, while Liverpool, Leeds, Luton and Edinburgh all set up vaccine establishments in the 1880s (Haygarth 1784: 151ff.). There were inquiries into Jenner's vaccination early in the nineteenth century (P.P. 1801–2) and a board was set up to distribute the vaccine across the country. Nevertheless, even smallpox did not really enter onto the plane of a *governmental* problematic; that is, perhaps since it was not held to be an environmentally determined condition (Pelling 1978: 18), it was not seen as posing particular problems for government (aside, for example, from questions of finance; P.P. 1810), even if it could be mobilized as a vehicle in party-political debate (Wilson 1990). All this is in some contrast to the mid-nineteenth century – vaccination was made compulsory in 1853 – when vaccination became such a prominent issue of political liberty (Porter & Porter 1988). But by then endemic disease had become a focus for government, and for public controversy.

The medicine of collective spaces

If we are looking for elements of a genealogy of nineteenth-century concerns, there was one particular eighteenth-century field in which endemic disease was an important focus of concern to the public and the power of government. This was the problem of fever in enclosed spaces. How did the eighteenth century spatialize fever? Medical government was concerned with disease as it affected public space, not in the sense of spaces open to the public but concerning that series of closed spaces that were constructed in the interests of the public. Although, nineteenth-century sanitary discourse was a discourse of cities or sectors of cities, the eighteenth-century discourse of fever was concerned with hospitals, prisons, naval vessels, military camps; closed sites of fever. These concerns fed into particular conceptual concerns: in particular, by the end of the eighteenth century, hospital fever (Aikin 1771), gaol fever (Howard 1777) and ship fever (Lind 1762, 1763, Blane 1799a, cf. Hudson & Herbert 1956). It was as if the Enlightenment – in its English variant at least – had become concerned about the closed sites of infection and putrefaction in its midst.

The eighteenth-century concern with fevers was not unnaturally tied to issues of public security. "Of all diseases, fevers were the ones most obviously related to the variables of geography and climate, and the constant expansion of the British Empire with the establishment of regular trading routes to India, the East and West Indies, the North American mainland, and parts of the African coast, together with the supporting military and civilian establishments, intensified the impact of fevers on the British consciousness" (Bynum 1981: 141). Hence the importance of fevers in the military context. In 1794–5 there were some 500 naval surgeons (and 700 by 1800) together with five major hospitals (the Haslar naval hospital being reportedly the largest brick structure in the country) (Lloyd & Coulter 1961: 210, Mathias 1975). The health of sailors and soldiers was a major concern, not least because the effect of disease on such communities could be enormous; the Walcheren expeditionary force, for example, reputedly had 40 times as many men killed by fever as by the enemy (Mathias 1975: 76). But there was also an epistemological side to these interests; "authoritarian communities" such as army camps and naval vessels acted, in effect, as experimental laboratories for the study of disease; as in, for example, the struggle against scurvy (ibid., cf. McNeill 1976: 246–7).

Historians have given us some excellent accounts of this eighteenth-century tradition, a true medicine of collective – but confined – spaces (Riley 1987: 89–112, 122–37, also Simon 1897, Buer 1926, Flinn 1965). This was a tradition concerned not with the provision of urban infrastructures but with the establishment of right conduct and discipline. Pringle, for example, emphasized that medicine was more or less useless in the prevention of malignant fevers even if it was equipped to diagnose them; the true prevention lay in inculcating good habits, proper practice and discipline (Pringle 1752: ix). The eighteenth-century writings are full of regimens and directions for hygiene; in at least the maritime and military domains epistemological considerations as to the actual nature of the fevers involved were of secondary interest to the known means of prevention. The work of Lind and Blane emphasizes "rules of conduct" on how to avoid ship fevers; and this without very much discussion as to what exactly such fevers are. Serious disputes amongst doctors tended to be over treatments not aetiologies. It is as if eighteenth-century fever possessed rather a precarious epistemological existence in that its coherence as an entity was inseparable from the practices and techniques that confronted it; fever was more easily manipulated than defined.

So in the eighteenth century, what is prioritized in the government of health is the individual (or the captain or commander) that has to attend to the rules of hygiene and govern his conduct with prudence, especially with regard to the so-called non-naturals (air, diet, motion and rest, sleeping and waking, excretions, passions of the mind, etc.). There was a kind of ascetic side to the preservation of health (Sinclair 1807: 19, 159ff.). In the nineteenth century, on the other hand, we have not so much rules to preserve individual health or health in locales as general regulations for preserving the collective health of the community. Here it was not a question of the government of individual conduct through fixed regimens and rules, and certainly not of an ascetic imperative (Simon 1897: 33), but rather of the provision of an infrastructure that would provide the individual and the collectivity with security in the face of threats to vitality. The eighteenth century met the sicknesses of collective space with ventilators and procedures of discipline; the nineteenth century posed the problem in terms of water and the proper government of towns and cities.

Urbanism and fevers

Towards the end of the eighteenth century there was, in fact, a moment of transition as to the understanding of fevers and their relation to government. Medical reformers such as Ferriar, Percival, Clarke, Currie, etc. turned towards a concern with fever in the urban context (especially Manchester, where we see the late-eighteenth-century experiments in Boards of Health) (Percival 1807: 1–67, Pickstone 1985). Here we have an undisputed precursor to nineteenth-century developments in urban hygiene. These endeavours rested on a spirit of philanthropy. They stemmed from the reform-consciousness of urban physicians (towns, said Percival, "are injurious to population" (Percival: 1807: 7)). Ferriar's work instances a no-doubt characteristic combination of motivations of charity, "improvement" and distrust of luxury (Ferriar 1810: 292, 265). Perhaps we see here for the first time the question of disease being posed as an obstacle to the provision of judicious and economically-minded assistance to the poor. In this process, a whole space – one that would have resonances in the nineteenth century – was opened up for matters relating to a specifically urban problematization of the question of the poor. To read Blane's comments on the virtues of sewers – those great instruments, as he put it, of "dryness" and "sweetness" – in his *Letters on the subject of quarantine* (Blane: 1799b: 19) is to feel transported forward by half a century; here one actually breathes, so to speak, the atmosphere of sanitary discourse. These kinds of endeavour and study certainly went some way towards a particular consciousness of the environment of infection as being characteristically *urban*. In short, there occurs here a definite, albeit undoubtedly limited, movement from consideration of closed spaces as a threat to security towards the urban space as a general environment for positive measures of security. What was involved in the inquiries and proposals of the late-eighteenth-century doctors was, in certain respects, an extension of the eighteenth-century discourse of enclosed space to the "open space" of the town. However, there were limits too with regard to the extent of this continuity of concerns. What exercised Percival and Ferriar's attentions most, for example, was the issue of lodging-houses as closed sites of infection; health regulation would consist, above all, in a system of inspection and registration of these dwellings of the poor. No doubt there was a large element of self-interest in such philanthropic exchange of charity for the poor and security for the middling classes; "it may excite the benevolence of some men . . . that acts of charity will not only serve them in another life, but promise them a longer enjoyment of the present" (Ferriar 1810: 172).

In some contrast to this, the nineteenth century tied the art of governing health to a positive art of governing the city. The city itself, or particular regions of it, came to be understood as the main crucible of fever, especially those domains given over to the poor; whole neighbourhoods become sites of fever or "fever districts" as Southwood Smith called them. The question now was not only that of the dwellings of the poor, or the state of lodging-houses, but one given grouping or sector of the population; those in poverty and those regions where the poorer classes are assembled in such numbers as to make the assemblages "quasi-public". This was not a medicalization of poverty. Rather, what was at stake was something more like a concern with the "de-pauperization" of disease coupled with a "naturalization" of poverty (Dean 1991, cf. Osborne 1994: 490–91). This theme is most visible in the work of Southwood Smith, which evinces a systematic concern with the relation between disease and poverty. He underlined the links between poverty and susceptibility to disease; that as much as a third of the working-class population was "deprived of the natural term of existence" by fevers (Smith 1854: 4). But Smith's work represented less an attack upon poverty itself than an attempt, as it were, to "purify" poverty from the distortions of disease (Smith 1839: 101–2, Smith 1854: 4, cf. Pelling 1978: 42). Smith's concern was to show that, in fact, poverty did not necessarily imply a diseased state. Or, at least, particular diseases such as typhus and the "continual fevers" only served to obscure the more natural processes of disease in the body. If the animal frame naturally tended to disease "by the very working of the machinery by which life is maintained" (Smith 1854: 13) then typhus only obscured these processes, being in fact preventable through sanitary regulation and hence not part of the essential "fate" of the poor. Of course, disease could lead to poverty, especially for the dependants of the stricken; by the prevention of disease one certainly contributed to a diminution of the burdens on the Poor Law Authorities. But the war against disease did not simply represent a war on poverty itself. No doubt this relative "de-pauperization" of disease did not originate with Southwood Smith. Aikin had already argued that the whole point of hospitals was that they were not almshouses for the poor but sites for the cure of disease (Aikin 1771). However, the separation of disease from the government of poverty also required a homogeneous – that is not to say necessarily "scientifically correct" – concept of fever.

The eighteenth-century discourse on fever and like diseases had been concerned typically with air, ventilation and cleanliness. Closed sites restricted air and led to putrefaction and the cultivation of pestilential vapours. The remedy almost invariably entailed the adoption of some version of Hales's celebrated ventilator (e.g. Pringle 1750: 46–52). The nineteenth-century discourse of public health, at least in its miasmatic version, also emphasized the role of putrified air. The difference – aside from the question of contagion that has so much impressed the minds of both contemporaries and historians of ideas – lay in the technology to hand; above all, that of the fever wards. By the early nineteenth century, fever had taken on a new homogeneity. Ferriar's conception of fever wards provided a distinct line of continuity through to Southwood Smith and others' work at the London Fever Hospital. Indeed, this hospital worked as a kind of apparatus for making fever visible as a homogeneous entity, receptive to theory (Bynum 1979: 99, also P.P. 1818, Rosen 1973: 630, Pelling 1978: 9–10). It was there that Southwood Smith did his pioneering work, walking the wards twice a day, keeping a rigorous journal of cases, performing autopsies on all fatalities; "In this manner, in the progress of years a mass of facts accumulates relating to the statistics, the types, the symptoms, the cases, the diagnosis, the pathology and the treatment of the disease" (Smith 1830: 6, Pelling 1978: 20). Observation of cases at the hospital lead Southwood Smith to argue that fever could not be understood in terms of an essence or genus. Fever, he argued, was "not an entity, not a being possessing a peculiar nature", but the name given to a characteristic "series of events", a series observable only through the techniques of autopsy (Smith 1830: 47, 39). In short, fever becomes that which is observable by virtue of the technology of analysis afforded by the fever hospital.

Of course, one might argue that Southwood Smith's work did not represent a particularly orthodox perspective in the early nineteenth century (cf. Pelling 1978: 61, 68). His work is, however, representative of a more general shift concerning the relation of fever to its environment; a shift that was no doubt made possible by the decoupling of fever from the notion of a genus (cf. Pelling 1978.: 21). In the eighteenth century, fevers were generalized in so far as they were representative of species. The different environments determined the singularity of fevers in the sense that the environment in which a fever appeared would impose a particular kind of deviation upon the genus of the disease (cf. Bynum 1981). In Southwood Smith's work, and in that of his fellow sanitarians the environment has taken on a more positive connotation in relation to the disease; not as something to be "subtracted", but as a determinant of the disease itself; witness Farr's claim that a fever was not the same entity in Whitechapel as compared to Westmorland (P.P. 1837–8: 63). This spatial concern also related to hydraulic matters. It was well known – a feature of the work of a Farr or a Simon fully as much as of a John Snow – that the location of the most fevered sectors of a city could be predicted from a glance at a map of the water supply (P.P. 1842: 160–61, 314–5, Briggs 1985b: 138–9). Hence the extraordinary emphasis in the nineteenth century on the spatial mapping of disease across urban environments.

Perhaps the empirical naturalism of the great Sanitary Surveys presupposed an implicit analogy whereby the mapping of disease across the geographical space of the city mirrored in macrocosm the meticulous clinical mapping of the disease across the spatial fabric of the body. In a striking way, too, it is noticeable how this naturalism of description was matched by a naturalism of conception with regard to sanitary matters. If the novelty of nineteenth-century sanitary discourse resided in its activism with regard to the environment – with the contention that the preservation of life requires a conscious strategy of defence against the hostility of the environment (Simon 1897: 2) – it is also the case that such activism was coupled, at least in the exemplary case of Chadwick, with a hostility to artifice as such. The hydraulic infrastructure was itself conceived naturalistically. Certainly sewers and other elements of the sanitary infrastructure could be classified, as they were by Farr, as "artificial agencies"

(P.P. 1837–8: 80). But sewers, drains, privies and the water supply were also "organic", in that they coupled themselves directly and literally to the vital economy of the body. Chadwick, with his "arterial-venous" project for the water system, literally envisaged a circular process whereby human excreta would be used in agriculture while agricultural drainage would supply towns with their water supply; hence tying body, city and economy together into one system. In short, in this model, the environment has ceased to designate an exterior; the hydraulic city has become a regulated milieu along with the body and the economy (Rabinow 1982: 276–7, cf. Armstrong 1993).

Drains and power

Much has been, and still could be, written on the novelty of this Victorian vision of the city; for example, with regard to the techniques with which the city was to be visualized, i.e. through reports, inspectorates, statistical investigations, Royal Commissions, journalistic reportage and so forth. A medical gaze had a certain, albeit limited, import here. Chadwick, for example, is well known for his rather negative attitude to the powers of the medical profession in dealing with sanitary issues, but doctors themselves were to be crucial at least as the eyes of sanitary science, distributed through the urban space, sending in reports (cf. Pelling 1978: 12). However, we also need to concern ourselves with the most mundane and material aspects of nineteenth-century sanitary regulation; not so much with medicine as with the real hero of the piece, sanitary engineering; focusing instead on what one might term the city's condition of existence – its subterranean and infrastructural elements; sewers, toilets, drainage, the government of nuisances.

These concerns might seem so mundane as to be better left beneath notice. But they actually reveal elements of a general political rationality. The Victorians seem to have been concerned with establishing a kind of free space of the city. Public health sought to free the city in order, so to speak, to leave it properly to itself as a kind of natural space; to exclude all dead matter from the space of the city. Hence the great process of clearing the city of the detritus that should be external to it – not just waste, sewage and nuisances but also "unhygienic" spaces that did not properly belong to the vital order of the city, above all places of death such as abattoirs and cemeteries. The city should be a space of vitality. And what do drains and sewers do? They function as the material embodiments of an essentially political division between public and private spheres; pipes, drains and sewers functioned to establish the sanitary integrity of the private home, yet without recourse to direct intervention. What was at stake was not just a Victorian fetish for cleanliness, but a strategy of indirect government; that is, of inducing cleanliness and hence good moral habits not through discipline but simply through the material presence of fast-flowing water in and through each private household. Compare this method to that of Ferriar and his colleagues in the Fever Hospital Movement, animated by the requirement that physicians should enter the houses of the sick to wash down the walls, burn clothes and so forth. In contrast to this, pipes are literally neutral and anonymous; they supply the home as a private space, and although by their presence they clearly have a certain moralizing impact upon conduct, this is achieved essentially through non-disciplinary means and not by imposing rules of conduct on the occupants but only by leaving the home and the family to itself; an emphasis that was later to be transformed by the neo-hygienic insistence upon the individual that was to become characteristic of early-twentieth-century public health (Rose 1985: 146–7).

Some time ago Karl Wittfogel made himself unpopular in some quarters by relating another form of hydraulic regulation to a – this time, totalitarian – political rationality (Wittfogel 1957). For Wittfogel, a hydraulic society meant an all-seeing, authoritarian society, one characterized by a system of "total power". Yet, the regulation of water can be used too for other means, albeit equally tied to a political rationality. The Victorians, too, established a kind of hydraulic society, albeit on different terms from the societies described by Wittfogel. And yet how lacking in a sense of the despotic or monumental is this liberal hydraulic endeavour; one cannot awe the populace with a drainage system, even if it is also true, as Buer observes (1926: 95), that instead of commemorating themselves with great cathedrals, the Victorians built magnificent drains.

Conclusions

Let us recap and briefly develop some of the points made in the discussion. Much of this chapter has turned upon a set of comparisons relating to the eighteenth and nineteenth centuries and the way they related health to the collectivity. The comparison had a purpose; it was to indicate that in some respects nineteenth-century public health partook of a liberal political rationality.

The first element of this was in fact a negative comparison, in that nine-teenth-century public health did not partake of a police rationality; that is to say that it was not a totalizing, all-enveloping, interventionist and disci-plinary rationality. Moreover, the actual desires of some of the medical profession notwithstanding, conceptions of a straightforward "medical-ization" of the State or social life would be largely inappropriate. This is partly for the relatively trivial reason that the medical profession were not greatly engaged as a body in the public health reforming mission, and partly because the notion of medicalization suggests normalization, and that too would be misleading, at least if we understand normalization in the negative sense usually ascribed to it. Certainly, the public health movement sought to establish and regulate sanitary norms, but this should not be understood as a despotic project. The setting up of techni-cal apparatuses in our societies designed to detect norms is part of a project, certainly of normalization, but also of co-ordination and pre-diction. Normalization expresses "the need, obscurely felt by society, to become the organic subject of needs recognized as such" (Canguilhem 1989: 248). What was to be at stake with sanitary intervention was not so much a normalization of vital capacities but the regulation of their normativity via the medium of environmental regulation; to free, so to speak, a space for vital normativity through a minimum standardization of the environment. What occurred was, in short, a realization that the establishment of biological normativity – the ability of the living being to levy norms on the environment – should be one of the aims of political rule. The famous social conscience of the Victorians was also a vital conscience.

But we also argued that there was something *liberal* about this vital con-science. This did not mean that public health, in all its diversity of per-spective, was in any way a conscious expression of liberal philosophy or dogma, and still less that it implies a non-interventionist strategy (cf. Smith 1979: 420–21). Rather, public health represented not so much a realization of a liberal philosophy but of a strategy of security appropriate to a liberal rationality of government. Of key importance here was the way in which public health and sanitary discourse sought to combine an emphasis on economy – that is, so far as possible (and this was the source of conflict), emphasizing economy of both finance and governmental intervention – with an emphasis on the *naturalism* of the processes to be regulated, i.e. a particular resistance to any kind of artifice of government. This naturalism was expressed at several levels. There was an assertion of the natural domain of vital laws that sanitary discourse took as its object;

a detachment of organic disease and poverty from the preventable circumstances of pathology directly due to the environment; the development of a sanitary infrastructure itself modelled on quasi-organic principles; a naturalization of the private space of the home as a domain sequestered from the direct impact of government; and even, abjuring all forms of theoretical closure, a naturalization of modes of describing sanitary and social conditions themselves. This series of naturalistic objectivations of the domain of government meant, of course, that the best government of these domains would necessarily be of a liberal character; that is, as free as possible from creating a disturbance of these natural norms of the vital sphere, beyond a certain basic system of regulation in the interests of their maintenance and security.

Nevertheless, in the end there can be no finite closure or reconciliation between the ideals of a liberal order and the mechanisms of security that are set in place to secure it. On the one hand, mechanisms of security by their very existence pose a threat to the integrity of the liberal order; there will always be claims that such mechanisms intrude too much upon what they are designed to secure. The historians are not wrong when they indicate the tension between interventionism and *laissez-faire*; but this tension, rather than being a contradiction between competing rationalities, represents a tension or dissonance within liberalism itself, one generated by liberalism. On the other hand, this very restlessness of liberal rationalities, and the contradictions they encounter with the technologies that they set in place, perhaps accounts for the very dynamism of liberalism, not as a political philosophy, but as a principle for the criticism of reality (Gordon 1991: 18). Liberalism fails endlessly, and generates interminable oppositions, but the solution to such failures tends to be a reconfiguration of liberal rationalities and principles themselves; liberalism, as a rationality of government, thrives upon its own failure.

Note

1. Thanks to Colin Gordon, Roy Porter and Nikolas Rose for sending me comments and criticisms on this chapter.

References

Aikin, J. 1771. *Thoughts on hospitals*. London: Joseph Johnson.

Armstrong, D. 1993. Public health spaces and the fabrication of identity. *Sociology* **27**(3), 393–410.

Blane, G. 1799a. *Observations on the diseases of seamen*, 3rd edn. London: Murray and Highley.

Blane, G. 1799b. *Letters on the subject of quarantine*. London: Philanthropic Forum.

Briggs, A. 1985a. Public opinion and public health in the age of Chadwick. In *Collected essays*, vol. II, 129–52. Brighton: Harvester.

Briggs, A. 1985b. Cholera and society in the nineteenth century. In *Collected essays*, vol. 2. Brighton: Harvester.

Brockington, C. Fraser 1965. *A short history of public health*. London: Churchill.

Buck, P. 1982. People who counted: political arithmetic in the eighteenth century. *Isis* **73**(1), 28–45.

Buer, M. C. 1926. *Health, wealth and population in the early industrial revolution*. London: Routledge & Kegan Paul.

Burchell, G. 1991. Peculiar interests; civil society and governing the system of natural liberty. See Burchell et al. (1991), 119–50.

Burchell, G, C. Gordon, P. Miller (eds) 1991. *The Foucault effect: studies in governmentality*. Hemel Hempstead, England: Harvester Wheatsheaf.

Bynum, W. 1979. Hospital, disease and community; the London Fever Hospital, 1801–1850. In *Healing and history*, C. Rosenberg (ed.). London: Dawson.

Bynum, W. 1981. Cullen and the study of fevers in Britain, 1760–1820. *Medical History Supplement* **1**, 135–47.

Canguilhem, G. 1989. *The normal and the pathological* (trans. C. Fawcett). New York: Zone Books.

Clokie, H. M. & J. W. Robinson 1937. *Royal Commissions of Inquiry*. Palo Alto, California: Stanford University Press.

Collini, S. 1980. Political theory and the "science of society" in Victorian Britain. *Historical Journal* **23**(1), 203–31.

Conrad, P. & J. W. Schneider 1980. *Deviance and medicalization*. St. Louis: C.V. Mosby.

Creighton, C. 1965[1894]. *A history of epidemics in Britain*, vol. II. London: Frank Cass.

Dean, M. 1991. *The constitution of poverty*. London: Routledge.

Eyler, J. 1979. *Victorian social medicine: the ideas and methods of William Farr*. Baltimore: The Johns Hopkins University Press.

Ferriar, J. 1810. *Medical histories and reflections* [2 volumes]. London: Cadell and Davies.

Flinn, M. W. 1965. Introduction. In *Report on the sanitary condition of the labouring population in Great Britain*. Edinburgh: Edinburgh University Press.

Foucault, M. 1979. *The history of sexuality*, vol. I. London: Penguin.

Foucault, M. 1989. *Résumé des cours*. Paris: Juillard.

Goldman, L. 1991. Statistics and the science of society in Britain; a social context for the G.R.O. *Social History of Medicine* **4**(3), 415–34.

Gordon, C. 1991. Governmental rationality: an introduction. See Burchell et al. (1991), 1–52.

Hacking, I. 1982. Bio-power and the avalanche of printed numbers. *Humanities in Society* **5**(3–4), 279–94.

Hacking, I. 1990. *The taming of chance*. Cambridge: Cambridge University Press.

Haygarth, J. 1784. *An inquiry how to prevent the smallpox*. Chester: J. Monk.

Hennock, E. P. 1957–8. Urban sanitary reform a generation before Chadwick. *Economic History Review* **10**, 113–20.

Howard, J. 1777. *The state of prisons in England and Wales*. Warrington: William Eyres.

Hudson, E. & A. Herbert 1956. James Lind: his contributions to shipboard sanitation. *Journal of the History of Medicine* **11**, 1–12.

Hutchins, B. L. 1909. *The public health agitation 1833–48*. London: Fifield.

Illich, I. 1976. *Medical nemesis*. New York: Pantheon.

Jones, D. D. 1931. *Edwin Chadwick and the early public health movement in England*. Iowa: University of Iowa Press.

Jordanova. L. 1980. Medical police and public health: problems of practice and ideology. *Society of the Social History of Medicine Bulletin* **27**, 15–19.

Keith-Lucas, B. 1953–4. Some influences affecting the development of sanitary legislation in England. *Economic History Review* **11**, 290–96.

Kneymeyer, F.-L. 1980. Polizei. *Economy and Society* **9**(2), 172–96.

Lambert, R. 1963. *Sir John Simon 1816–1904 and English social administration*. London: MacGibbon and Kee.

Lewis, R. A. 1952. *Edwin Chadwick and the public health movement 1832–1854*. Harlow, England: Longman.

Lind, J. 1762. *An essay on the most effectual means of preserving the health of seamen in the Royal Navy*. London: Wilson.

Lind, J. 1763. *Two papers on fevers and infection*. London: Wilson.

Lloyd, C. & J. L. S. Coulter 1961. *Medicine and the Navy 1200–1900*, vol. III: *1714–1815*. Edinburgh: Livingstone.

McNeill, W. 1976. *Plagues and peoples*. London: Penguin.

Mathias, P. 1975. Swords and ploughshares: the armed forces, medicine and public health in the late eighteenth century. In *War and economic development*, J. M. Winter (ed.). Cambridge: Cambridge University Press.

Mead, R. 1720. A discourse on the plague. In *Medical works* (1767). Dublin: Thomas Ewing.

Minson, J. 1985. *Genealogies of morals; Nietzsche, Foucault and the eccentricity of ethics*. London: Macmillan.

Navarro, V. 1986. *Crisis, health and medicine: a social critique*. London: Tavistock.

Nikiforuk, A. 1991. *The fourth horseman*. London: Fourth Estate.

Osborne, T. 1993. Liberalism, neo-liberalism and the liberal profession of medicine. *Economy and Society* **22**(3), 345–56.

Osborne, T. 1994. Sociology, liberalism and the historicity of conduct. *Economy and Society* **23**, 484–501

Pasquino, P. 1991. "Theatrum Politicum": the genealogy of capital – police and the state of prosperity. See Burchell et al. (1991), 105–18.

Pelling, M. 1978. *Cholera, fever and English medicine*. Oxford: Oxford University Press.

Percival, T. 1807. *Works* [4 volumes]. London: Richard Cuttwell.

Pickstone, J. 1985. *Medicine in an industrial society*. Manchester: Manchester University Press.

Porter, D. & R. Porter 1988. The politics of prevention: anti-vaccination and public health in nineteenth century England. *Medical History* **32**, 231–52.

Porter, T. 1986. *The rise of statistical thinking*. Princeton, New Jersey: Princeton University Press.

P.P. 1801–2. *Report from the committee on Dr Jenner's petition*. (75), II, 267–315.

P.P. 1810. *Report from the national vaccine establishment*. (330), II, 259–61.

P.P. 1818. *Contagious fever in London*. (332), VII, 1–52.

P.P. 1837–8. *Appendices and supplements to 4th Annual Report of the Poor Law Commission* (147), XXVIII.

P.P. (House of Lords) 1842. *Report into the sanitary condition of the labouring population of Great Britain*. XXVI.

P.P. 1844. *First report on the state of large town and populous districts*. (572), XVII.

Pringle, J. 1750. *Observations on the nature and cure of hospital and jayl fevers in a letter to Doctor Mead*. London: Miller and Wilson.

Pringle, J. 1752. *Observations on the diseases of the army in camps and garrison*. London: Miller, Wilson and Payne.

Rabinow, P. 1982. Ordonance, discipline, regulation: some reflections on urbanism. *Humanities in Society* **5**(3–4), 267–78.

Redlich, J. & F. W. Hirst (eds) 1958[1903]. *History of local government in England* (ed. B. Keith-Lucas). London: Macmillan.

Riley, J. C. 1987. *The eighteenth century campaign to avoid disease*. London: Macmillan.

Risse, G. 1992. Medicine in the age of enlightenment. In *Medicine in society*, A. Wear (ed.), 149–95. Cambridge: Cambridge University Press.

Rose, N. 1985. *The psychological complex*. London: Routledge.

Rose, N. 1991. Governing by numbers. *Accounting, Organization and Society* **16**(7), 673–92.

Rose, N. 1994. Medicine, history and the present. In *Reassessing Foucault*, C. Jones & R. Porter (eds), 48–72. London: Routledge.

Rosen, G. 1953. Cameralism and the concept of medical police. *Bulletin of the History of Medicine* **27**(1), 21–42.

Rosen, G. 1957. The fate of the concept of medical police. *Centaurus* **5**, 97–113.

Rosen, G. 1958. *A history of public health*. New York: M. D. Publications.

Rosen, G. 1973. Disease, debility and death. In *The Victorian city*, vol. II, H. J. Dyos & M. Wolff (eds). London: Routledge & Kegan Paul.

Rumsey, H. Wyldbore 1856. *Essays on state medicine*. London: John Churchill.

Simon, Sir J. 1897. *English sanitary institutions*, 2nd edn. London: John Murray.

Sinclair, J. 1807. *The code of health and longevity* [4 volumes]. Edinburgh: Constable.

Small, A. 1909. *The Cameralists: pioneers of German social policy*. Chicago: University of Chicago Press.

Smith, F. B. 1979. *The people's health 1830–1910*. London: Croom Helm.

Smith, T. Southwood 1825. Plague – typhus – quarantine. *Westminster Review* **3**, 499–530. In *Public health in the Victorian age*, vol. II, R. Hodgkinson (ed.). Westmead, Gregg International 1973.

Smith, T. Southwood 1830. *A treatise on fever*. Harlow, England: Longman.

Smith, T. Southwood 1839. *Report on the prevalence of fever in the Metropolitan Unions*. In P.P. XX (239), Appendix C, No. 2, 100–106.

Smith, T. Southwood 1854. *Results of sanitary improvement*. London: Charles Knight.

Szreter, S. 1991. Introduction: the G.R.O. and the historians. *Social History of Medicine* **4**(3), 401–14.

Wilson, A. 1990. The politics of medical improvement in early Hanoverian London. In *The medical enlightenment of the eighteenth century*, A. Cunningham & R. French (eds). Cambridge: Cambridge University Press.

Wittfogel, K. 1957. *Oriental despotism*. Oxford: Oxford University Press.

Young, G. M. 1936. *Portrait of an age*. Oxford: Oxford University Press.

Zola, I. 1986. Medicine as an institution of social control. In *Basic readings in medical sociology*, D. Tuckett & J. Kaufert (eds), 254–9. London: Tavistock.

Chapter 6

Lines of communication and spaces of rule

Andrew Barry

. . . how is it that . . . there has never arisen a medical science concerned with nations and with international communities? (Husserl
1965: 150)

Analyses of government and discipline have generally had little to say
about the development of the physical – as distinct from the biomedical
or psychological – sciences. Perhaps this is not surprising. Physics, in itself,
does not have any direct relation either to the regulation of individual
conduct or the bio-political management of population, and knowledge
of the physical universe does not appear to bear any traces of the political
(Latour 1988). Moreover, if there is a clear connection between, for example, the ethical practice and training of medical practitioners and the
development of a liberal mode of government (Osborne 1993), the same
cannot be said of the practice of physicists.

Paradoxically, it is precisely in effecting a separation from politics and
society that physics acquired some general political utility. In the nineteenth century the development of reliable and effective technologies, and
communication technologies in particular, became a critical point of
mediation between development of physics and the security and the
economy of empire (Wise 1988). It also made enormous demands on the
discipline of physical scientists and engineers. The figure of the modern
natural scientist – a person whose activity is at once too technical and too
practical to be considered intellectual or philosophical, and too divorced
from social reality to be considered political – emerges at this moment.
Physics became political but not politicized. The scientist became, as Max
Weber noted, a technician (Weber 1948).

Electrical communications developed in the mid-nineteenth century in
relation to a complex set of military, commercial and administrative
demands. Yet, however "illiberal" their origins, communications networks

have come to provide the perfect material base for liberal government. They are pervasive and yet do not possess a centre. They appear to increase the density of contacts within society without any unnecessary intervention by the State. They have made possible the reconfiguration of territorial space in a manner compatible with the requirements of liberal rule. They have enabled threats to be responded to rapidly and effectively *without* the necessity of creating a detailed system of surveillance (cf. Virilio 1977, Giddens 1985). They also have appeared to enable the press to exercise a liberal and critical gaze on the *day-to-day* conduct of government. Yet the acquisition of these benefits has entailed an intensification of regulation both at the local level of the laboratory and the enterprise, and at the global level of international relations. Certainly, as Foucault's work suggests, the mechanisms and techniques of discipline help to provide the subjective conditions necessary for the exercise of liberal forms of freedom (Pizzorno 1992: 207). But discipline and regulation, it seems, have played a vital role in reconfiguring the material infrastructure on which liberal forms of government are also thought to rely.

Writing the history of physics

To be sure, the history of the physical sciences has often been written without reference to politics. It is a history of theoretical innovation: a history of the progressive movements from the mechanistic forces of the Newtonian cosmos, to the nineteenth-century electromagnetic theories of the ether, to the statistical universe of quantum mechanics of the mid-twentieth century. It is a history of paradigm shifts, revolutions and epistemological breaks. Attempts to understand this narrative in the context of a broader analysis of economic, cultural or discursive shifts have always been problematic. Boris Hessen's suggestion in 1931 that the "scientific revolution" of the seventeenth century was associated with the origins of capitalism has provided generations of critics of Marxism with a suitable object to attack (Schaffer 1984). Meanwhile, Paul Forman's claim that the rise of quantum mechanics in Weimar Germany needed to be understood in terms of the philosophical and political commitments of German physicists appears methodologically crude and historically inaccurate (Forman 1971). And Michel Serres's explorations of the roots of (and routes between) literature and science have been largely ignored by uncomprehending Anglo-Saxons (Serres 1982). For Michel Foucault, the analysis of relations between those sciences, such as physics, which possessed the strongest epistemological structure and political and economic forms was simply too complex to consider (Foucault 1980: 109).

Here, however, I want to move beyond the rather restricted epistemological problematic defined by the philosophy of science and the sociology of knowledge. I want to argue that, far from being of interest only to the specialist, the study of physics and other "exact" sciences is of importance to those engaged in any broader theorization of modern forms of political power. In order to effect this re-examination of the significance of physics to the study of politics, two shifts in perspective are necessary. The first shift involves some change in our perception of the natural sciences in general, and physics in particular. It involves focusing not on the history of theory, but rather examining the history of physics more broadly as a history of experimental, measurement and engineering practices and standards – as a history, in other words, of practices concerned with defining and manipulating the properties of objects and devices (Latour 1987, Schaffer 1992, Barry 1993a). Physics can be considered not just as a "fundamental" discipline but as one element of a complex set of technological assemblages.

The second shift in perspective that is necessary is temporarily to abandon the attempt either to attempt to write the history of the physical sciences in terms of revolutions or epistemological breaks or to try to account for the development of such sciences in terms of deeper economic and social transformations. Instead, the focus of this chapter is on the relation of the "exact" physical sciences to the problems of government. Under what conditions did the apparently *asocial* physical sciences become an important technical resource for government? To what extent, if at all, is there a relation between the conduct of the physical sciences and specific forms of governmental rationality? And in what ways did the articulation of physics with the objectives of government have implications for the practice of physics itself?

Territory, architecture, communications

One way of understanding the significance of the physical sciences to government is suggested by Foucault's account of the relation between territory and the government of the State. According to Foucault, the police theorists of the eighteenth century often conceived of the royal territory in terms of the model of the city (Gordon 1991: 20). Although the notion of police applied, in principle, "only to the set of regulations that were to assure the tranquillity of the city" (Foucault 1989b: 260), in practice police became the form of political rationality that could be applied to the whole territory. In this context the city was no longer conceived of as an exceptional space within the overall space of the territory. Rather, "the cities, with the problems that they raised . . . . served as the models for the governmental rationality that was to apply to the whole of the territory" (ibid.: 259).

The privilege accorded to the city in the political rationality of police had, according to Foucault, particular significance for the politics of architecture. Prior to the eighteenth century architectural practice had not acquired any general political dimension. However, from the eighteenth century onwards "every discussion of politics as the art of government of men necessarily includes a chapter or a series of chapters on urbanism, on collective facilities, on hygiene, and on private architecture" (ibid.: 259, Foucault 1986: 240). Although architecture could, in principle, be articulated with a number of different political projects, in practice it acquired particular centrality within the political discourse of police.

The end of the eighteenth century saw the emergence of a rather different series of reflections on territorial space. According to Foucault, the figure of Napoleon stands at the break between "the old organisation of the eighteenth-century police State and the forms of the modern State, which he invented" (Foucault 1989b: 260). The preoccupation of earlier political theorists with the urban and the territorial was, if not entirely absent, none the less displaced (Foucault 1989a: 99). At the centre of the concerns of the forms of political rationality that developed in the nineteenth century was not the city or the territory but *society*. The governmental State was no longer defined in relation to its physical territory, its surface area, but in relation to its social geography, its population and its economy (Foucault 1991: 104). Government, in this context, "not only has to deal with a territory, with a domain, and with its subjects, but that it also has to deal with a complex and independent reality that has its own laws and mechanisms of reaction, its regulations as well as its possibilities of disturbance" (Foucault 1986: 242).

If territorial space was an object that was intrinsically more opaque, more problematic and more social than the theorists of police had imagined, how then was it possible to organize, defend and manipulate this space? How was it possible to ensure its integrity against possible disturbances? And what implications did this shift in governmental rationality have for the political significance of technology? Was it still appropriate or possible to organize territory using the methods of architects?

126

At one level, the development of a variety of forms of "social" expertise provided one technical solution to the problems posed by government. Expertise in social and economic statistics, in particular, acted as a mediator between the decisions and calculations of administrative authorities and the complex reality of social and economic processes (Rose 1993). Liberal government had to comprehend the dynamics of the economy and yet to respect the autonomy of society from any possible action by the State. In brief, liberal government strove to engage in a process of continual self-examination. It had to ensure that its actions were, in every sense, economical.

But although social expertise played a vital role in the practice of liberal government it could not, none the less, directly effect the spatio-temporal conditions within which political power could be exercised. How could the territorial space of the nation be effectively policed without intruding into the daily lives of its citizens? How could public authorities respond rapidly to external or internal threats to the nation? How could the flow of persons and messages be managed in a way that did not restrict unduly the liberty of the individual? And how could the volume and speed of communication be both regulated and intensified to meet the growing demands of industry and administration? No doubt there is no simple answer to these questions. Liberalism has deployed many different methods in an effort to reconfigure the space of the nation into an appropriate form. Foucault notes, for example, the importance of the naval hospital as a mechanism for filtering and regulating the flow of alien objects across territorial boundaries (Foucault 1977: 144, Deleuze 1988: 42). However, from the nineteenth century onwards it was not architecture but communications technology that came to have a critical role in regulating the flow of objects, information and persons, thereby facilitating the development of a liberal political and economic space. This relation between liberalism and communications had two dimensions.

First, communications networks came to provide a necessary link between the deliberations of public authorities and the dispersed space of the national territory; appearing to enable the authorities both to direct and to trace the course of distant events *in real time*, however imperfectly. In principle, it would become possible for the various branches of the State to know of and to act rapidly on any serious disturbance in the social body, establishing a complex feedback between such disturbances and the exercise of more or less subtle forms of administrative or military action. Thus, communication networks created what Deleuze & Guattari have called a *striated* space: a space within which movements and flows are regulated in ways which enable authorities to act; a space that is measured, directed and standardized as opposed to nonmetric, rhizomic and acentred (Deleuze & Guattari 1987: 474–500). This was seen as important for liberal as well as for more traditional or authoritarian forms of State organization (Foucault 1989b: 262). If liberalism was suspicious of excessive State intervention and of the capacity of government to act, an effective communication and information system enabled the public authorities to judge the minimum level of action necessary. And if the national territory were too complex an object to be policed in detail, it none the less enabled the educated members of the public to judge for themselves the urgency and necessity of intervention by the State. The government of a liberal society depended not just on the existence of an educated population, but on citizens who kept themselves informed.

The association between government, the public sphere and the speed of administrative and military action was of considerable significance (Virilio 1977). From the nineteenth century onwards public agencies have sought to make a rapid response to any apparent risk to the wellbeing of the population, whether this risk be military, economic or biomedical. At the same time, one of the most common criticisms of government (at whatever level), has been that it is insufficiently *alert* to the existence of a possible danger. Although liberalism recognized the dangers of governing too much, it was also aware of the urgent necessity of intervention in times of crisis. Liberal government was expected to respond rapidly, and yet with caution.

Secondly, communication networks have increasingly been seen as enhancing the self-governing capacities of society itself. If, as Foucault argues, the new science of political economy arose "out of the perception of new networks of continuous and multiple relations between population, territory and wealth" (Foucault 1991: 101), then communication networks provided the material and informational base on which such complex superstructural relations could grow. In effect, the communications infrastructures came to function as perfect embodiments of the liberal political imagination: maximizing the density, intensity and spatial extension of interactions within the social body itself while, at the same time, minimizing the direct demands made by the state on the people. They enabled society to come to know itself and to govern itself on the basis of its own knowledge. Thus, communications technologies were an instrument of, and not a constraint on, the exercise of freedom; the technological foundations of a liberal public space.

In what follows I focus on the development of the electric telegraph, drawing on a rich body of recent work by historians of science, including Simon Schaffer, Crosbie Smith and Norton Wise. It is in the development of the telegraph that a certain kind of relation between politics, physics and engineering is most clearly established in the latter half of the nineteenth century. Physics, along with other sciences and technologies of communication came to be seen to have a key role in reconfiguring national and imperial space. In the next section I trace some of the ways in which the development of the electric telegraph was thought to have political significance. In the subsequent sections I examine how the development of the telegraph network was associated with the changes in the practice of physics and engineering and in the regulation of international space.

Telegraphic politics

From its beginnings in the mid-nineteenth century the electric telegraph was perceived as an instrument of administrative surveillance and internal political security (Briggs 1988: 375). In 1845, for example, the telegraph entrepreneur, Richard Brett, suggested to Sir Robert Peel, that:

> the advantages of the [telegraph] plan applied to police arrangements throughout the UK and to the Army and Navy departments must be obvious to government. By its operation instructions might be conveyed instantaneously and the movements of forces so regulated that any available number might be brought together at a given point in the shortest possible time necessary for their convergence. (quoted in Bright 1898: 6)

As early as 1846 the Home Secretary reserved the right to take possession of the telegraphic apparatus during periods of internal unrest reflecting, in part, an anxiety that the telegraph would become an instrument of political agitation (Mather 1953: 49). By and large, however, attempts to turn the telegraph into a tool of the State were resisted. The telegraph was perceived as a technology for individuals and firms; not exclusively of the public authorities. When the telegraph companies were eventually nationalized in 1870 a clear separation was made between the management and ownership of the telegraph, and its utilization by the police and the armed forces. The telegraph network was expected to be operated, along with the rest of the Post Office, in the interests of the population as a whole with a minimum of interference from the security apparatus of the State. The network did have a vital role in ensuring the economic and political unity of the nation, but the successful fulfilment of this role required the *minimum* level of direct interference by the authorities (Kieve 1973: 146). Although many argued otherwise, it was accepted that there was no contradiction between the policy of nationalization and the objectives of a liberal administration.

In France the development of the electric telegraph was associated more closely to the demands of administration and security. In the 1790s, the Republican government had seen the mechanical forerunner to the telegraph, the semaphore, as a means of exercising its control immediately over its dispersed population. The Committee of Public Safety was instructed to map semaphore routes and authorized the construction of a national network. News of the instructions of the French government, it was hoped, could be spread simultaneously every day, or every hour, in order that the government could exercise "its influence over the whole republic" (Attali & Stourdze 1977: 97). When, in 1850, Napoleon III accelerated the construction of an electric telegraph network, he gave it the priority of "promptly carrying the government's orders throughout the territory" (Bertho 1985: 25). In short, the telegraph was understood as an instrument of public authority but not as part of the infrastructure of a civil society (Attali & Stourdze 1977). As Attali & Stourdze argue: "communication, as understood by the French centralized state, was primarily a lecture which the State, with professorial wisdom, delivered to society" (ibid.: 97).

In the latter half of the nineteenth century attention was focused not just upon the more specific and local problems of directing the dispersed activities of military and police forces and local government administrators or the role of telegraph in the national economy (Mather 1953, McNeill 1982: 249), but upon the global problems of ensuring the unity and strength of the imperial community against the threat of disintegration. The creation of a secure telegraphic network was perceived as essential to imperial security. When the electric telegraph line was completed between Calcutta and Bombay, Governor-General Dalhousie wrote to a friend: "The post takes ten days between the two places. Thus in less than one day the Government made communications which, before the telegraph, would have occupied a whole month – what a political reinforcement this is!" (quoted in Headrick 1988: 97).

The threat posed to imperial cohesion was seen as both external and internal. Internally, the telegraph was thought to be important for maintaining the civic unity of a geographically dispersed, and socially and culturally fractured community (Bright 1914: 134, Marx 1973 [1853]: 320). In terms of the cohesion of the empire, the telegraph enabled the margins to keep in contact with the centre, thereby uniting "all the free countries in different parts of the world" (Bright 1914: 135, Marvin 1988). Later, these functions were given an explicitly liberal form with the development of broadcasting (Donald 1992: 71–87). For John Reith, the BBC's first director, radio had the potential to be "an integrator" for democracy and a contributor to the intellectual and moral happiness of the community. "We believe", he wrote, "that a new national asset has been created . . . the asset referred to is of a moral and not the material order – that which, down the year, brings the compound interest of happier homes, broader culture and truer citizenship" (Reith 1949: 116). In practice, argued Reith, this asset would function not through the broadcast of propaganda to a passive audience, but through encouraging the audience to engage with the programmed material, and "to discriminate" (Frith 1988: 24–44). The internal cohesion of the national and international community could only be achieved through free and active participation. In this context, the function of the BBC's World Service was to advance the cause of freedom and liberty not through propaganda, but by simply *telling the truth*, thus making it possible for individuals to judge for themselves (Mansell 1982, Barry 1993b).

In terms of external threats to nation and empire, the imperial communication networks came to have a central role in maintaining political and military order, ensuring that any threat could be responded to immediately. The empire was, it seemed, a fragile and unstable conglomeration whose health and stability needed constant vigilance. The telegraph enabled the imperial government to optimize its response to any signs of crisis in the imperial body, thereby economizing on the use of scarce military resources. At the same time, from the Crimean War onwards, the press was able to exercise a critical gaze on the conduct of the imperial government. During the Indian Mutiny of 1858 *The Times*, in particular, was convinced of the value of the new technology, noting that "better than numerous reinforcements, better than any confused energy in counsel would have been clear and accurate knowledge, day by day of what was passing at either end of the telegraph wire" (*The Times*, 21 May 1858).

If the telegraph was a technology that enabled both the public authorities and their critics to monitor the course of distant and dispersed events, its ability to inscribe the reality of such distant events was imperfect. In the late nineteenth century the Foreign Office frequently complained that the telegraph, far from enabling long-distance control, encouraged local officials to exaggerate the urgency of the crises that they faced (Kubicek 1969, Kennedy 1971). More generally, the telegraph was limited by its capacity to transmit only the shortest messages. Thus businessmen, for example, had to resort to an elaborate set of codes to ensure that even routine price information could be easily communicated (Bright 1898: 176). The history of communications since the end of the nineteenth century has been a history of attempts to increase the capacity, reliability, speed and geographical coverage of the network.

Measurement, precision and empire

Ian Hacking has noted how in the period after 1820 there was a huge growth in the quantity of numbers being published concerning the state of the population (Hacking 1991). Statistics, as has been noted elsewhere, became an important technical feature of liberal forms of government. However, the interest in greater quantification was not confined to the social sciences. Charles Babbage, for example, in his *Economy of machinery and manufactures* argued that: "it is the science of calculation – which becomes continually more necessary at each step of our progress and must ultimately govern the whole of the application of science to the arts of life" (Babbage 1989: 266).

At this time measurement was not necessarily considered an important task for natural scientists. When Lord Kelvin, in his now famous address on "electrical units of measurement", laid out what he was to call "a philosophy of measurement", his claim that measurement had a central place in the conduct of science should be read as an argument rather than as a statement of the contemporary practice of the physical sciences (Wise & Smith 1986, Hacking 1990, Smith & Wise 1990, Schaffer 1992). Echoing Kelvin's philosophy, Robert Clifton, the Professor of Experimental Philosophy at Oxford, suggested in 1871 that "at the present time the progress of physics seems to me to depend on the progress of methods of exact measurement" (quoted in Gooday 1990: 25).

While the value of measurement was a significant theme in the writings of some Victorian physicists, it was also of central importance to the educational practice and moral order of the late Victorian laboratory. Professors at the new physics laboratories of the 1860s and 1870s placed great emphasis on teaching the importance of precision, skill and patience in experimental practice (Gooday 1990). This concern with the discipline of the experimenter marked a significant shift away from the gentlemanly codes that had dominated laboratory practices in the seventeenth and eighteenth centuries (Schaffer 1988). The late Victorian laboratory expected both high moral and technical standards. As Simon Schaffer has argued, "a culture convinced of the need for accurate data and surveillance as the right means for social management and reform would also see precision measures as a ethical good" (Schaffer 1992: 25). Following its initial development in the physics laboratories, the emphasis on measurement diffused to other fields such as chemistry, physiology and engineering (Gooday 1990). However, it was not until 1902 that the British government opened its own specialized laboratory for precision measurement and standardization, as a response to the economic and political threat posed by the formation of a major standards laboratory in Germany – the *Physikalisch-Technische Reichanstalt*.

The significance of electrical measurements and standards for the reliable and economic operation of the telegraph was recognized by physicists and engineers in the 1850s and 1860s. After the disastrous failure of the first Atlantic cable in 1858, electrical research and political action were united and were increasingly directed towards the problems of predicting and controlling the behaviour of the expensive submarine cables (Smith & Wise 1990: 670). The parliamentary committee that was formed to investigate the causes of the failure of the submarine cable was quite clear that it was due to the absence both of adequate electrical measurements and standards, and of appropriate standards of engineering practice. They concluded:

> We attribute the failure of this enterprise to the original design of the cable having been faulty owing to the absence of experimental data, to the manufacture having being conducted without proper supervision, and to the cable not having being handled with sufficient care. (Submarine Telegraph Committee 1860: ix)

The next decade saw a series of debates concerning the relative merits of different techniques of measurement, and of different electrical standards. Werner Siemens, the German telegraph entrepreneur, suggested that a practical electrical resistance standard based upon his standard mercury column would be sufficient for the purposes of telegraph engineering. British physicists disagreed with Siemens and argued for basing electrical standards on what they called an "absolute" system of units based upon fundamental principles of physics (Schaffer 1992: 27). The physicists won the debate, and as a result telegraph engineers needed to appreciate the value of the discipline of physics for their work. In effect, the Standards Committee for the British Association for the Advancement of Science became an institution of government lying outside of the central organization of the State. Moreover, British standards became world standards.

Thus, precision measurements and electrical standards performed a complex role. First, they were seen to be crucial in ensuring that the electrical telegraphic connections between the distant parts of the empire were secure against the hazards of technical failure. As Schaffer argues, the integrity of the imperial cable network came to be based on a vast apparatus of electrical standards, teaching laboratories and precision workshops. Electrical instruments and procedures developed in London, Cambridge and Glasgow provided the standards against which the rest of the imperial telegraph network could be assessed, and towards which the procedures of telegraph engineers had to be adjusted (Schaffer 1992). During the same period, in 1884, Greenwich was defined as the world centre for the measurement of space and time (Howse 1980, Giddens 1985: 175), British laboratories became centres for measurements of the speed and energy of information transmitted along the telegraphic cable. Together, Greenwich and the electrical laboratories provided the basis, in principle, for calculating the exact spatial and temporal co-ordinates of any event in the world (Kern 1983: 16, Barry 1994: 45).

Secondly, electrical measurements provided the basis for a field of research in "fundamental" electromagnetic theory. According to the physicist William Thomson (Lord Kelvin), the development of electrical standards had started "a train of investigation which now sends up branches into the loftiest region and subtlest ether of natural philosophy" (Thomson 1894, quoted in Schaffer 1992). As Norton Wise has argued, the telegraph came to function as a *mediating machine*, articulating a relation between the most abstract and fundamental areas of physical science and the most practical and urgent problems facing the empire (Wise 1988: 101).

Thirdly, while the electrical laboratories were seen as exemplars of good scientific conduct, they did not have a complete monopoly, and a broader interested public became fascinated by scientific and engineering practices. The late nineteenth century is marked by a proliferation of journals read by telegraph engineers, operators and the general public with names like *The Engineer*, *The Telegraph Journal*, *The Electrician* and *The Electrical Review*. Later, in the 1920s and 1930s, a similar spate of publications developed in connection with the growth of wireless. These journals, while they published reports of developments in the electrical industries, also sought to encourage awareness amongst their readership of scientific principles and methods, the latest discoveries in electrical science, and relations between electrical science and engineering practice. Today, publications of this kind would be discussed within studies of "the public understanding of science" or "the popularization of science". However, these terms are rather misleading – as they indicate a somewhat neutral or passive relation between the public and science. One way of reconceiving of the public/science relation, at least in relation to this historical material, is to examine the ways in which non-scientists came to expect themselves to embody the self-discipline of science: workers and members of the public who came to employ established procedures of laboratory conduct and, thus, to adopt the highest standards of imperial science.

Interference and regulation

If the standardizing and measuring work of the physics laboratories was thought to be a necessary condition for the development of a reliable communications system, it was not a sufficient one. Telegraphy, like its more recent replacements telephony and radio, was prone to interference or disruption. In order for the telegraph network to work it was necessary to take care of these sources of interference, whether they were "social" or "natural" in origin. The electrical signals that passed along the telegraph wires could become distorted, irregular and unstable. They needed to be filtered, managed and monitored.

Some forms of interference to telegraphic communications proved difficult to control. As late as the 1890s, for example, fishing boats provided a constant source of damage to the cable line between Britain and Ireland. Moreover, despite technical improvements, it required skill and attention to record the faint signals ("the mysterious wavy line") that were often received by telegraph and later by wireless (*The Telegraph Journal* 1 July 1890: 8). Long-distance communication involved the highest degree of concentration on the part of operators (*The Telegraph Journal* 15 May 1890: 6). Telegraph companies and the government sought to establish minimum standards of performance and reliability. According to government regulations on wireless telegraphy:

> every ship fitted with wireless apparatus must also have a telegraphist licensed by government to whose authority the ship is subject;

> and in order to allow him to be licensed he must have a competent knowledge of the adjustment of the apparatus, able to transmit and read by sound at a speed of at least 20 words a minute . . . In addition, his certificate testifies that the Government has bound the telegraphist to an obligation of preserving secrecy of correspondence. (Select Committee on the Radio Telegraphic Convention 1907: xxxvii)

Other sources of interference were internal to the telegraphic industrial apparatus. The telegraph was to suffer considerable industrial disruption throughout the late nineteenth century (Kieve 1973: 186). It was also the first industry that involved the geographical dispersion of large numbers of employees, which created new problems of co-ordination. As a result of its geographical dispersal, as Alfred Chandler has argued, the telegraph companies were the first (together with the railways) to develop a bureaucratic management structure, along with a trained class of managers who could be delegated to exercise local supervision over provincial telegraph offices (Chandler 1977, see also Weber 1978: 349). By the late 1860s the four senior executives of the aptly-named "Western Union" administered over 3,000 telegraph stations throughout the United States. The company's annual report for 1869 described the elaborate array of figures that needed to circulate throughout this organization in order that activities of every manager could be made accountable.

> Each station is in charge of a Manager, who has control of his office, and is accountable to the Direct Superintendent for the proper performance of his duties and of those of his subordinates. The District Superintendents are accountable to the General Superintendents and the latter to the Executive Committee. On the first of every month each office forwards to the District Superintendent a report, showing the number of messages sent and received, and gross receipts, the amounts received on messages for each office with which business was done; the amounts received at all other offices with which messages were exchanged; the amounts received for or paid to other lines, and all expenditure in detail. (annual report of the Western Union Telegraph Company for 1869, quoted in Chandler 1977: 198)

Yet there were problems of perhaps more fundamental significance than trade union agitation or the difficulties of network management. These were problems associated with the need for international regulation of communication, both in order to promote the formation of international communication and information networks and in order to protect national security. How could the fragile cables of the electric telegraph maintain their integrity in passing across from one national space to another when each was organized along different lines with different priorities? How could governments prevent the authorities or inhabitants of other countries from intercepting telegraphic communications? How was it possible to regulate the *flow* of information across international space? The idea of a permanent international organization emerged as one solution to these problems. Since 1865, when Napoleon III instigated the formation of the first international organization, the International Telecommunications Union, communications has been at the forefront of the development of international organizations (Mulgan 1990: Ch. 9). The establishment of global standards of measurement and engineering practice was only able to occur through the development of international agreements, guaranteed by the disciplined procedures developed during the later nineteenth century within British, German and US laboratories. Precision measurement and standardization were at the centre of international agreements in communications. The Anglo-German Cable Agreement of 1911, for example, noted that: "Each conductor shall be formed of a strand of seven copper wires all of equal diameter, shall weigh 1071 lbs per N.M. and shall at a temperature of 75 F have a resistance not higher than 11.65 ohms and lower than 11.18 ohms per N.M." Physical measurement became, in other words, both the technology and object of international organization.

While the international regulation of communications has always been characterized by the ambition of universal coverage, this ambition has been in tension with the concern, discussed earlier, to maintain the security of the nation against external threats. International organization was not the means by which global space might be reconfigured and *striated*. During the late nineteenth century the British government took great pains to reduce its dependency on foreign cables. As early as the 1860s, for example, expensive submarine cables were laid in the Red Sea in order to avoid using land routes that were administered by "unreliable" and poorly trained Turkish officials and constantly disrupted by snow (Headrick 1988: 100–101). By the end of the century there had developed a widespread concern that the economic and cultural wellbeing of the empire depended upon the existence of an imperial communications network. Any gap or break in the telegraphic network signified a potential fracture in the imperial body. Significantly the first and second "Imperial Conferences" in the 1890s were preoccupied with demands to establish "an all-red route". This would lead, according to Earl Grey, to "an electric bond of empire" (Jebb 1911: 392). By the end of the century over half of the world's international telegraph system was British owned (Interdepartmental Committee on Cable Communications 1902, Kennedy 1971: 740). The empire, it seemed, was united by wires (cf. Callon & Latour 1981).

Conclusions

There is, no doubt, nothing essentially "liberal" about the technology of the electric telegraph, or the science of electromagnetism, or the idea of a communications network. Telegraphy developed in the nineteenth century as a commercial industry and as an instrument of national and imperial security. It was employed by the emerging commercial news agencies such as Reuters, by business, by the military and by colonial administrators. It played an increasingly key role in the conduct of war from the 1860s onwards. Its development depended, moreover, on an intensification of regulation both at the local level of the individual laboratory and the global level of international organization. None the less, the telegraphic network came to provide perhaps a certain kind of liberal solution to what Harold Innis called "the problem of empire" (Innis 1950). On the one hand, it enabled the imperial administration to economize on its use of military resources and to maximize their application at the appropriate moment. It served to establish the conditions for the maintenance of national and imperial security while, at the same time, minimizing the need for the *physical presence* of the police or the military. Electrical communications are, after all, a necessary precondition for the development of the ultimate "liberal" military technology: the *invisible deterrent* (cf. Deleuze & Guattari 1987: 478). On the other hand, the idea of a national or global communications network has come to provide both a symbol and an instrument of a liberal order; a *virtual community* within which anyone should be able to participate. Far from developing simply into instruments of State surveillance or elements of some kind of "super-panopticon", communications networks have become, it seems, "technologies of freedom" (Pool 1983).

References

Attali, J. & Y. Stourdze 1977. The birth of the telephone and the economic crisis: the slow death of monologue in French society. In *The social impact of the telephone*, I. de Sola Pool (ed.). Cambridge, Mass.: MIT Press.

Babbage, C. 1989. *Economy of machinary and manufactures*. In *Charles Babbage: collected works*, vol. 8, M. Campbell-Kelly (ed.). London: William Pickering.

Barry, A. 1993a. The history of measurement and the engineers of space. *British Journal for the History of Science* **26**, 459–68.

Barry, A. 1993b. Television, truth and democracy. *Media, Culture and Society* **15**(3), 487–96.

Barry, A. 1994. Harmonisation and the art of European government. In *A new Europe? Social change and political transformation*, H. Davis & C. Rootes (eds), 39–54. London: UCL Press.

Bertho, C. 1985. *Histoire des telecommunications en France*. Toulouse: Editions Eres.

Briggs, A. 1988. *Victorian things*. London: Penguin.

Bright, C. 1898. *The submarine telegraph*. London: Crosby Lockwood.

Bright, C. 1914. Inter-imperial telegraphy. *Quarterly Review* **220**, 134–51.

Burchell, G., C. Gordon, P. Miller (eds) 1991. *The Foucault effect: studies in governmentality*. Hemel Hempstead, England: Harvester Wheatsheaf.

Callon, M. & B. Latour 1981. Unscrewing the big Leviathan: how actors macrostructure reality and how sociologists help them do so. In *Toward an integration of micro and macro sociologies*, K. Knorr Cetina & A. Cicourel (eds), 277–303. London: Routledge & Kegan Paul.

Chandler, A. 1977. *The visible hand: the managerial revolution in American business*. Cambridge, Mass.: Harvard University Press.

Deleuze, G. 1988. *Foucault*. London: Athlone Press.

Deleuze, G. & F. Guattari 1987. *A thousand plateaus: capitalism and schizophrenia*. Minneapolis: University of Minnesota Press.

Donald, J. 1992. *Sentimental education: schooling, popular culture and the regulation of liberty*. London: Verso

Forman, P. 1971. Weimar culture, causality and quantum theory 1918–27. *Historical Studies in the Physical Sciences* **3**, 1–116.

Foucault, M. 1977. *Discipline and punish: the birth of the prison*. London: Penguin.

Foucault, M. 1980. Truth and power. In *Power/knowledge*, C. Gordon (ed.), 109–33. Brighton: Harvester.

See Gordon (1980), 109–33.

Foucault, M. 1986. Space, knowledge and power. In *The Foucault reader*, P. Rabinow (ed.). London: Penguin.

Foucault, M. 1989a. *Résumé des cours*. Paris: Juillard.

Foucault, M. 1989b. An ethics of pleasure. In *Foucault live*, S. Lotringer (ed.), 257–74. New York: Semiotext(e).

Foucault, M. 1991. Governmentality. See Burchell et al. (1991), 87–104.

Frith, S. 1988. *Music for pleasure*. Cambridge: Polity.

Giddens, A. 1985. *The nation-state and violence*. Cambridge: Polity.

Gooday, G. 1990. Precision measurement and the genesis of physics teaching laboratories in Victorian Britain. *British Journal for the History of Science* **23**, 25–51.

Gordon, C. 1991. Governmental rationality: an introduction. See Burchell et al. (1991), 1–52.

Hacking, I. 1990. *The taming of chance*. Cambridge: Cambridge University Press.

Hacking, I. 1991. How should we do the history of statistics? See Burchell et al. (1991), 181–96.

Headrick, D. 1988. *The tentacles of progress: technology transfer in the age of imperialism.* Oxford: Oxford University Press.

Howse, D. 1980. *Greenwich and the discovery of the longitude*. Oxford: Oxford Univeristy Press.

Husserl, E. 1965. Philosophy and the crisis of European man. In *Phenomenology and the crisis of philosophy*. New York: Harper & Row.

Innis, H. 1950. *Empire and communications*. Oxford: Clarendon Press.

Interdepartmental Committee on Cable Communications 1902. *First Report of the Interdepartmental Committee on Cable Communications*. Cd 958. London: HMSO.

Jebb, R. 1911 *The imperial conference*, vol. I. London: Longman, Green.

Kennedy, P. 1971. Imperial cable communications and strategy 1870–1914. *English Historical Review* **86**, 728–52.

Kern, S. 1983. *The culture of time and space, 1880–1918*. London: Weidenfeld & Nicolson.

Kieve, J. 1973. *The electric telegraph: a social and economic history*. Newton Abbot: David & Charles.

Kubicek, R. 1969. *The administration of imperialism: Joseph Chamberlain and the Colonial Office*. Durham NC.

Latour, B. 1987. *Science in action*. Milton Keynes, England: Open University Press.

Latour, B. 1988. A relativistic account of Einstein's relativity. *Social Studies of Science* **18**, 3–44.

McNeill, W. 1982. *The pursuit of power: armed forces and society since A.D. 1000.* Chicago: University of Chicago Press.

Mansell, G. 1982. *Let truth be told: 50 years of BBC external broadcasting*. London: Weidenfeld & Nicolson.

Marvin, C. 1988. *When old technologies were new: thinking about communications in the late nineteenth century*. Oxford: Oxford University Press.

Marx, K. 1973 [1853]. The future results of British rule in India. In *Surveys from exile*. London: Penguin.

Mather, F. 1953. The railways, the electric telegraph and public order during the Chartist period. *History* **38**, 40–53.

Mulgan, G. 1990. *Communication and control*. Cambridge: Polity.

Osborne, T. 1993. On liberalism, neo-liberalism and the "liberal" profession of medicine. *Economy and Society* **22**(3), 345–56.

Pizzorno, A. 1992. Foucault and the liberal view of the individual. In *Michel*

Foucault: philosopher, T. Armstrong (ed.), 204–14. Hemel Hempstead, England: Harvester Wheatsheaf.

Pool, I. de Sola, 1983. *Technologies of freedom*. Cambridge, Mass.: Belknap Press.

Reith, J. 1949. *Into the wind*. London: Hodder & Stoughton.

Rose, N. 1993. Government, authority and expertise in advanced liberalism. *Economy and Society* **22**, 283–99.

Schaffer, S. 1984. Newton at the crossroads. *Radical Philosophy* **37**, 23–8.

Schaffer, S. 1988. Astronomers mark time: discipline and the personal equation. *Science in Context* **2**(1), 115–46.

Schaffer, S. 1992. Victorian metrology and its instrumentation: a manufactory of ohms. In *Invisible connections*, R. Bud & S. Cozzens (eds). Washington State: Bellingham.

Select Committee on the Radio Telegraphic Convention 1907. *Report from the Select Committee on the Radio Telegraphic Convention*. Cd 246. London: HMSO.

Serres, M. 1982. *Hermes: literature, science and philosophy*. Baltimore: The Johns Hopkins University Press.

Smith, C. & N. Wise 1990. *Energy and empire: a biographical study of Lord Kelvin*. Cambridge: Cambridge University Press.

Submarine Telegraph Committee 1860. Report of the Submarine Telegraph Committee. *Parliamentary Papers* **62.**

Virilio, P. 1977. *Speed and politics* (trans. M. Polizzotti). New York: Semiotext(e)

Weber, M. 1948. Science as a vocation. In *From Max Weber*, H. H. Gerth & C. Wright Mills (eds), 129–56. London: Routledge & Kegan Paul.

Weber, M. 1978. The development of bureaucracy and its relation to law. In *Max Weber: selections in translation*, W. Runciman (ed.), 341–56. Cambridge: Cambridge University Press.

Wise, N. 1988. Mediating machines. *Science in Context* **2**(1), 77–113.

Wise, N. & C. Smith 1986. Measurement, work and industry in Lord Kelvin's Britain. *Historical Studies in the Physical Sciences* **17**, 147–73.

Chapter 7
Assembling the school

Ian Hunter

Introduction

Foucault's later work has, to date, had relatively little influence on educational research.[1] There may be aspects of the field of academic educational research itself that make it fairly impervious to Foucauldian insights. This field has been largely divided between an educational psychology characterized by its functional integration with the school system, and a "progressive" educational sociology characterized by its critical disavowal of the system. Given that Foucauldian genealogy entails neither integration nor disavowal – and instead, in the case of education, aspires to an analysis strongly restrained by the contingency and intractability of the school's historical emergence – it is perhaps not so surprising that the existing field has found little need to accommodate such an approach. This conjecture receives some confirmation in the continuing marginality of educational history. Further, while educational psychology has itself been the object of Foucauldian investigation (Donzelot 1979, Rose 1985), educational sociology has not.

This state of affairs helps to explain the fact that the few genealogical investigations of school systems have largely fallen on deaf ears. Such has been the fate of the path-breaking reconstruction of the British elementary school undertaken by Jones & Williamson (1979) that rejects both the traditional "Whig" account of State schooling as a vehicle of social enlightenment, and the more recent "critical" account of it as an instrument of capitalist social control. Instead, Jones & Williamson locate the emergence of the elementary school in terms of the governmental construction of a series of problematic "moral topographies" – statistical profiles of dangerous and endangered populations – and the disciplinary technology of the school itself, improvised as a means of moral management. In thus disengaging itself from the ethical passions of both liberal and Marxian discourse, this work seems to have rendered itself unintelligible to most students of education.

Where Foucault's work has been taken up in education, it has been largely as a supplement to existing "critical" sociological approaches. Usually it is *Discipline and punish* (Foucault 1977) that fills this role. A number of studies have thus used Foucault's description of the monitorial classroom to provide a finer-grained account of the manner in which the school allegedly reproduces social relations, by detouring human capacities into the forms required by middle-class hegemony, capitalism, racism, patriarchy and other enemies of complete human development. One can see this use in some recent English works (Ball 1990, Donald 1992), but it is more pronounced in the American-based "critical pedagogy" movement. Here, in the proliferating literature of ethical activism – for example, Giroux & McLaren (1989, 1994), McLaren (1989), Kincheloe (1993) – one finds Foucault effortlessly absorbed into the progressive emancipatory project. It is precisely Foucault's criticism of the notion of emancipation that critical pedagogy absorbs into its emancipatory project; and it is his insistence on the interdependency of power and knowledge that it uses to criticize the educational "ideologies" of capitalism, patriarchy, racism. But such uses ignore Foucault's stress on the "productivity" of disciplinary power in augmenting human attributes; and his account of the "technical" character of government, as an ensemble of technologies and aims irreducible to the "logic" of capital or the "will" of the state.

Foucault neither possesses a theory of society in the conventional sense, nor does he employ a theory of the formation of the subject comparable with those found in psychoanalysis, phenomenology or semiotics. Hence Foucault cannot himself produce an account of the school as an apparatus for the disciplinary formation of subjects, wielded in the interests of social domination. One response to this state of affairs is to join Nancy Fraser and Jürgen Habermas in saying "so much the worse for Foucault". One can then set about using *Discipline and punish* as a supplement to such an account in the manner already indicated. This wastes the opportunity that his work provides to reopen the question of whether the school is in fact an apparatus for the social domination of subjectivity. It also misses a chance that Foucault's work holds out to educational theorists themselves: namely, to reconsider their own ethical and political relation to the actually existing school system. The remarks that follow address both of these issues.

From educational principles to school premises

Contemporary educational theory is highly principled, in two different but related senses. First, it approaches the school system as if it were an attempt – typically a failed one – to actualize certain fundamental under-lying ethical and political principles such as equality, liberty and rational-ity. For liberal educational theory – whose recent resurgence owes much to the work of the American scholar Amy Gutmann (1980, 1987) – these principles are invested above all in the rational and moral capacities of free individuals. Such capacities will apparently allow a society of rational individuals to use the school system as the democratic means to form itself as a society of rational individuals. For Marxian educational sociol-ogy – for example, Williams (1961), Thompson (1963), Bowles & Gintis (1976, 1977, 1989), Bowles (1977), Apple (1980), Connell et al. (1982), Green (1990) – it is not rational individuals that matter but classes and their economic interests; and the school is typically treated as the instru-ment by which the dominant class has imposed its interests, thereby reproducing social inequality.

These rival theories may not be as far apart as they seem. Even for Marxian theory, the school system *should* be a means for realizing the principles of equality, liberty and rationality. And while liberals opt for a notion of individual development through political participation, Marxists pin their faith in a notion of collective development through socio-historical transformation. Bowles & Gintis encapsulate both the difference and the closeness of liberal and Marxian educational theory:

> . . . the liberal concept of human nature forces us to separate what are in fact integrally interrelated aspects of human welfare: learning (human development) and choosing (human freedom). By so doing, liberal educational theory justifies schooling as a form of domina-tion in which the freedom of the student is subordinated to an insti-tutional will. An adequate conception of human nature must recognise that learning occurs through the exercise of freedom. Such a concept allows the fulfilment of the liberal vision and cor-responds to the notion of progressive social change as the full democratisation of social life. (Bowles & Gintis 1989: 24)

Here the central point to be observed is that both Marxian and liberal theories derive the principles of education from a certain image of the person. This is a conception of the person as a self-developing subject, who "learns" through freedom, and for whom the school is thus only an instrument of the person's own self-realization or *Bildung*, as the Germans would say.

Secondly, current educational theory is principled in the intellectual and ethical demeanour of its theorists. These theorists typically conduct their intellectual selves in a highly principled manner. Educational policies and institutions are often criticized and opposed "on principle". The principle invoked is of course that of the complete development of the person. And this means that no matter what definite and limited improvements might be promised by particular educational reforms, they can always be criticized for failing to realize this principle. Hence, because they obey other imperatives, such reforms – aimed, for example, at improving literacy, increasing participation and retention rates, improving the scholastic performance of girls or minorities – are routinely criticized as "instrumental", "technocratic", "managerialist"; that is, as failing to realize the principle of complete personal development. But it is not difficult to show that no actually existing State school system has ever been based on this principle. This fact, however, appears no impediment to principled educational theory. On the contrary, it is *because* no actual system has ever been governed by this principle that theorists can conduct themselves as principled persons: rejecting the actual State system as merely empirical; denouncing attempts to describe it without critique as "positivist"; and forming their own intellectual conduct on the basis of an uncompromising insight into what this system should be or will be, when history finally realizes the ideal: a hypercritical and prophetic intellectual fundamentalism.

This play between the ideal and the real can imbue educational theory and history with a curious kind of ambivalence to the school system. Connell and his collaborators, for example, describe State schooling as a bureaucratic imposition on working-class culture, designed to reproduce class differences by ensuring that working-class students and families systematically fail to meet the academic and behavioural demands of a middle-class curriculum. In the same book, however, the authors argue that the comprehensive secondary school – surely the pinnacle of the State's bureaucratic intervention in education – was not "imposed on the working class" but "grew in response to a powerful demand from the working class, and . . . represented an egalitarian reform" (Connell et al. 1982: 170). Similarly, from the liberal side, Gutmann argues both that the school system fails to function as a democratic institution and that mass schooling is a historical legacy of democratic polities. With regard to the latter point, for example, she claims that: "Judging from historical experience, it seems implausible that nondemocratic institutions are more reliable in establishing adequate education for every child than are democratic ones" (Gutmann 1987: 138).

These of course would be important claims if they were true. The central empirical concern of this chapter is to show that they are not. On the one hand, I argue that the modern school system is not the historical creation of democratic polities or of popular political struggle. Neither, on the other hand, can it be understood as the instrument through which the aspirations of rational individuals or self-realizing classes have been defeated, through the cold calculations of the State acting on behalf of an inhuman economic system. Empirically, I suggest that the school system can be neither as good as its critics wish it were, nor as bad as they think it is.

But this empirical concern also has a theoretical edge, for it is driven by the genealogical approach to disciplinary institutions exemplified in *Discipline and punish*. One of the striking consequences of this approach is that historical phenomena are seen to emerge not as realizations of underlying principles or developmental laws, but as contingent assemblages put together under "blind" historical circumstances. In *Discipline and punish* this shift in the axis of analysis is marked in the subordination of educational principle to a concern with what might be called the *habitus* of the school itself. Foucault's concern is to describe not the ideals of education or its hidden class functions but the detailed organization of the (monitorial) school as a purpose-built pedagogical environment assembled from a mix of physical and moral elements: special architectures; devices for organizing space and time; body techniques; practices of surveillance and supervision; pedagogical relationships; procedures of administration and examination.

There had been earlier books on the architectural and disciplinary organization of the school, such as Malcolm Seaborne's (1971) important study *The English school*. And there had of course been many earlier theoretical and historical accounts of the principles of education and of the ways these principles had been betrayed by the social reality of schooling. But while the focus of the former studies tended to exclude discussion of the profound social and moral consequences of the school milieu, the latter accounts tended to ignore the school as a built-environment altogether, treating it as the pliable instrument of larger forces or deeper principles.[2] Foucault's intervention in *Discipline and punish* was thus to insist that it is not educational principles that are central to the role of education systems but school premises. Foucault's argument implies that both the formation of the person carried in modern education, and the social uses to which education can be put, are inseparable from the actual historical assemblage of the school as a moral and physical milieu dedicated to the mass training of children.

Foucault's genealogical approach is distinguished most radically from liberal political philosophy and dialectical social theory because it allows for an analysis of social institutions that is unprincipled in both of the relevant senses. On the one hand, Foucault's genealogies show us how to avoid treating the modern school system as a failed attempt to realize the principle of complete personal development. They allow us instead to approach the school as an improvised historical institution – assembled from the moral and material grab-bag of Western culture; providing a means of dealing with specific exigencies; and capable of nothing more than contingent solutions to limited problems. On the other hand, the Foucauldian analyst is less likely to claim to speak on behalf of a principle of humanity that the school supposedly fails to realize. Hence, rather than conducting themselves on the basis of unrealized and uncompromising principles, analysts are given the opportunity to temper their demands of the school system, and to situate their analysis in relation to the kinds of problems that the system has actually been improvised to cope with.

Two elements of the historical milieu in which the "popular" school emerged are of particular importance. The first of these consists of the political objectives and governmental technologies of the early-modern administrative territorial State. In his later essays on the theme of "governmentality" Foucault has characterized the novelty of these states in terms of a new rationale and practice of government. This rationale of government, *raison d'état*, conceived of the State as its own end. It rationalized a form of government whose objects were the security and prosperity of the State itself, and which identified the welfare of the citizens with the achievement of these ends. At the same time, under the umbrella of this rationale the domains and objectives of government in fact began to multiply. Once government was conceived in terms of an optimal management of a territory and its population, it multiplied into a number of discrete domains – government of the economy, internal and external security, welfare, moral discipline – each increasingly controlled by its own expert personnel. These were the circumstances in which, during the eighteenth century, statesmen and bureaucrats in a State like Prussia first began to propose the building of a State school system: as a means for the mass moral training of the population with a view to enhancing the strength and prosperity of the State and thereby the welfare of the people.

The second historical "surface of emergence" of the modern school was provided by the institutions and practices of Christian pastoral guidance. States may wish to transform their populations for "reasons of state", but this does not mean that they can simply whistle the means of moral training into existence. In western Europe, the administrative State borrowed these means from the Christian pastorate. Indeed, under the banners of the Reformation and the counter-Reformation, the churches had begun to develop their own school systems independently of the State, as instruments of massive campaigns to Christianize and "confessionalize" the daily life of the laity (Hinrichs 1971, Laqueur 1976, Delumeau 1988, Hsia 1989). As James Melton (1988) has shown, the Pietists of the Prussian city of Halle had begun to improvise a school system, conceived as a means of mass moral training, as early as the late seventeenth century, while Prussia was still a rurally based agricultural society, albeit administered by an increasingly sophisticated and powerful bureaucratic government. While Prussian statesmen might see the pastoral school as a handy instrument for the social training of a citizenry, they were also taking up the forms of pastoral training and expertise of a religiously based institution of spiritual guidance.

Let me be as provocative as possible. The school system, I suggest, is not bureaucratic and disciplinary by default, having betrayed its mission of human self-realization to a repressive State or a rapacious economy. It is positively and irrevocably bureaucratic and disciplinary, emerging as it does from the exigencies of social governance and from the pastoral disciplines with which the administrative State attempted to meet these exigencies. This does not mean that the school system has been inimical to the goal of self-realization. On the contrary, one of the most distinctive characteristics of the modern "popular" school – the one that makes it so difficult for its critical theorists to understand – is that, in adapting the milieu of pastoral guidance to its own uses, State schooling made self-realization into a central disciplinary objective.

The pedagogical state

One of the first parliamentary initiatives of the newly established Australian Colony-State of Victoria was to lay plans for a popular school system. It was the task of the Select Committee of 1852 "to inquire into and report upon the workings of the present systems for the Instruction of Youth in this Colony" (Hunter 1994: 38). In this, as in so many things, the colony was echoing the institutions of its parent State. Here the models were the great parliamentary Select Committees on education. These were the instruments through which the British government had brought to bear the technical expertise and the political force that made the education of the population thinkable as a State objective. Faced with the task of establishing the infrastructure of civil governance in a settler society, the Victorian parliamentarians and notables had to solve problems something like those that had confronted the emerging States of western Europe in the seventeenth and eighteenth centuries. One of the differences, of course, was that the Australian colonists could borrow ready-made the political and intellectual technologies that European States had improvised to overcome such problems. We should not be surprised then that the school system developed in Victoria – its administrative apparatus, architecture, pedagogy, methods of teacher training and some of its leading personnel – were taken directly from the system of popular education that the British State had been building since 1839.

The colonists had also inherited a particular way of thinking about education that, while it was in fact historically quite recent and still controversial, had become commonplace. Thus in his testimony to the Select Committee, the Reverend James Clow – betraying no awareness of the momentous history lying behind his words – could affirm that: "as the educated citizen is much more valuable to the State than an uneducated one, the State should do all in its power to further education" (Blake 1973 I: 24). About a century earlier, much closer to the emergence of this style of thought, Johann von Justi had elaborated a similar theme with regard to university education:

> It will be enough if we attend to [the universities'] ultimate purpose. This, in so far as they are public foundations of the state, can be no other than that of affording to youth properly prepared in the lower schools adequate instruction in all intelligence and science which will be needful for them, in order that they may some time, as servants of the state and upright citizens, render useful services to the common-wealth [*dem gemeinen Wesen*], and be in a position fully to discharge their duties. (Small 1909: 299)

Justi's remarks appeared in a comprehensive textbook on State management, his *Staatswirtschaft*, whose full title might be loosely translated as "a systematic treatise on all economic and administrative sciences necessary for the government of a country".

It might seem incongruous to juxtapose the views of a notable in a colony-state that was "born democratic" with those of a bureaucratic adviser to the absolute States of Prussia and Austria. But for all the differences in their political complexions, the liberal clergyman and the statist administrator are the bearers of a common governmental rationale for State schooling. Both of them think of education as a cultural transformation of the population carried out in the interests of the State. They argue that the State should intervene in education as a means of enhancing its corporate wealth and prosperity, and *thereby* the wellbeing of its citizens.

This is the political mentality that Foucault (1991) has dubbed "governmentality". We must resist the intellectual temptation to explain this away as the result of a utilitarian philosophy, or an "instrumental" bureaucracy acting on behalf of an exploitative economy; to treat it as a mere subtraction from a more complete form of development oriented to the moral perfection of the person. Such responses are literally incapable of contemplating the possibility that the emergence of the governmental State has made the State's calculation of its own interests into a permanent and legitimate feature of political reflection and morality. Two features of the administrative State, and the circumstances in which it emerged, help us to comprehend this.

First, far from "failing" to base itself on such absolute moral principles as moral perfection or the "just state", the administrative State emerged, in part, from a sustained intellectual and political campaign to banish such principles from the sphere of government. Drawing on such diverse intellectual sources as neo-Stoicism, Dutch natural law, and the ethics of Gracian, and articulated by writers as different as Lipsius and Pufendorf, Hobbes and Thomasius, this movement waged a long battle to detach political reflection from theology and reconstitute it on civil grounds (Oestreich 1969, 1982, Brückner 1977). Reinhart Koselleck (1988) has taught us to see this as a profound moral and political achievement. The administrative State, as an object of political reflection and as an objective of political activity, emerged during the period of religious civil war that decimated European societies during the seventeenth and early eighteenth centuries. This warfare, argues Koselleck, was driven by a supramundane "politics of conscience" that indeed claimed to derive government from absolute moral principles. This was a politics that saw the prince as God's representative on earth and that saw the just State as an expression of divine will, committed to "unifying the faith" and defending the "true religion" at all costs. Koselleck describes how the unprecedented civil carnage fuelled by such non-negotiable principles eventually discredited their claim to provide ultimate foundations for government, at least in the eyes of practising statesmen and administrators.

These were the circumstances under which a new rationale for government appeared. The survival and flourishing of the State itself emerged as the prime directive of political thought and action. The doctrine of *Staatsraison* thus treated the security and prosperity of the State as ultimate in relation to all other political ends. As the only agency capable of standing above the warring sects and factions, the State became "absolute". It did so not in the name of a new political philosophy, or as an expression of the arbitrary will of the prince, but as the circumstantially-driven instrument for ending religious slaughter and imposing civil peace (Koselleck 1988: 23–34). The State's achievement of social peace thus emerged as an ultimate horizon for political morality, producing the inescapable "worldliness" or mundanity of the administrative State's political objectives.

Koselleck (1988: 36) credits Hobbes with providing the first systematic formulation of the moral and political consequences of these developments. The emergent ethical autonomy of the State meant that the "citizen" could no longer be thought of as identical with the "man". The citizen was defined by public obedience to the law which was the condition of social peace. The "man", on the other hand, might freely follow the light of his conscience as long as this did not interfere with his public duty to the law. The persona of the citizen as an inhabitant of the administrative State, and the persona of the reflective subject as practitioner of religious self-governance, now represented two distinct kinds of ethical comportment. Historical circumstances, moreover, required their sequestration in two distinct realms, of "public" and "private" conduct. The manner in which this protracted and incomplete elaboration of different modalities of conduct was embodied in official policy is represented well enough in Wöllner's Edict on Religion, issued by the Prussian justice minister at the end of the eighteenth century:

A subject of the Prussian state is declared free to hold what religious views he likes, so long as he quietly performs his duties as a good citizen of the state and so long as he keeps any peculiar opinion to himself and carefully guards himself from spreading it or persuading others, making them uncertain in their faith or leading them astray. (Gregor 1979: x)

This policy had been in force throughout the century and, as the practical cornerstone of religious toleration, was itself regarded as a symbol of "enlightenment". It was typical of policies tempered in the furnace of religious civil war, and was symptomatic of the State's "atheist" attempt to detach itself from all confessional ideals and to subordinate the latter to civil peace and prosperity.

Those who think that the administrative State lacks a defensible conception of social wellbeing as the result of a moral disintegration that has split political administration from individual conscience should perhaps think again. Without this separation – that was a hard-won differentiation of adjacent spheres of life and forms of personal comportment – the imposition of a politically binding conception of public good on confessionally divided communities would have been impossible. Significant private freedoms associated with "liberal" societies – in this case religious toleration and freedom of worship – far from being the expressions of democratic institutions or popular resistance, were means by which the administrative State pacified and governed fratricidal communities. Above all, the mundane objectives of the administrative State – social order, economic prosperity, social welfare – emerged as an authentic moral and political response to the "political situation" and they remain quite irreducible to the conscience of the "reflective person".

The second feature of the administrative State that makes it irreducible to the moral and intellectual physiognomy of the person, is the manner in which it combines the exercise of power with the development of knowledge or expertise. It became possible to think of the tasks and scope of government in a new way because new "faculties" of governmental reflection had been improvised. These faculties were neither housed in the "human subject", nor were they expressions of its historical evolution. They comprised instead an archipelago of calculative institutions – statistical societies, administrative bureaux, university departments – where governmental analysis and decision were the product of particular kinds of procedural expertise. A conception and apparatus of government emerged that, as Foucault (1991: 88–96) has shown, differed from both machiavellian *Realpolitik* and legal–constitutional reflection on the rights and duties of sovereignty. This is a conception of government as an art and the state as an "enterprise" (*Betrieb*) conceived in terms of an optimal management of the various domains of government and grounded neither in the legal or moral right of its citizens, nor in the arbitrary sovereignty of its prince, but in "fundamental and special knowledge" of the governmental domains themselves.

The typical and perhaps central form of such knowledge was statistics: an invented intellectual technology that, as Georges Canguilhem (1978) and Ian Hacking (1975, 1982) have shown, was responsible for a specific historical transformation and augmentation of human intellectual capability. Because of its capacity to represent reality in terms of quantifiable and manipulable domains, the technology of statistics creates the capacity to relate to reality as a field for government. It was through the technology of social statistics therefore that the German Cameralists were able to reconstruct the objectives of government as a series of problems requiring expert management.

In England, James Kay-Shuttleworth – who was to become the head of the State's first education bureau – was typical of those who used social statistics to transform the meaning of popular education. His survey, *The moral and physical condition of the working classes of Manchester in 1832,* was perhaps the single most influential British argument for State intervention in popular education. Kay-Shuttleworth's (1973) "perception" of Manchester's social problems, and of State education as their corrective instrument, was formed through a series of statistical correlations linking the poverty, criminality, morbidity, alcoholism and immorality of Manchester's working classes to their "ignorance" or illiteracy. A specific political and intellectual technology allowed Kay-Shuttleworth and others similarly positioned to have access to a new object of political perception and action. This object was the population. The population thus emerged as the bearer of an array of conducts and capacities that had been rendered problematic through the application of statistically determined norms or standards of living.[3] The knowledge of the "moral and physical conditions" of Manchester's working classes produced by Kay-Shuttleworth's social survey was neither science nor ideology. It was neither a neutral representation of social facts nor a representation whose distortion by class interests meant that the true facts had been obscured. This is because the role of social statistics is not so much to represent reality as to problematize it: to call it into question; to hold it up for inspection in the light of what it might be; to picture its reconstruction around certain norms of life and social wellbeing – norms derived of course from the social, economic and political objectives of government.

The new political and intellectual technologies of government – whose organizational form is the bureau – thus allowed the life and labour of national populations to be known in a form that opened them to political calculation and administrative intervention. Government thus unites the application of knowledge and the exercise of power not in the negative form of ideology, but in definite technical problematizations and interventions that help to bring new departments of social life into being. State-administered elementary education emerged as a new domain of government in which the school would take shape as an instrument for training whole populations in the capacities required for participation in more sophisticated forms of social, economic and political life. The emergence of "popular" education as a governmental objective can thus be attributed neither to liberalism's community of rational individuals nor to Marxism's dialectic of opposed classes. Instead, State schooling emerged as the instrument and object of a technically formed, institutionally-organized and circumstantially driven governmental expertise, whose social distribution was inescapably limited and will remain so.

The school system cannot be treated as the (compromised) expression of educational principle. State schooling emerged from particular historical exigencies confronting administrative States, and from the intellectual and political technologies that these States happened to have at their disposal for addressing such exigencies. While the exigencies varied – we have mentioned civil war and rural backwardness in Prussia, the chaotic populations of industrial cities in England, the untutored colonial population of Australia – the technology of statistical survey and social intervention tended to be portable across different States, imposing a common "statist" intelligibility on education no matter what the state-form. Popular education was not an attempt to realize the individual's inner self but a means of enclosing populations in a purpose-built pedagogical milieu capable of creating socially disciplined persons. This milieu was provided not by the State but by the Christian pastorate, which was indeed dedicated to forming morally self-governing individuals. To understand why the ethic of self-realization, while not the *foundation* of popular education is yet one of its central *disciplinary goals*, we must consider the role of the pastoral milieu in State schooling.

Spiritual discipline and "subjectification"

For Johann von Justi, eighteenth-century statesman, bureaucrat and administrative intellectual, the happiness or highest good of the citizens and of the State were inseparable. They consisted in three things: "freedom, assured property, and flourishing industry" (Small 1909: 331). For Immanuel Kant, moral philosopher and privileged citizen of one of the absolute States that Justi helped to administer, the highest good was moral

155

enlightenment. In its political form this consisted in individuals throwing off the "self-incurred tutelage" of external governance and beginning the task of self-realization, relying only on their own faculties of conscience and consciousness. According to the philosopher any State that did not democratically embody this rational and self-determining moral will was illegitimate. In the name of the freedom of the self-reflective person, Kant launched the moral problematization of government whose echo we can still hear in today's theorists of democratic education.

Kant was, however, less than clear about how the State could be transformed into the expression of individual reason. In fact he happily acknowledged Frederick the Great as the democratic embodiment of the will of his people. Indeed Kant was somewhat more aware than his modern followers of the complex relation between the tutelary training of the population and the capacity for rational self-government, for at one level, he acknowledges that the latter may depend on the former:

> But only one [that is, Frederick] who is himself enlightened is not afraid of shadows, and who has a numerous and well-disciplined army to assure public peace, can say: "Argue as much as you will, and about what you will, only obey!" A republic could not dare say such a thing. Here is shown a strange and unexpected trend in human affairs in which almost everything, looked at in large, is paradoxical. A greater degree of civil freedom appears advantageous to the freedom of the mind of the people, and yet it places inescapable limitations upon it; a lower degree of civil freedom, on the contrary, provides the mind with room for each man to extend himself to his full capacity. (Kant 1986: 269)

Those tempted to see Kant's defence of an army-backed enlightenment as an aberration, or as an unessential concession to circumstance, are missing the point. Ensconced in the bosom of a newly pacified "police" State, and thereby able to engage in philosophical and religious speculation without fear of religious butchery, Kant is no less beholden to the separation of civic duty from private conscience than was Hobbes. Yet, because of the mix of rationalism and Pietism informing his philosophy, Kant remains committed to both the unity of the person and to the supremacy of individual conscience, as expressed in the categorical imperative. Unlike Hobbes and Pufendorf, Lipsius and Thomasius, Kant did not allow civic or governmental interests to have an ethical standing equivalent to that of the inner moral sense. Indeed, he denied such interests the status of morality altogether, calling them merely "prudential".

Kant's ethical individualism and universalism thus make it impossible for him to reach a positive historical understanding of the separation of the governmental and intellectual–spiritual (*geistlich*) spheres. If Kant does acknowledge the difference between the civic comportment of the citizen and the inward bearing of the rational subject, it is only as a disfiguring split – between prudence and morality, tutelage and self-realization, the empirical and the ideal. This is why "history" for Kant – and indeed for all post-Kantian historicisms – is a developmental process governed by the mission of healing the split in man's ethical nature. Hence it is to history that Kant appeals when he imagines that the state's creation of rational capacities in its citizens will eventually reflect back on the State, transforming it into the expression of its citizens' capacity for reason.

Kantian political and moral philosophy thus juxtaposes two incompatible views: a *de facto* acknowledgement that rational conduct is an effect of the State's pacification and training of the population; and the unblinking faith of an intellectual elite that such conduct arises from intellectual self-reflection alone. The best that Kant can manage is to treat the flourishing of intellectual reflection within Frederick's "warfare-welfare" State as a "paradox". The only resolution that Kant can find for this "paradoxical" situation – that was generated when supramundane intellectuals became citizens of radically mundane administrative states – is to posit a circular relation between the State's disciplinary creation of a rational citizenry and the citizenry's intellectual creation of a rational State. In this regard Kant is the intellectual godfather of today's liberal and Marxian educational theorists. For the liberal paradox of a community of rational individuals that uses schooling to form itself, and the Marxian dialectic of "learning (human development) and choosing (human freedom)", are latter-day variants of the Kantian circle. Like Kant's, these views are incapable of reflecting on the school system as one of the arational, disciplinary means through which states began to form populations capable of civic conduct.

Kant's presumption of the morally ultimate character of self-reflective personhood has not gone unchallenged. A project to "historicize" Kant – by tying the development of the person to that of "society" – began with Schiller and passed through Hegel to Marx, and then on into the proliferating dialectical anthropologies of our own time. But the role of history in these anthropologies – to complete the development of the person by reconciling man's material determination and his reflective intellect – is far too Kantian to succeed in its mission. Thus a number of scholars, including Foucault in his late work on ethics, have sought genealogies for personhood in the non-dialectical disciplines of ethical anthropology and the historical-sociology of religion, and it is not difficult to detect the late Foucault's dependence on the work of such scholars as Pierre Hadot (1981, 1990) and Paul Rabbow (1954). These lines of inquiry reject the Kantian view of the moral subject as its own foundation and are equally hostile to Hegelian and Marxian historicist accounts of the "formation of the subject". The object of their investigations is neither the self-reflective subject nor the historical dialectic that promises to synthesize this subject, but the specific spiritual practices and disciplines through which individuals become ethically self-concerned and seek to compose themselves as the "subjects" of their own conduct. The reflective subject is understood as a particular practice or comportment of the person, deriving ultimately from Western "spiritual disciplines".

For these studies the individual is seen as the raw material for various kinds of "ethical work", including the kind of self-problematizing and self-reflective work that results in that comportment of the person that we call "the subject". Two features of this cultural labour through which individuals are "subjectified" are of particular concern to us. The first is that before individuals can begin to reflect on themselves as the subjects of their own conduct – before they can take an ethical interest in themselves – they must undergo a certain kind of problematization. They must first cross a "threshold of interrogation", and this is only done through initiation into specific practices of self-problematization (Jambet 1992). Greco-Roman and Christian cultures are rich with such practices. Whether in the form of Stoic self-testing or in that of the Christian "interrogation of the flesh" – whether through the Catholic confessional or Protestant self-examination – we are the heirs to a whole series of inventions for taking an interest in ourselves as the subjects of our conduct.

Secondly, the particular ways in which individuals can conduct themselves as persons – the ways in which they can "be themselves" – are the product of the forms of ethical labour through which they perform a certain "work of the self on the self". Once again classical and Christian spiritual practice is the source of a repertory of such forms: self-examination, sexual austerity, fasting, practices of self-integration, mystical disciplines. These provide the "ascetic" means by which individuals can "practise themselves", disciplining and comporting themselves as the responsible agents of their own (sexual, visionary, dietary) personhood, in pursuit of a self-imposed spiritual goal.

The persona of the subject – the model of the person as a reflective agent – is thus analyzed as a particular comportment of the individual made available to European populations by Christian spiritual discipline and pastoral guidance. If this preliminary genealogy proves tenable then it will be necessary to give up the idea that the subject might freely choose its own form, through a rational inspection of moral principles or competing versions of the good life. Freedom becomes a characteristic of individual action only after conduct has undergone moral problematization. One can seek to free oneself from carnal desire, for example, but only after one's sexual conduct has been problematized as a shackle on the soul or as an impediment to true vision. Or, to take a Kantian example, one can seek to free oneself from "sensuous inclinations" and self-interest, but only after one has been compelled to problematize these as encumbrances on the pure will. What individuals cannot do is freely choose the form in which they will undergo moral problematization and cross the threshold of interrogation into a particular way of relating to themselves and living the good life.

Seen from this angle, Weber's (1930) account of the rise of the Protestant ethic in the sixteenth and seventeenth centuries is a description of a massive exercise in spiritual training. Like so-called "Muslim fundamentalism" today, early-modern Protestantism was an attempt to spiritualize church and society through the systematic transfer of ethical disciplines from the priesthood to the lay population. This transfer involved the systematic use of devices for mass spiritual problematization – in particular the doctrine of predestination that, as Weber argues, destroyed the certitude of salvation that had come from collective participation in the sacraments of the true church. And it involved the systematic transmission of particular forms of ethical labour: practices of self-watchfulness and self-control, special forms of devotional reading and writing, through which the faithful monitored and reassured themselves of their ethical standing. The result was a profound dissemination and individualization of Christian spirituality, as ordinary members of the flock were inducted into a practice of ethical life that made them "personally" responsible for their own salvation. Jean Delumeau (1988) has given a parallel account of the counter-Reformation, as a systematic distribution of prestigious and previously esoteric spiritual compartments to large lay populations.

Perhaps it will now seem less surprising that the first popular school systems in Europe were established by the churches as instruments for the intensification and dissemination of Christian spiritual discipline and pastoral guidance. Although this movement reached its highest point under the impetus of eighteenth-century Pietism and Puritanism (Laqueur 1976), it began in the continental European states during the sixteenth and seventeenth centuries (Melton 1988). The emergence of popular education in states like Prussia and Austria thus coincides with neither capitalism nor industrialization, nor with any of the other poles of the great dialectic. While the appearance of Christian school systems may have roughly coincided with the emergence of the administrative State, such systems were, in their initial inspiration and organization at least, the product of an autonomous history. This was a specifically religious effort by the Reformed Churches to Christianize European peasantries, using first parish Sunday schools and then parochial day schools in a project to transfer spiritual discipline into daily life.

What Christian pedagogy contributed to the development of mass school systems was something far more important and permanent than that dismissed by critical historians as religious brainwashing. It contributed the organizing routines, pedagogical practices, personal disciplines and interpersonal relationships that came to form the core of the modern school. No doubt it will seem implausible to suggest that at the centre of the modern school we find a "psychagogy" or pedagogics of spiritual discipline. When we look at the core structure of the modern school, however, we see a carefully crafted formative milieu that first appeared in the Christian schools of the seventeenth and eighteenth centuries. The classroom is a space of ethical formation in which the students are placed under the continuous ethical supervision and problematization of a teacher who embodies both moral authority and pastoral care (Laqueur 1976, Jones & Williamson 1979, Hunter 1988, 1994: 62–87).

The object of this pastoral pedagogy was not to produce docile workers or social automatons. Instead, as we have seen, it was to form the capacities required for individuals to comport themselves as self-reflective and self-governing persons. There is no doubt that the disciplines required for this comportment were not themselves reflectively and freely chosen. But this is a fact about "subjectification" that critical theory has not yet understood. In criticizing pedagogy for failing to make the disciplines of reflective freedom into freely reflected disciplines – and in claiming this achievement for itself – educational critique fails to grasp that the capacities of the reflective person emerge only *after* individuals have been initiated into the arts of self-concern and self-regulation. In transmitting the disciplines of ethical self-concern and ethical labour into the daily life of the laity – in creating what Weber calls a "worldly asceticism" – Christian pedagogy was a means by which larger sectors of the European population began to conduct themselves as reflective persons:

> The Puritan, like every rational type of asceticism, tried to enable a man to maintain and act upon his constant motives, especially those which it taught him itself, against the emotions. In this formal psychological sense of the term it tried to make him into a personality. Contrary to many popular ideas, the end of this asceticism was to be able to lead an alert, intelligent life . . . All these important points are emphasized in the rules of Catholic monasticism as strongly as in the principles of conduct of the Calvinists. On this methodical control over the whole man rests the enormous expansive power of both. (Weber 1930: 119)

It is, therefore, not to a pure Kantian intellect that we must look if we are to understand the dissemination of self-reflective personhood, but to the construction of that special pedagogical milieu in which such personhood is formed as a disciplined comportment.

Social training and spiritual discipline

By the middle of the eighteenth century in most western European states two different and autonomous rationales for educating the population lay side by side. One had emerged from a movement that had succeeded in deleting moral perfection from the goals of political administration – that had placed the State's survival above the soul's salvation – and in doing so had achieved a purely worldly or mundane reconstruction of the objectives of government: "freedom, assured property, and flourishing industry". From the political rationality and "expert systems" of the emerging governmental State emerged the imperative for a bureaucratically organized system of mass education. This was a system designed to discipline and enhance the social capacities of "problematized" populations in accordance with a number of governmental objectives: the social disciplining of agrarian peasantries as in Prussia and Austria; the "moral and physical" training of chaotic urban sub-proletariats as in Britain; the "modernizing" of the colonized Irish peasantry. The other programme emerged from the historic efforts of the reformed Protestant and Catholic churches to Christianize lay populations, through a dedicated transfer of spiritual discipline into the routines of daily life. This Christian pedagogy was indeed designed to secure the soul's salvation, in the form of the self-reflective and self-perfecting moral personality. Yet it consisted of an ensemble of quite "material" ethical practices and techniques, transmitted through the institutional organization of a new type of pastoral school.

The manner in which "critical" educational theory and history has sought to efface the "statist" and Christian lineages of the modern school system suggests a systematic attempt to "transcend" historical actuality. If our initial sketch of these genealogies can be sustained then we will have to give up the idea that the bureaucratically organized pastoral school is a temporary phenomenon, created to serve the interests of an exploitative economy, and destined to be democratically transformed once this economy is brought under the popular control of an emancipated working class or a community of rational individuals. State schooling is not the expression of the interests and capacities of a collective person, temporarily divided and alienated by the class structure of society, and therefore open to a democratic distribution once class divisions are overcome. On the contrary, it is the product of those historically invented technical faculties of the administrative State whose institutional form is the bureau. As Weber insists, it was the expert–technical ethos of the bureaucratic office that made it possible – indeed a point of honour – for individuals to renounce their "personal" religious and ethical commitments and to participate in "impersonal" State-centred decision-making. In attempting to base their professional conduct on their "habitual virtuosity" as procedural experts – and not in their relation to themselves as reflective persons – bureaucrats thus represent an autonomous and indispensable persona of our civic existence. Far from being a temporary alienation of the democratic community's capacity for self-determination, the bureaucratic character of State schooling is the instrument and the effect of that historical transformation that separated the worldly government of the population from the spiritual politics of conscience.

Equally, we will have to give up the belief that the "subjectivizing" or "religious" character of pedagogy is symptomatic merely of the school's "hidden curriculum" and ideological mission; and that it will one day be replaced by a "critical pedagogy" in which the reflective person is created through an act of personal reflection. We have seen that the self-reflective ethical subject produced by Christian pedagogy was not an ideological detour on the way to a true consciousness. Neither was the Christian formation of the person a down-payment that will be fully redeemed when secular rationality finally permits a free choice among "good lives". To the contrary, this subject was and is the result of an unchosen initiation into a spiritual discipline that equips individuals to comport themselves as reflective subjects. Indeed, it is the fact that Christian pedagogy existed as a discipline, rather than as an ideology, that allowed it to slip its theological moorings and to reappear in the form of secular moral education. In fact this latter "humanist" pedagogy employs practices of problematization and forms of ethical labour adapted from its Christian prototype. The self-reflective, self-regulating students that it forms are thus no less the result of an unconditional initiation into the disciplines of conscience.

Bureaucratic administration and pastoral-disciplinary pedagogy thus emerge as permanent and inescapable features of the modern school system. No doubt there will be many who will find such a conclusion to be at best implausible and, more likely, politically and ethically misguided, perhaps even culpable. After all, it might be said, today we live in liberal or social democratic societies in which citizens no longer require the protection of a paternalist State, and where they possess the political capacities to run their own affairs, including the school system. Moreover, it seems clear that, in the most advanced sectors of society at least, the capacity to conduct oneself as a rational reflective person has long since displaced the rites of Christian pastoral guidance.

I have not been questioning these facts, however, only the theory that treats them as signs of a process in which a collective subject – the working class, the democratic community – is supposed to be transforming the school system into the instrument of its self-realization. I have provided a historical argument to the contrary: that the liberal and democratic virtues of the school system are in fact the direct outcome of its bureaucratic organization and its pastoral pedagogy. Following Koselleck, I have argued that it was the administrative State that created a non-violent, tolerant and pragmatic sphere of political deliberation, by forcefully separating the civic comportment of the citizen from the private persona of the man of conscience, and by subordinating spiritual absolutes to governmental objectives. Perhaps the foremost instrument and effect of this historic development was the education "bureau", through which states conceptualized and organized that massive and ongoing programme of pacification, discipline and training responsible for the political and social capacities of the modern citizen. Further, I have argued that it was Christian pastoralism that disseminated the comportment of the self-reflective person so prized by critical theorists, and that it did so via a pedagogy of moral "subjectification" that remains at the heart of modern schooling.

The school system thus emerged through a piecemeal series of exchanges between a State that conceived of the school as a bureaucratic instrument for the social governance of citizens, and a Christian pastorate that saw it as a means for the spiritual disciplining of souls. These exchanges, whose end is still not in sight, occurred in the form of a whole series of improvisations at the level of architecture, pedagogy, administration. If we speak then of the "rarity" of the school, this is a way of indicating the fragility and contingency of the process that brought it into being, and the scarcity of the basic pedagogical rituals that our culture happens to have at its disposal.

Notes

1. This chapter draws on materials published in my *Rethinking the school* (Hunter 1994). Its writing was made possible by the award of an Australian Research Council Fellowship, for which I am grateful. I should also like to thank the editors for their helpful commentary on the first draft and Simon During who suggested the title.
2. A notable exception to this tendency is Laqueur (1976), a study that combines analysis of the social and cultural forces driving the movement for popular education with a detailed treatment of the Sunday school as a specific organization of space, time and activity.
3. For discussions of this and related issues, see Canguilhem (1978), Miller & Rose (1990) and Foucault (1979).

References

Apple, M. 1980. *Education and power*. London: Routledge & Kegan Paul.

Ball, S. J. (ed.) 1990. *Foucault and education: disciplines and knowledge*. London: Routledge.

Blake, L. J. (ed.) 1973. *Vision and realisation: a centenary history of state education in Victoria* [2 volumes]. Melbourne: Education Department of Victoria.

Bowles, S. 1977. Unequal education and the reproduction of the social division of labour. See Karabel & Halsey (1977), 137–53.

Bowles, S. & H. Gintis 1976. *Schooling in capitalist America: educational reform and the contradictions of economic life*. New York: Basic Books.

Bowles, S. & H. Gintis 1977. I.Q. in the U.S. class structure. See Karabel & Halsey (1977), 215–32.

Bowles, S. & H. Gintis 1989. Can there be a liberal philosophy of education in a democratic society? See Giroux & McLaren (1989), 24–33.

Brückner, J. 1977. *Staatswissenschaften, Kameralismus und Naturrecht: ein Beitrag zur Geschichte der politischen Wissenschaft im Deutschland des späten 17. und frühen 18. Jahrhunderts*. Munich: Verlag C. H. Beck.

Canguilhem, G. 1978. *On the normal and the pathological*. Dordrecht: D. Reidel.

Connell, R. W., D. J. Ashenden, S. Kessler, G. W. Dowsett 1982. *Making the difference: schools, families and social division*. Sydney: Allen & Unwin (Australia).

Delumeau, J. 1988. Prescription and reality. See Leites (1988), 134–58.

Donald, J. 1992. *Sentimental education: schooling, popular culture and the regulation of liberty*. London: Verso.

Donzelot, J. 1979. *The policing of families*. New York: Pantheon Books.

Foucault, M. 1977. *Discipline and punish: the birth of the prison*. London: Penguin.

Foucault, M. 1979. *The history of sexuality*, vol. 1. London: Penguin.

Foucault, M. 1991. Governmentality. In *The Foucault effect: studies in governmentality*, G. Burchell, C. Gordon, P. Miller (eds), 87–104. Hemel Hempstead, England: Harvester Wheatsheaf.

Giroux, H. A. & P. L. McLaren (eds) 1989. *Critical pedagogy, the state, and cultural struggle*. New York: State University of New York Press.

Giroux, H. A. & P. L. McLaren (eds) 1994. *Between borders: pedagogy and the politics of cultural studies*. London: Routledge.

Green, A. 1990. *Education and state formation: the rise of education systems in England, France and the USA*. London: Macmillan.

Gregor, M. J. 1979. Translator's introduction. In *The conflict of the faculties*, I. Kant. Lincoln, Nebraska: University of Nebraska Press.

Gutmann, A. 1980. *Liberal equality*. Cambridge: Cambridge University Press.

Gutmann, A. 1987. *Democratic education*. Princeton, New Jersey: Princeton University Press.

Hacking, I. 1975. *The emergence of probability: a philosophical study about early ideas of probability, induction and statistical inference*. Cambridge: Cambridge University Press.

Hacking. I. 1982. Biopower and the avalanche of printed numbers. *Humanities in Society* **4**, 279–95.

Hadot, P. 1981. *Exercises spirituels et philosophie antique*. Paris: Etudes augustiennes.

Hadot, P. 1990. Forms of life and forms of discourse in ancient philosophy. *Critical Inquiry* **16**, 483–505.

Hinrichs, C. 1971. *Preußentum und Pietismus: der Pietismus in Brandenberg-Preußen als religiös-soziale Reformbewegung*. Göttingen: Vandenhoeck & Ruprecht.

Hsia, R. Po-Chia. 1989. *Social discipline in the Reformation: central Europe 1550–1750*. London: Routledge.

Hunter, I. 1988. *Culture and government: the emergence of literary education*. London: Macmillan.

Hunter, I. 1994. *Rethinking the school: subjectivity, bureaucracy, criticism*. Sydney: Allen & Unwin.

Jambet, C. 1992. The constitution of the subject and spiritual practice: observations on "L'Histoire de la sexualité". In *Michel Foucault, philosopher*, T. J.

Armstrong (ed.), 233–47. New York: Harvester Wheatsheaf.

Jones, K. & K. Williamson 1979. The birth of the schoolroom. *Ideology and Consciousness* **6**, 58–110.

Kant, I. 1986. What is Enlightenment? In *Philosophical writings*, E. Behler (ed.), 267–81. New York: Continuum.

Karabel, J. & A. H. Halsey (eds) 1977. *Power and ideology in education*. Oxford: Oxford University Press.

Kay-Shuttleworth, J. 1973. *The moral and physical condition of the working classes of Manchester in 1832*. In his *Four periods of public education*. Brighton: Harvester.

Kincheloe, J. L. 1993. *Towards a critical politics of teacher thinking*. Westport, Connecticut: Bergin & Garvey.

Koselleck, R. 1988. *Critique and crisis: enlightenment and the pathogenesis of modern society*. Oxford: Berg.

Laqueur, T. W. 1976. *Religion and respectability: Sunday schools and working class culture 1780–1850*. New Haven, Connecticut: Yale University Press.

Leites, E. (ed.) 1988. *Conscience and casuistry in early modern Europe*. Cambridge: Cambridge University Press.

McLaren, P. L. 1989. On ideology and education: critical pedagogy and the cultural politics of resistance. See Giroux & McLaren (1989), 174–204.

Melton, J. van H. 1988. *Absolutism and the eighteenth-century origins of compulsory schooling in Prussia and Austria*. Cambridge: Cambridge University Press.

Miller P. & N. Rose 1990. Governing economic life. *Economy and Society* **19**, 1–31.

Oestreich, G. 1969. Fundamente preuâicher Geistesgeschichte: Religion und Weltanschauung in Brandenburg im 17. Jahrhundert. *Jahrbuch Preussischer Kulturbesitz* **1969**, 20–45.

Oestreich, G. 1982. *Neostoicism and the early modern state*. Cambridge: Cambridge University Press.

Rabbow, P. 1954. *Seelenführung: Methodik der Exerzitien in der Antike*. Munich: Kösel-Verlag.

Rose, N. 1985. *The psychological complex: psychology, politics and society in England 1869–1939*. London: Routledge.

Seaborne, M. 1971. *The English school: its architecture and organisation 1370–1870*. London: Routledge & Kegan Paul.

Small, A. W. 1909. *The Cameralists: the pioneers of German social polity*. Chicago: University of Chicago Press.

Thompson, E.P. 1963. *The making of the English working class*. London: Pelican Books.

Weber, M. 1930. *The Protestant ethic and the spirit of capitalism*. London: Allen & Unwin.

Williams, R. 1961. *The long revolution*. London: Chatto & Windus.

Chapter 8

Governing the city: liberalism and early modern modes of governance

Alan Hunt

Liberalism and governmentality

One of the interesting questions that has come to fore in the sociology of governance is the neo-Foucauldian approach to the understanding of liberalism (Gordon 1991, Burchell 1993, Rose 1993). What is distinctive about this line of thought is that it self-consciously avoids discussing liberalism as either a political philosophy or as a constitutional configuration. Drawing on Foucault's late and scattered comments, liberalism is explored as a form of governmental rationality or governmentality. Much that is original and insightful about modern forms of liberalism is emerging. This chapter explores one possible weakness in this line of inquiry, namely, that tends to take Foucault's schematic characterization of pre-modern forms of government at face value. Foucault expressed two general periodizations of the forms of government; the first contrasted absolutism (characterized by sovereignty and law) with the disciplinary society; the second strand contrasted an administrative state ("police"/ "Polizei-ordnungen", Cameralism) and liberalism ("governmentalization of the state", "society of security").

Nikolas Rose observes that "governmentality, for Foucault, is specified in opposition to a notion of police" (1993: 289). The core claim is that liberalism constructs itself in the form of limits on the domain of politics and the recognition of a civil society "outside" the state. Liberalism is presented as a form of governance that succeeds the form associated with "police". I will argue that this view does not sufficiently recognize the role of governmentality in the early cities of Europe between the fourteenth and seventeenth centuries. It should be noted that I make no attempt to arrive at a general account of my own, let alone a periodization, of the forms of city government. Rather, I argue that in so far as governmentality is about the mentalities and rationalities associated with the practices of governing, there was far greater continuity between the governance of the European cities and modern liberalism than is often recognized. I illustrate this theme by exploring the part played by one distinctive form of early modern regulation, namely, the sumptuary laws directed at a wide range of forms of personal consumption.[1] These laws typically regulated what could be worn and by whom, what food could be consumed, and what hospitality provided. Sumptuary laws have generally been regarded as irrational attempts to buttress an already-waning feudal hierarchy.[2] This is, I suggest, a mistaken view and I will argue that these laws attest to the existence of projects of governance that are distinctly modern in their trajectory and, furthermore, show interesting links to those areas of urban governance that have widely been regarded as harbingers of modernity such as sanitary regulation and plague measures.

Urbanism and sumptuary regulation

The city and the experience of urban existence are important components of profound shifts in social life. In the classic formulation of the connection between modernity and urbanization voiced by Ernst Troeltsch, towns have been "a preparation and foundation for the modern world" (Troeltsch 1931 I: 255). Although the city itself is not quintessentially modern, some of the most distinctive developments in the forms of social life occurred in an urban environment. And it is possible to push this a stage further by saying that these developments probably could only have occurred within cities.

Projects of sumptuary regulation were found throughout medieval and early modern Europe; a brief survey will help to locate the subsequent discussion.

Regular sumptuary regulation begins to appear by the end of the twelfth century (1157 in Genoa, 1188 in France) and becomes more frequent in the thirteenth century (1234 in Aragon, 1249 in Sienna, 1250 in Florence, 1256 in Castile). In the thirteenth century, sumptuary enactments came from both Church and State; in 1274 Pope Gregory X issued an edict banning "immoderate ornamentation" throughout Christendom. Thereafter sumptuary law became increasingly secular. By the second half of the fourteenth century, sumptuary laws were present in significant numbers over most of Europe (in 1363 England had its first significant sumptuary enactment). By the middle of the fifteenth century

Scotland and the German cities and principalities had established sumptuary legislation.

Some patterns are detectable in European sumptuary law. Continuity with ancient societies is evident in the widely imposed restrictions on conspicuous consumption in connection with funerals and weddings and other public celebrations of private rites of passage (births, christenings, etc.). The regulation of dress is also present from the beginning, but it becomes increasingly important; it comes to be the typical target of medieval sumptuary law, to such an extent that the term sumptuary law itself becomes almost synonymous with the regulation of dress and ornamentation.

Dress regulation took two distinctive forms, the first being the imposition of expenditure limits. The second form was to reserve particularly significant types of cloth or style of dress for designated categories; this was done either by granting a privilege to a social category (e.g. "only nobles may wear ermine") or by negative prohibition (e.g. "no female servant may wear a train"). There was a complex articulation alongside hierarchical considerations in the use of sumptuary dress provisions to regulate gender relations; sometimes it was men who were targeted and at other times it was women; those statutes that target women frequently employed strongly misogynistic attitudes and language. For present purposes, it is sufficient to comment that, on balance, medieval sumptuary *rules* were directed against men more often than against women.[3] Although women only came to be the privileged object of sumptuary regulation in the early modern period, there is abundant evidence to show that *enforcement* had always been directed more rigorously against women than it was against men.

Sumptuary laws were found in virtually every type of political regime in medieval and early modern Europe; they were as prevalent in highly centralized nation-states already well on the way to absolutism as they were in the relatively democratic cities and communes. A few broad generalizations are possible. The paradigm cases of protracted State unification, France and Spain that went on to become highly centralized absolutist States, had sumptuary laws by the late twelfth or early thirteenth centuries and there was a more or less continuous history down until the eighteenth century. The fragmented city-states of Italy and Germany exhibit a mass of sumptuary legislation for much the same period. There was surprisingly little difference between both the temporal span and the general characteristics of the sumptuary law of such divergent cases as England, the great Italian cities, such as Venice and Florence, and in

German city-states, as well as the intensely Protestant Swiss towns. There seems to have been little difference in either the volume or the character of sumptuary regimes in Protestant or Catholic societies.

The contrasting cities of Florence and Venice epitomize the long duration of sumptuary legislation through their rise to mercantile and political power and subsequent decline. In Venice sumptuary laws stretched from the end of thirteenth century until the end of the eighteenth (Newett 1907). By the late fifteenth century enforcement officials, "*Provveditori sopra le Pompe*" (supervisors of luxury), had been appointed to enforce the sumptuary ordinances. As the rate of fashion change increased, legislation became more complex, striving for comprehensive restrictions on the latest fashions. In 1511 the Senate went so far as to order that "all new fashions are banned" (Okey 1907: 281). Legislative activity persisted into the eighteenth century; the last Venetian edict that I have record of – from 1781 – continued to complain about the wasteful living of citizens, the destruction of fortunes and the loss of government revenue (Davis 1962: 45, cf. Hazlitt 1900).

In Florence, sumptuary laws commenced in 1281. The city produced prolific sumptuary legislation and its records have been well preserved (Hughes 1983, Kovesi-Killerby 1993) and from the very beginning the Commune adopted the distinctive strategy of allowing the purchase of licences to wear otherwise forbidden apparel; this fiscal tactic tied sumptuary rules closely to the "gabelle" tax that already existed on salt and wine (Kantorowitz & Denholm-Young 1970: 358).

Florentine sumptuary legislation became more complex; one in 1356 ran to 43 chapters. Their content was directed mainly against women's apparel, in particular, against luxury clothes and extravagant ornamentation. There is evidence of a general connection between the perception of military and economic crises and the resort to renewed sumptuary endeavours. Sumptuary ordinances were increasingly linked to misogynistic denunciations of women. During a debate in 1433 in the Signoria women were rebuked for their "reprobate and diabolical nature" by which means they forced their husbands to indulge them in luxury. This trope is a common element in the politics that surrounds the political economy of marriage; what motivated the city fathers to regulate luxury and control the size of dowry payments was the populationist concern with the age of marriage, the key determinant of the size of families, and hence of the Florentine population (Brucker 1971: 181).

Sumptuary law was in evidence in Nürnberg from the late thirteenth century (Greenfield 1918, Strauss 1966). Early sumptuary law had as its central focus the regulation of the public celebration of private ceremonies, in particular, weddings and funerals. Later there was a shift of focus, funerals attracted less attention, while weddings became the primary target. The marriage laws of Nürnberg were subject to a series of cumulative prohibitions; restrictions were placed on the number of wedding guests, out-of-town fiddlers were prohibited and wedding presents were limited by value or by number. It was not until the end of the sixteenth century that there is evidence of a new concern, with the maintenance of social class distinctions in dress (Greenfield 1918: 126).

In Switzerland sumptuary laws spanned nearly 500 years from the very beginning of the fourteenth century until the end of the eighteenth century (Vincent 1935). In the fourteenth century the focus was, as elsewhere, on the regulation of expenditure on weddings and funerals. Later the same century there is a shift of attention to dress, a typical concern being with female *décolletage*, while requiring that a man's coats should be sufficiently long to cover "his shame" (Vincent 1897: 360). Significantly, during the height of the Calvinist ascendancy, although there was vigilant enforcement of sumptuary law, there was little new legislative activity. The mix of moral and economic considerations (sin and waste) in the attempt to hold fashion at bay persisted through the sixteenth and seventeenth centuries.

There are grounds for stressing the generality of European sumptuary law; a generality that transcends differences in political organization, economic system and dominant religious ideology. Sumptuary laws provided a versatile technology with no necessary political or doctrinal allegiances. The city exhibited a tendency towards solidarity and cohesion that united diverse populations as having distinctive urban interests. In the first place the towns were counterposed to feudal interests, but more importantly cities were constituted from the constellation of co-operative and competitive relations between autonomous social groups, of which the guilds provided the paradigm case. Weber gave sharp focus to this relationship in his formulation that cities did not originate in guilds, but rather that guilds originated in cities (Weber 1978 II: 1239–40). The guilds were significant in that they both required alliances between economically independent groups while, at the same time, they focused and objectified competition. It was thus the twin poles of competition and co-operation that laid down much of the distinctive character of the urban experience. The nature of the socio-economic relations involved is captured by the idea of guilds as "sworn confraternities" with a capacity for both self-regulation and for collaborative legislative activity.

The urban experience was one of considerable anxiety and danger, alongside its obvious advantages and attractions. Of the dangers one only has to recall the experiences of fire and plague. Less dramatic anxieties were associated with the difficulties attendant upon the concern with recognizing others in the jostle of the urban streets or in their night-time gloom that Lofland has captured as a "world of strangers" (Lofland 1973). With urbanization came an intensification of the public/private divide, while its boundaries underwent radical and perplexing shifts. While drawing attention to the risks that were characteristic of the urban experience it is important to keep firmly in mind that towns and cities acted as magnets, not least because they offered a positive expectation of choice and self-determination, that was absent in rural society. One of the significant manifestations being the complex interplay between the government of others and government of the self.

Elizabeth Wilson gets it just right when she refers to prostitution as the metaphor for urban disorder (Wilson 1992: 91). The encounters on the streets were uncontrolled; there is a sense of both promiscuity and alienation in the daily contacts of urban life that bred an anxiety about the mixing across social rank and across occupation, of young men and women. One consequence is the proliferation of anxieties about social breakdown, immorality, contagion, risk and excitement (Berman 1982, Corbin 1990). Prostitution, for example, was a signifier of both men's voyeuristic mastery of the streets and, at the same time, the freedom of, and familiarity with, the streets exhibited by prostitutes that gave them a partial autonomy rarely gained in the increasingly closed domestic world that women came to inhabit (de Swaan 1990). The streets became and remained sexually charged public spaces that elicited strong and continuing regulatory impulses. The growing sense that "something must be done" and the concern with urban disorder were important well-springs of the sumptuary impulse. Prostitutes were subject to extensive temporal and spatial regulation. Typical were attempts to keep brothels outside the city walls or, at least, confined to specific locations.[4]

Urban sumptuary law?

How do we explain the prevalence of sumptuary law in the great cities that were the harbingers of modern capitalism? Although some have suggested that sumptuary laws were an irrational feudal relic, this cannot account for the volume of sumptuary law in so many of the cities that sprang up in post-feudal Europe. One obvious and attractive possibility is to distinguish different varieties of sumptuary law and to propose the existence of a distinctively urban sumptuary law.

This strategy has been pursued by Diane Hughes who explicitly links the expansion of sumptuary law with those cities of northern Italy that were forced to admit the popular classes of merchants and guild artisans into government. In the course of developing this theme, she introduces the idea that a distinction is needed between "urban sumptuary law" and "aristocratic sumptuary law". Urban sumptuary law takes one of two possible forms: it is either universalistic (imposes the same restraint on all, e.g. "No person shall wear rings containing more than two ounces of gold") or, alternatively, it is employed by the contending classes of patricians and merchants in fighting out their conflicts of interest as a form of fighting with property. Aristocratic sumptuary law associated with the great monarchical States, was directed at the regulation of dress and other forms of consumption according to social hierarchy (Hughes 1983: 73).

I proceed with some caution to criticize Hughes's distinction because there is no doubt that this model is intuitively attractive. There is also no doubt either that it covers some cases; the best fit is between Hughes's "aristocratic" category and the absolute monarchies of, for example, early modern France and Spain. My reservation is that the distinction does not succeed in capturing sufficient of the historical record. The main problem is that the hierarchical sumptuary ordering that Hughes associates with the "aristocratic" category is just far too persistent. Too many thoroughly respectable non-aristocratic societies persisted with hierarchic dress codes – for example, in Puritan New England, sumptuary regulation was strongly hierarchic (Shurtleff 1968). Conversely, there were few cities that practised the universal sumptuary legislation that imposed uniform restrictions across social classes. Even more problematic is the fact that the hierarchic form of sumptuary law most frequently succeeded (rather than preceded) the more universalistic forms of sumptuary rules. Conversely, it was in societies that corresponded most closely to a hierarchic model of fixed social ranks that were more likely to have universalistic sumptuary rules. Thus the detailed evidence concerning the history of sumptuary laws in European urban life suggests that the distinction between "urban" and "aristocratic" sumptuary law cannot be sustained.

The perspective of governance provides an alternative approach to understanding the part played by sumptuary laws in the projects of urban government.[5] It insists that governance is not only the work of "governments", but that it arises from the mundane activities of people grappling

173

with the exigencies of life. Such practices have no necessary coherence. Governance focuses attention on the content of the processes of governing, it brings to the fore the "how" of governing, what gets done, by whom, what means are employed, and with what consequences. In coming close to a technical interest in the mechanics of governance, the approach needs to be very insistent upon the "limits of governance". Governance is always incomplete; it consists of attempts and is always subject to avoidance, evasion and resistance.

Sumptuary law can be understood in terms of a number of persistent and distinctive "sumptuary projects" that combine in diverse ways. It is possible to identify a small number of general sumptuary projects that are concerned with expenditure, appearance, gender, luxury and trade. What constitutes the distinctive features of particular historical forms of sumptuary regulation are the combination of these elements that are explored in what follows.

From the ordering of appearance to the ordering of space?

Lyn Lofland has argued that urban history is marked by a shift from an "appearential order" to a "spatial order" (Lofland 1973); in the premodern city, appearance was the key to social identity while the modern city is subject to spatial segregation. It is my contention that the urban experience has always involved an interaction between "appearential" and spatial ordering rather than a transition from one to the other. The regulatory practices that developed within the medieval city were from an early stage concerned with spatial ordering. This is true of both sumptuary and other forms of regulation. There was widespread spatial regulation of economic activity through the positive designation of market locations or, negatively, the prohibition of specific economic activities from designated locations; prostitutes and beggars were key targets of such regulation.

The orthodox account views sumptuary law as involving the project for the production and reproduction of social closure. It may be worth thinking of social closure and enclosure as being connected with a more modern project, namely, the first stages of citizenship associated with the "communal citizenship" of the medieval city understood as a two-fold process. On the one hand, the circle of participation widens; the lower-orders become "enclosed" within the space of the "social body" (a metaphor approaching literalness within the physical space of the city walls). On the other hand, mechanisms of social closure change their form, from "blood" and birth, via symbols (shields, livery, etc.) to more exclusively economic participation via guilds. As Maffesoli (1991) argues, groups constitute themselves through the "formism" of the symbolism that attaches itself to a sign (a garment, a habit, a taste, etc.). The implication of this is that sumptuary law operates on, and is implicated in, both the mechanisms of "enclosure" and "closure".

What now needs to be considered is whether there occurred an intensification of urban governance in the early modern period. Such an intensification might involve some combination of extension and intensification. Extending governance involved activities that previously had not been controlled coming to be regulated. Sumptuary law may well have been just one of an expanded range of such activities. The intensification of governance involved the forms of regulation practised becoming more rigorous or more thorough and efficient. The severity of regulation, in contrast to its volume, is more difficult to judge. Mere harshness of sanctions might be an indicator but would not necessarily get to grips with its intrusiveness, how much difference it made to everyday life. Nor is it a matter of the efficiency of the regulatory capacity of the authorities, for it was rarely technical questions alone that determined the degree or intensity of regulation.

My own view is that sumptuary laws appear to have failed to penetrate significantly into the everyday world. A cross-section of diaries from the periods of high sumptuary activity provides few signs of any immediate anxiety about such rules. The diaries generally attest to the everyday importance of dress; many describe garments that would almost certainly have been proscribed by the sumptuary law of the day. This impression is supported by the dearth of evidence of prosecution for sumptuary offences from most of the jurisdictions involved, but absence of evidence of systematic enforcement does not of itself establish that sumptuary law was ineffectual or unimportant.

Sumptuary law was one element of a process in which more and more aspects of social life were becoming objects of disciplinary or regulatory activity. But there was little sense that the regulatory screw was being tightened. Why, then, did a significant expansion in governance occur? Because much of this expansion occurred in the cities of Europe, it seems likely that it was connected with some of the distinctive social changes that came about with urbanization, for example, the increased density of urban life, the shifting boundary between public and private or the commodification of economic relations (phenomena that are themselves internally connected).

For present purposes it is sufficient to note that sumptuary activity occurs at much the same time as the urban authorities were busily engaging in a wide range of other regulatory projects. Consider, for example, the governance of public health. Typical were the attempts to regulate what kind of waste could be disposed of in the streets, public thoroughfares and water systems, and what animals could be kept and where. Pigs in particular were a significant point of intersection between a concern with waste and a concern with the place of animals in urban space. The ambiguous location of pigs in the history of urban regulation was further compounded by the fact that they had come to play the dramatic role of defendants in criminal trials where they were accused, tried and executed for a wide range of offences; the most common offence being assault or causing the death of a child (Evans 1906).

A note of caution should be entered against a widespread tendency to attach a developmental significance to this expansion of regulation. It does not follow that a quantitative expansion of regulatory intervention means that this activity becomes more coherent and systemic. Marc Raeff's important study of the German city ordinances (*Landes-* and *Polizei-Ordnungen*) was more prepared than I think his material justified to conclude that the new "codified" ordinances involved a conscious effort to bring about "coherence, regularity, and continuity" that characterized the cities whose politics he captured in his title as "well-ordered police states" (Raeff 1983: 21).

In contrast to this far-sighted vision, it seems more likely that the ordinances were only "codified" in the sense that they brought together many discrete regulatory initiatives. In other words, it is risky to assume that anything more than administrative convenience was involved in the production of these ordinances. The ordinances read much like modern city ordinances and by-laws that do not aspire to coherence, but merely convenience, in that they bring together sets of rules and regulations on related topics.[6] It is generally unsound to attribute long-range and large-scale projections to people grappling with the immediate pressures of daily life and its government in difficult and confusing times.

This more contextual evaluation of the expansion of governance is well captured by Jeffrey Minson. One should not understand strategies of "police" as harbingers of modernity or the Welfare State. What is significant is that sumptuary interventions such as the reform of manners and "medical police" bear on the specificity of personal life; thereby personal and domestic life became matters of political and economic moment. This regulation of personal life was the product of changes in the "police" projects associated with the rise of liberal forms of government that involved both political and non-political modes of regulation (Minson 1985: 106).

What remains indisputable, from the evidence of Raeff and others, is that extensive and self-conscious regulatory projects were an important feature of the governance of the early modern cities of Europe. Further, it is also clear that sumptuary ordinances were associated with a wide range of other regulatory initiatives. Distinctively sumptuary projects became entwined increasingly closely with public health matters, moral regulation, the control of the labour market and of vagrancy and, perhaps most important of all, with the burgeoning field of economic policy. This makes it possible to argue that, as these arenas of modern governmental activity became more clearly elaborated and distinguished one from the other, the purely sumptuary dimension did not so much die away, but became dispersed within a range of more or less self-contained fields of both public and private regulation that constituted some of the distinctive features of liberal governance.

It is with the rise of the city that there occurs what Le Goff and others have seen as an intensification of governance (Le Goff 1988). The prevalence of sumptuary laws in significant periods of the expansion of European cities is an early manifestation of this regulatory impulse. Increasing social differentiation no longer makes it possible for people to know and to agree upon precisely how they must eat or dress in every situation, or the gestures they must perform. As Durkheim made clear, "moral and legal prescriptions lose clarity and preciseness, they no longer regulate any save the most general forms of behaviour, and these only in a very general way, stating what should be done, not how it should be done" (quoted in Lukes & Scull 1983: 55). Sumptuary law came to the fore in the pre-modern and early modern city as a mechanism that partially closed the gap between the pre-modern and the modern. Sumptuary regulation might be said to be a form of legal regulation focusing on the visible face of everyday life. These considerations seem to suggest that the presence of sumptuary laws in the cities can be seen as facing both ways, as both a manifestation of the rise of modernity and as form of resistance thereto.

Governmentality and State formation

So far my consideration of the place of sumptuary law in the emergent cities of Europe has focused on changes in the nature of governmental activity. I will now consider whether it is possible to identify more closely the connection between sumptuary law and the forms of government characteristic of urban Europe. In his paper on "governmentality" Foucault drew a distinction between two forms of government. The first, "the state of justice" of the Middle Ages, he characterized as a "society of laws". The second, the "administrative state" of the fifteenth and sixteenth centuries, corresponded to a "society of regulation" (Foucault 1979: 21). These forms precede the distinctively modern forms of government through "surveillance" and liberalism. Foucault's typology suggests the question: Should we regard the prevalence of urban sumptuary law as confirmation of the increasing importance of regulation in the "administrative state"?

In the first place this connection between regulation and administration fits with another distinctive Foucauldian theme, namely, that of his expanded conception of "policing" that revolves around the thesis that the "police's true object is man" (Foucault 1981: 248). Policing thus conceived has a dual characteristic; on the one hand to provide the city with adornment, form and splendour and, on the other, to stimulate productive working and trading relations in order to expand the wellbeing and prosperity of the city, measured primarily by the weight of its coffers. This conception of policing resonates with what might be called the economic side of sumptuary regulation, with its concern that resources should not be wasted, that people should apply both their capital and their labour purposefully both for their individual benefit and for that of the community.

It is instructive to compare Foucault's analysis of early modern regulation with Gerhard Oestreich's account of "social discipline" in early modern Europe. Central to Oestreich's argument is the identification of discipline as having two dimensions, that of individual self-discipline (the Eliasian conquering of passion and emotion) and social discipline. In the process of State formation it is social discipline that is more important than sovereignty; the central concern is to intensify, revitalize and discipline public life. Here we encounter Foucault's conception of police in a new guise. "Police", for Oestreich, encompassed the whole of "civil organization" and "the regulation, discipline, and control of a community" and thus linked a technology and a rationality of discipline (Oestreich 1982: 156).

This conception of police developed in urban Europe from the late medieval period. It is a response to an increased demand for labour, the drift from country to towns and increased social density; all of which generate pressures towards "new modes of life" that were characterized by greater variation in lifestyle that, in turn, generated a perceived need for more discipline. These projects are manifested in an enormous regulatory productivity that was exemplified in the police ordinance for the city of Strasbourg from 1628. What is significant is to note how its regulatory range covers both the public and the private spheres, the criminal and the civil. It included moral regulations (Sunday observance, sorcery, blasphemy, cursing), many public health rules, child-rearing practices, control of servants, and relations between innkeepers and guests. It contained extensive sumptuary regulations (dress, funerals, festivities, weddings, drinking, etc.); begging, almsgiving and vagrancy; the status of Jews; and, finally, economic regulation (weights and measures, usury and monopolies) (Oestreich 1982: 158).

Viewed from the standpoint of State formation, such mechanisms of urban governance attest to the considerable space that existed for forms of authority below the level of the central State, from the governments of communes, to the councils of the guilds, to patriarchal familial power. At the same time there were significant continuities with pre-modern social relations, exemplified in the persisting importance of pre-modern forms of communal activity. Festivals, processions and carnivals were central features of the public participation of the inhabitants of urban communities. Similarly, fairs and markets were not only a major form of exchange relations, but also of communal experience; they were also closely linked to libidinal pursuits and to "excitement" (O'Malley 1992). The disciplinary response, manifested particularly in the governance of the self, the preoccupation with decency, diligence, gravity, modesty, orderliness, prudence, reason, self-control, sobriety and thrift, was epitomized by the concern to effect the "triumph of Lent over carnival" (Burke 1978). The guilds sustained a governmental role, to some extent independent of whether they held formal political power; they continued to engage in local legislation until, in the case of most German cities, well into the eighteenth century, when their judicial and legislative powers were stripped by imperial decree (Wegert 1981).

Down to the present, consumption has continued to expand its association with pleasure and self-realization. One significant consequence has been that, in the course of the extension of commodification, discipline, apparently so essential for production oriented to the market, is always at

179

risk of being undermined by the hedonistic culture of consumption, the "society of the spectacle", that systematically eats away at the culture of work and production. This provides one way of understanding the tensions between modernization and continuity that surrounded urban governance. This tension was strongly reflected in the discourses surrounding sumptuary law, which sought both to preserve tradition whilst at the same time striving to inculcate a new economic rationality of thrift, investment and self-sufficiency.

While urban life rendered social relations more transparent, even though impersonal, it was accompanied by the dramatic "privatization" that sketched out the new monochrome configuration of public and private zones within urban space. The study of everyday life has rightly become a serious and rigorous enterprise, as exemplified by the studies brought together by Philippe Ariès & Georges Duby (1987–91). The discovery of silent, and thus private, reading is only one surprising revelation concerning the transformation of everyday life towards the end of the Middle Ages (Chartier 1989). This intense privatization of life brought with it not only an ever more sharply defined separation between public sumptuousness and private luxury that had profound impact on the controversies over conspicuous consumption, but also a protracted interrogation of the proper scope of governance.

From different standpoints, religious and secular, economic and moral, those who governed seemed always to be faced with a sense of the "disorder" that must have seemed endemic to urban existence. This sentiment seems easy to understand from the vantage point of the late twentieth century when, after seeming to have learned to live with urban and then suburban life, we have been going through a period of dramatically increased insecurity about the very viability of urban life. For those charged with governing late medieval cities the sense of disorder was manifest not only in the disorder of social appearances, but also in the dislocations threatened by the ubiquitous figures of "masterless men", the transients, vagrants and beggars whose arrival in the cities was evidence of the break-up of the old order and appeared such a threat to the new. These anxieties and preoccupations link with the focus on the regulation of appearance since both strands provided a powerful stimulus to the practices and ideologies of moral regulation. Beggars were either to be driven out of town by the whip or classified, counted, badged or branded; all techniques partaking of both spatial and "appearential" ordering.

The towns gave rise to a collective capacity formed as centres of solidaristic action by otherwise powerless individuals (Poggi 1978: 37).

One important feature of this process was the securing of "free" legal status for individuals as citizens and the corporate status of the guilds that became the primary form of self-organization of economically decisive sections of the population. Urban guilds and corporations were like nurseries in which self-respect and dignity emerged, along with feelings of fellowship and mutual respect, and thus effected a radical break from the dependencies of the lord–vassal relations of feudalism (Gurevich 1985).

Not only was self-organization important, but also the mechanisms that brought together the different "estates" or strata of self-organized citizens. The distinctive political expression was the emergence of the late medieval assemblies or "parlements" that Poggi sees as the key institutional expression of this stage of development. For present purposes the most important consequence was the emergence of a distinct process of "legislation", that Poggi correctly describes as a "momentous innovation" (Poggi 1978: 55). Legislation came to be conceived as a process of self-conscious deliberation in contrast to a conception of legislation as edict or as an expression of royal command. In a significant respect these deliberative interventions can be viewed as the birth of "politics", leading to an expanding range and diversity of regulatory activity. Most cities undertook a considerable expansion of what is perhaps best regarded as distinctively "urban legislation". Much of it was directly "economic", guaranteeing market conditions and practices, weights and measures, price and quality controls. Another important arena was that of sanitary regulation dealing with the keeping of animals, disposal of refuge, preservation of water supply and the upkeep of highways. Such urban regulation also included aspects of the regulation of private life (dowries, marriages, servants, apparel) and matters relating to the expansion of "civic public life" exhibiting elements of town planning with regard to the construction of churches, town halls and public spaces (Black 1984).

There are a number of things that should be noted about this expansion of governance. In the first place it frequently occurred with little or no attention to the possibility of enforcement. There remains a persisting sense in which legislation was conceived as a form of public exhortation. This feature is significant in accounting for the low level of enforcement of sumptuary laws. The absence of sustained enforcement is typically regarded as evidence that this variety of regulation was not "for real" and was doomed to failure. It may be that this conventional view is not simply a misunderstanding of sumptuary law, but is more generally a misapprehension of the early forms of regulatory legislation. Poggi offers the instructive example of the activity of the Parlement of Franche-Comté that in the opening decades of the sixteenth century embarked upon a broad range of regulation that included amongst its targets: general security, crime, heresy, access to pasturage and vineyards, the seasons for hunting, control of craft skills and product standards, weights and measures, the maintenance of roads and waterways, control over the export of salt, iron, wine and wheat, and the fixing of prices at inns. The simple, but fundamental point to be made, is that sumptuary law was one amongst an extraordinary expansion of projects of governance.

Paternalism, urban government and the Reformation

A frequent explanation of the prevalence of sumptuary laws in the late medieval and early modern city was that it manifested a predisposition towards a paternalistic mode of government. Some commentators also suggest that urban paternalism was associated with the coming of the Reformation in the first half of the sixteenth century. Kent Greenfield, in one of the most thorough studies of urban sumptuary law, argued that medieval sumptuary regulation was neither "police regulation" nor "economic regulation", but rather stemmed from a "paternal" conception of government that manifested itself in an "impulse to care for intimate processes of the citizen's life" (Greenfield 1918: 133), exemplified in attempts to regulate marital relations and other household relations. His concept of paternalism was one that viewed the State as assuming responsibility for economic thrift and the moral standard of family life, a concern that went hand in hand with the minute regulation of such matters as prices, wage rates and the like. Greenfield's account of the government of Nürnberg identifies a persistent paternalism that, significantly, reached across the most important political and intellectual upheaval, namely, the coming of the Reformation. Thus he rejects a causal connection between the advent of the Reformation and sumptuary laws.

Gerald Strauss, who like Greenfield has focused on Nürnberg, likens paternalism rather literally to the voice of "an offended, sometimes outraged parent correcting his prodigal offspring" (Strauss 1966: 112). His description of paternal governmentality is striking. "Affluent and confident though the city was, it peered into the future with concern and suspicion" (Strauss 1966: 114). Yet this formulation, and maybe the concept "paternalism" itself, only engages with the backward-looking gaze of city government. The city fathers are presented as only wanting to preserve a society functioning through the operation of a mutually beneficial system of co-operation and interdependence.

Merry Weisner (1988) argues that urban paternalism in Germany became increasingly concerned with morality. This resulted in both an extension of regulation into the household, but also an exclusion of certain groups from "the public good". These trends manifested themselves in increasingly interventionist regulation of domestic servants, of beggars and of prostitutes. By the end of the sixteenth century, control over servants reached its strictest and this coincided with the intensification of sumptuary clothing laws. This regulation was much concerned with the maintenance of the visible distinctions between mistresses and their maidservants. From the end of the fifteenth century, there were attempts to hide the visibility of prostitution. Prostitutes were forbidden, for example, to sit outside the brothel and from occupying the front pews at church. During the first half of the sixteenth century, throughout Germany city ordinances closed the brothels. The ideology of concern with the "good of the community" came to demand a wider scope and increasingly embraced an expanding concern for decorum, order and morality. Evidence from Nördlingen into the late seventeenth century suggests the existence of a wide and intrusive moral regulation. A wide range of popular activities and recreations were forbidden in moves that were typical of projects to reform popular morals: nude swimming, night revelry, "tobacco-drinking" and the throwing of snowballs were all forbidden (Friedrichs 1979).[7]

The Reformation wrought profound changes with respect to who held power and the forms of constitutional relations between Church and State, but there was a remarkable degree of continuity with respect to the objects of governance (Davis 1975, Ozment 1975). Thus the regulatory activities of the city governments of northern Europe after the Reformation reveal a significant continuity with their predecessors. Sumptuary regulation persisted, but at a somewhat reduced frequency and intensity. This suggests, that at least for present purposes, any discussion that places a significant reliance on the identification of urban government as "paternalist" tends to emphasize only its conservative face, significant though this was, at the expense of the stuttering and unplanned steps into the future that also marked the practices of city government.

With these considerations in mind, it seems more fruitful to rely on the conception of discipline rather than paternalism as an organizing theme. It will be recalled that one of Foucault's most significant contentions is that "power" is never entirely negative, but must be understood as having a positive dimension. Similarly it is necessary to free "discipline" from

183

exclusively negative attributes. Programmatically Foucault was committed to such a treatment, though it is significant that given the preponderant emphasis he placed on the connection between discipline and surveillance, especially apparent in his studies of asylums and prisons, in practice he tended to reproduce a negative conception of discipline. In contrast, my exploration of the trajectory of urban government points to a conception of discipline as a set of practices traversed by both positive and negative dimensions, in the concern for predictability and efficiency, and negative dimensions, concerned with the preservation of the old ways and of imposing moralistic restrictions.

One of the major features of this shifting form of discipline was a profound change in the role of government with respect to economic protectionism. The emergence of distinct urban economies was marked by a wide range of protectionism, both internal and external. Examples of this internal regulation were restrictions on the number of apprentices, on the admission of new masters, prohibition on "putting-out", and restrictions on forestalling and other manipulations of the market. External regulation was epitomized by tax or other restraints on the import and export of goods. Concern with "the economy" was, however, not something confined to the cities, but was just as evident in the centralized States. Sumptuary law was gradually and unintentionally submerged by increasingly explicit "economic" projects. Cities had an abiding fiscal motive in the light of which it came to make good economic sense to refrain from prohibiting certain styles of dress or ornamentation, but instead to impose a tax or to grant exemptions against contributions to the city's coffers. By extension it became increasingly frequent for what started out as sumptuary restraints to become import restrictions (e.g. restrictions on wearing of silk become prohibitions on Italian silk). It was not a big step to the positive promotion of domestic industries on import substitution grounds. It was through such mechanisms, that may provisionally be identified as protectionist, that the "government of the economy" became transformed. Sumptuary laws underwent a metamorphosis and remerged in various forms of protectionism.

Conclusion

The history of urban sumptuary regulation provides just one of many possible avenues from which to explore the characteristic of urban governance. The most significant conclusion is that it provides evidence of a complex of governmentalities that transect all accounts constructed in terms of a stark division of pre-modern and modern. The second general conclusion is that the significance of each project of governance lies not so much in any intrinsic characteristics, but rather in its combination with other projects of governance. I do not contend that early modern sumptuary laws were manifestations of liberalism, but I do suggest that we should be cautious about assuming that there is some clearly identified pre-liberal form of governance from which the exploration of modern liberalism can launch itself.

Notes

1. This study forms part of a wider project on the governance of consumption: Hunt, *Governance of the consuming passions: a history of sumptuary regulation* (1995).
2. Some key texts on the history of sumptuary law are cited below; for extended sources on their analysis see Hunt (1995).
3. Many enactments simply made no reference to women; this probably attests to the greater public role of men and the concomitant privatization of women.
4. Given the current interest in the figure of the *flâneur* it is worth noting that I have come across no evidence of attempts at regulating the mobility of urban males in general, although apprentices were a very common regulatory target.
5. For fuller elaboration of a sociology of governance see Hunt & Wickham (1994).
6. There was undoubtedly a more general systematization involved in the production of the texts of the "science of police" (Scribner 1987).
7. I follow Peter Burke in viewing projects of the "reform of popular culture" as occurring where a social cleavage between classes or other social positions widens such that the dominant group seek first to moralize and then to regulate or prohibit characteristic recreational and other activities of the subordinate group (Burke 1978).

References

Ariès, P. & G. Duby (eds) 1987–91. *A history of private life* [5 volumes]. Cambridge, Mass.: Harvard University Press.
Berman, M. 1982. *All that is solid melts into air: the experience of modernity*. New York: Simon & Schuster.
Black, A. 1984. *Guilds and civil society in European political thought from the twelfth century*

to the present. London: Methuen.

Brucker, G. (ed.) 1971. *The society of Renaissance Florence: a documentary study.* New York: Harper & Row.

Burchell, G. 1993. Liberal government and techniques of the self. *Economy and Society* **22**(3), 267–82.

Burke, P. 1978. *Popular culture in early modern Europe.* London: Temple Smith.

Chartier, R. 1989. The practical impact of writing. In *A history of private life* vol. III: *Passions of the Renaissance*, R. Chartier (ed.), 111–65. Cambridge, Mass.: Harvard University Press.

Corbin, A. 1990. *Women for hire: prostitution and sexuality in France after 1850* (trans. Alan Sheridan). Cambridge, Mass.: Harvard University Press.

Davis, J. 1962. *The decline of the Venetian nobility as a ruling class.* Baltimore: The Johns Hopkins University Press.

Davis, N. 1975. *Society and culture in early modern France.* London: Duckworth.

de Swaan, A. 1990. The politics of agoraphobia. In *The management of normality: critical essays in health and welfare.* London: Routledge.

Evans, E. P. 1906. *The criminal prosecution and capital punishment of animals.* London: Heinemann.

Foucault, M. 1979. Governmentality. *Ideology and Consciousness* **6**, 5–21.

Foucault, M. 1981. Omnes et singulatim: towards a criticism of "Political Reason". In *The Tanner Lectures on Human Values*, vol. II, S. McMurrin (ed.), 223–54. Cambridge: Cambridge University Press.

Friedrichs, C. 1979. *Urban society in an age of war: Nördlingen, 1580–1720.* Princeton, New Jersey: Princeton University Press.

Gordon, C. 1991. Governmental rationality: an introduction. In *The Foucault effect: studies in governmentality*, G. Burchell, C. Gordon, P. Miller (eds), 1–52. Hemel Hempstead, England: Harvester Wheatsheaf.

Greenfield, K. 1918. *Sumptuary law in Nürnberg: a study in paternal government.* Baltimore: The Johns Hopkins University Press.

Gurevich, A. 1985. *Categories of medieval culture.* London: Routledge & Kegan Paul.

Hazlitt, W. C. 1900. *The Venetian Republic: its rise, its growth, and its fall, 421–1797.* London: Adam & Charles.

Hughes, D. 1983. Sumptuary laws and social relations. In Renaissance Italy. In *Disputes and settlements: law and human relations in the West*, J. Bossy (ed.), 69–99. Cambridge: Cambridge University Press.

Hunt, A. 1995. *Governance of the consuming passions: a history of sumptuary regulation.* London: Macmillan.

Hunt, A. & G. Wickham 1994. *Foucault and law: towards a new sociology of law as governance.* London: Pluto.

Kantorowitz, H. & N. Denholm-Young 1970. *De Ornatu Mulierum: a consilium of Antonius de Rosellis with an introduction on fifteenth century sumptuary legislation* [1933]. In *Rechtshistorische Schriften von Dr. Hermann Kantorowicz*, H. Coing & G. Immel (eds), 341–76. Verlag C. F. Müller.

Kovesi-Killerby, C. 1993. Practical problems in the enforcement of Italian sumptuary law, 1200–1500. In *Crime and disorder in Renaissance Italy*, K. Lowe (ed.). Cambridge: Cambridge University Press.

Le Goff, J. 1988. *The medieval imagination* (trans. Arthur Goldhammer). Chicago: University of Chicago Press.

Lofland, L. 1973. *The world of strangers: order and action in urban public space*. New York: Basic Books.

Lukes, S. & A. Scull 1983. *Durkheim and the law*. London: St. Martin's Press.

Maffesoli, M. 1991. The ethics of aesthetics. *Theory, Culture and Society* **8**, 7–20.

Minson, J. 1985. *Genealogies of morals: Nietzsche, Foucault, Donzelot and the eccentricity of ethics*. London: Macmillan.

Newett, M. M. 1907. The sumptuary laws of Venice in the fourteenth and fifteenth centuries. In *Historical essays*, T. F. Tout & J. Tait (eds), 245–78. Manchester: Manchester University Press.

Oestreich, G. 1982. *Neostoicism and the early modern state*. Cambridge: Cambridge University Press.

Okey, T. 1907. *The old Venetian palaces and the old Venetian folk*. London: Dent.

O'Malley, P. 1992. Containing our excitement: commodity culture and the crisis of discipline. In *Studies in law, politics and society*, vol. XIII, S. Sibley & A. Sarat (eds). Greenwich, Connecticut: JAI Press.

Ozment, S. 1975. *The Reformation in the cities: the appeal of Protestantism to sixteenth century Germany and Switzerland*. New Haven, Connecticut: Yale University Press.

Poggi, G. 1978. *The development of the modern state: a sociological introduction*. London: Hutchinson.

Raeff, M. 1983. *The well-ordered police state: social and institutional change through law in the Germanies and Russia, 1600–1800*. New Haven, Connecticut: Yale University Press.

Rose, N. 1993. Government, authority and expertise in advanced liberalism. *Economy and Society* **22**(3), 283–99.

Scribner, R. 1987. Police and the territorial state in sixteenth-century Württemburg. In *Politics and society in Reformation Europe*, E. I. Kouri & Tom Scott (eds), 103–20. London: Macmillan.

Shurtleff, N. (ed.) 1968. *The records of the Governor and Company of the Massachusetts Bay Company* [1853] [5 volumes]. American Medieval Society Press.

Strauss, G. 1966. *Nuremburg in the sixteenth century*. Chichester, England: John Wiley.

Troeltsch, E. 1931. *The social teaching of the Christian churches* [2 volumes]. London: Allen & Unwin.

Vincent, J. 1897. European Blue Laws. *Annual Report of American Historical Association*, 355–73.

Vincent, J. 1935. *Costume and conduct in the laws of Basel, Bern and Zurich 1370–1800*. Baltimore: The Johns Hopkins University Press.

Weber, M. 1978. *Economy and society: an outline of interpretive sociology* [2 volumes], G. Roth & C. Wittich (eds). Berkeley: University of California Press.

Wegert, K. 1981. Patrimonial rule, popular self-interest, and Jacobinism in Germany, 1763–1800. *Journal of Modern History* **53**, 440–67.

Weisner, M. 1988. Paternalism in practice: the control of servants and prostitutes in early modern German cities. In *The process of change in early modern Europe*, P. Bebb & S. Marshall (eds), 179–200. Ohio University Press.

Wilson, E. 1992. The invisible flâneur. *New Left Review* **191**, 90–110.

Chapter 9
Risk and responsibility

Pat O'Malley

Risk society

Almost the defining property of Foucault's conception of disciplinary power is that it works through and upon the individual, and constitutes the individual as an object of knowledge. In the disciplines, the central technique is that of normalization in the specific sense of creating or specifying a general norm in terms of which individual uniqueness can be recognized, characterized and then standardized. Normalization in the disciplinary sense thus implies "correction" of the individual, and the development of a causal knowledge of deviance and normalization. Within strategies of regulation, rejection of the focus upon individuals and on causation therefore would signal not merely a redirection of particular policies but rather a shift away from the disciplinary technology of power itself.[1] In the field of crime and crime control, for example, such a development has been detected in programmes and policies based on the regulation of behaviours and their consequences – in which "actuarial" (Cohen 1985) or "insurance"-based (Reichman 1986, Hogg 1989) assumptions and techniques are brought into play. Thus Stan Cohen (1985) observes that the conception of a mind-control society envisaged in Orwell's *1984* is mistaken, for although such key Foucauldian elements as surveillance continue to develop, there is little or no concern with individuals as such. In situational crime prevention, one of the fastest-growing techniques of crime control, concern is with the spatial and temporal aspects of crime, thought out in terms of the opportunities for crime rather than its causal or biographical origins:

> What is being monitored is behaviour (or the physiological correlates of emotion and behaviour). No one is interested in inner thoughts . . . "the game is up" for all policies directed to the criminal as an individual, either in terms of detection (blaming and

punishing) or causation (finding motivational or causal chains) . . .
The talk now is about "spatial" and "temporal" aspects of crime,
about systems, behaviour sequences, ecology, defensible space . . .
target hardening. (Cohen 1985: 146–8)

Crime increasingly comes to be understood not as a matter of personal
and social pathologies in need of correction, but as a set of risks, more or
less inevitable in some degree, but predictable and manageable in aggre-
gate terms. Prevention and risk-spreading (e.g. insurance) become more
central than detection and correction (Reichman 1986).

While such writers are concerned primarily with understanding the
management of crime, there is a considerable literature that identifies this
as merely one instance of the displacement of disciplinary techniques by
actuarialism, across a very broad spectrum of social sites (e.g. Ewald 1986,
1990, 1991, Simon 1987, 1988, Castel 1991, Defert 1991, Donzelot
1991). Prominent among these interpretations is a view that such actuarial or insurantial techniques of power are displacing discipline because
of their heightened efficiency in regulating populations. In the following
pages this position will be critically assessed, and an alternative position
developed in which actuarialism is viewed as a technology that varies very
greatly in its nature and in its articulation with other technologies,
depending on its nexus with specific political programmes. In turn, in
place of an inevitable expansion of actuarial power to create a "risk society", and concomitant displacement of the disciplines and sovereignty (as
actuarial theorists tend to claim), it will be suggested that the relative
prominence and roles of different social technologies depends rather on
the political rationalities ascendant in any social setting.

One of the clearest and most developed elaborations accounting for the
rise of actuarialism as a social technology is given by Jonathan Simon
(1987, 1988). Following leads from Donzelot (1979) and Ewald (1986)
Simon regards these risk-based, insurance or actuarial techniques as
becoming dominant because they function to intensify the effectiveness of
power. In his view the movement from normalization (closing the gap
between distribution and norm) to accommodation (responding to variations in distributions) "increases the efficiency of power because changing
people is difficult and expensive." (Simon 1988: 773, see also Cohen
1985). Such increased efficiency is seen to derive from the fact that
actuarial techniques are more subtle in their operation, consequently are
less likely to generate resistance, and thus require lesser expenditure of
political resources. In Simon's interpretation, this subtlety arises out of

three primary characteristics of actuarial techniques. First, unlike the disciplines, they act by manipulating the environment or the effects of problem behaviours, rather than by attempting to correct errant individuals. Secondly, they act on categories derived from risk analysis that need not overlap with the categories of everyday experience, and which thus are less likely to be recognized and resisted. Thirdly, they act *in situ* rather than by separation or exclusion of deviant cases, and as a by-product have less need to be coercive.

In related accounts, actuarial technologies lower resistance to social regulation because – as in the example of insurance – they are seen to provide security by managing the risks to health, employment, legality, etc. Through deployment of insurantial processes such as risk-spreading, they thus appear to act technically rather than morally. Moreover, because of its "technical" concern with managing the effects of targeted categories of action or event, rather than a political or moral concern with faults or causes, actuarial practice

> results in the dedramatization of social conflicts by eliding the
> question of assigning *responsibility* for the origin of "social evils" and
> shifting the issue to the differing technical options . . . required to
> optimise employment, wages, allowances, etc. (Donzelot 1979: 81,
> see also Simon 1988, Ewald 1991, Gordon 1991)

Overall then, actuarialism appears as incorporative rather than exclusionary, meliorative rather than coercive, statistical and technical rather than moral and individualized, tolerant of variation rather than rigidly normalizing, covert rather than overt and so on.

These interpretations of actuarial technologies resonate strongly with a number of other accounts that have become influential, notably that of the "dispersal of social control" (e.g. Cohen 1979, Abel 1982). While key differences exist between these interpretations (for example over the integration of the whole into a control "system", as opposed to a fragmented array of regulatory agencies), in each there is a clear case being made that a more efficient form of power has been developed – efficient that is in terms of a political and economic cost–benefit calculus. Correspondingly, in such accounts, there is also a very strong tendency towards a totalizing vision of regulation. Largely because of its greater efficiency, actuarial power is seen to permeate virtually all social fields, replacing "the punitive city" (Cohen 1979) with the "risk society" (Simon 1987, Gordon 1991) or "post-disciplinary order" (Castel 1991).

These accounts imply that technologies of power can be ranked hierarchically in terms of efficiency, and even that there is a kind of natural selection among technologies such that the most efficient survive. Despite their claims to a Foucauldian lineage, such interpretations run against Foucault's insistence on the fragmentary nature of social relations across time and space. Moreover, they collide with his (1984) recognition of discipline and regulation as "two poles of development linked together by a whole intermediary cluster of relations", characterized by "overlappings, interactions and echoes" (Foucault 1984: 149). Thus, rather than there being an implied redundancy, there comes into being a dynamic interaction:

> We must consequently see things not in terms of substitution for a society of sovereignty of a disciplinary society and the subsequent replacement of a disciplinary society by a governmental one; in reality we have a triangle: sovereignty-discipline-government, which has as its primary target the population and as its essential mechanism apparatuses of security. (Foucault 1979: 19)[2]

Such instances do not imply any hierarchy of efficiency, nor competition between forms of power, although such forms may be expected to collide as well as to collude. The clear implication is not to map out the unfolding of an evolution, but to understand the dynamics of such triangular relations and the conditions that affect the roles taken by the various elements in specific combinations. With respect to the nature and impact of actuarial techniques therefore we need to think out their relationships with sovereign and disciplinary forms, in terms of articulations and alliances, colonizations and translations, resistances and complicities between them rather than in terms of their unilinear development.

From power to political programmes

In order to avoid the difficulties associated with creating Power as a new subject, motor or logic of history, Donzelot (1979) suggests that it be reconceptualized in terms of technologies, political programmes and strategies. In this conceptualization, technologies, of which the panopticon and insurance are examples, emerge as "always local and multiple, intertwining, coherent or contradictory forms of activating and managing a population" (Donzelot 1979). Technologies, although they have their own dynamics, nevertheless develop primarily in terms of their role in relation to specific political programmes. Political programmes focus upon doing something about a "practicable object", for example the reduction of levels of unemployment, rates of crime or youth homelessness. They are recipes "for corrective intervention . . . [and] redirection". In turn, such programmes are formed in terms of more abstract strategies – "formulae of government, theories which explain reality only to the extent that they enable the implementation of a program" (Donzelot 1979: 77). Keynesianism and *laissez-faire* liberalism provide examples of the latter.

Moving on from Donzelot's sketchy position, it can be argued that technologies do not simply come into being as a result of a logic of power, but are developed with specific purposes in mind (Miller & Rose 1990).[3] Subsequently they may be generalized to other purposes and fields. Institutional risk-management planning, for example, developed initially in relation to insurance and was adapted unevenly to distinct purposes in relation to the formation of programmes such as welfarism. However, the continued spread of technologies is by no means assured once commenced. The appeal of technologies may be based on a variety of criteria other than perceptions of effectiveness, and even the latter are subject to fluctuations not easily accounted for in any deterministic narrative – as the continuing oscillation between institutionalizing and de-institutionalizing tendencies in the field of mental health policy suggests (Scull 1975, La Fond & Durham 1991).

What influences the spread of technologies is most likely to be their appropriateness to particular ends, and this in large measure will be related to political struggles that establish programmes on the social agenda. The history of disciplinary or of actuarial techniques in specific fields such as health management, unemployment policy or crime control, this suggests, is not to be understood as the gradual encroachment of a more efficient technology of power, but the uneven, negotiated and partial implementation of a political programme and the consequent (equally partial) installation of the appropriate social techniques. The development of public benefit welfarism may thus be understood as the outcome of struggles between political programmes, informed by broader "strategies" such as Keynesianism, in each national instance taking different forms shaped by local conditions and the outcomes of struggles and negotiations.

This familiar manner of thinking about technologies of power leads to a more overtly political understanding of the developments reviewed so far. Further, it has major consequences for an understanding of risk-based techniques. These may initially be examined with respect to three key issues – the amorality of actuarial technology, its efficiency and its articulation with other social technologies.

Morality, risk and the free market

In the analyses of Simon, Ewald and others reviewed above, it is clear that they identify the practices of welfarism and the interventionist State as the exemplars of actuarialism as a contemporary technique of rule. Because in their day-to-day operations these techniques work bureaucratically and on categories rather than individuals, it is argued that they are thought by the populace to work amorally. As seen, this amoral or technical characteristic is interpreted as a source of efficiency, as it reduces opposition. However, in few Western industrial states in the present day can it be thought that "actuarial" welfarism is publicly understood to be made up of amoral and apolitical programmes. An equally available construction of such programmes sees them as the outcomes of moral and political struggle, which still continue to be the objects of major conflict. The establishment of workers' compensation, of graduated income taxes and of such various schemes of social insurance as unemployment relief, public health schemes and legal aid, has normally been achieved against considerable resistance in the political arena. Even their formation in the discourses of actuarialism has been fought out in moral and political terms, for example with respect to actuarialists building into social insurance specific safeguards against the assumed moral laxity of the working class (Cuneo 1986). As must be self-evident in the current era, the preservation of social insurances is still a matter of bitter moral conflict, notably in the face of neo-liberalism and economic rationalism. Certainly within the strategic vision of neo-liberalism, such opposition takes on the form of the moral crusade against the coils of the Welfare State that is sapping the energy and enterprise of individuals (Gamble 1988). Moreover, the moral banner under which it carries forward this fight is that of the free market – the free market that reinstates the morally-responsible individual and sets it against the collectivization and social dependency said to be inherent in socialized risk-management techniques.

This is not to deny that in many instances socialized risk-management techniques work invisibly and amorally, as Simon and his colleagues argue. Rather, it is to deny that they can be reduced to merely instrumental techniques for managing masses, the success of which is attributable in large measure to certain intrinsic characteristics or automatic effects. I would argue that such matters are always problematic. As objects of political struggle, not only are actuarial techniques both overtly political and moral issues, but currently their socialized applications (i.e. the welfarist social insurances) are on the retreat as a result of distinctly moral interventions.

Simon interprets this latter shift in terms of an actuarial restructuring of welfarism, as "access to public benefits is increasingly distributed through methods of risk-assessment" (Simon 1987: 78). In view of the enormous contraction of public benefit welfare and related strategies that has occurred under economically rationalist regimes in many Western States, this claim seems a rather determined attempt to rescue a thesis of hegemonic socialized security that is forced upon such writers by their identification of actuarialism with welfarism. It is admittedly evident that risk-based "targeting" of benefits is increasingly a feature of welfarism. For example, the short-term unemployed may be targeted for "retraining" or "redeployment" while the long-term unemployed may be excluded from benefit or put on a lower rate of benefit. However, were attention paid to the neo-liberal political environments of these technical processes, it would become fairly obvious that actuarial discourses are being used as means not simply of redistributing benefits, but primarily as a technique for downscaling welfare, and as a way of justifying this contraction. This surely is something different to theorizing actuarial technologies in terms of their ascendancy through the necessary centrality of the "hegemony of welfare" (Simon 1987) or the "society of security" (Gordon 1991).

Efficiency: governance and market relations

Can power be more or less efficient, as is assumed in the above readings of Foucauldian accounts? In a recent paper, Miller & Rose (1990) point out that one of the peculiarities of discourses of governmentality is that they are eternally optimistic, assuming

> that a domain or a society could be administered better or more effectively . . . [and as a result] the "failure" of one policy or set of policies is always linked to attempts to devise or propose programs that would work better. (Miller & Rose 1990: 4)

Such optimism may thus appear as an important characteristic of governmentality, but as such it should be distinguished sharply from the idea that governmentality (or any other manifestation of "power") can *objectively* perfect itself. Rather, programmes incorporate discourses of success and failure as part of their political character.

> The imperative to evaluate needs to be viewed as itself a key component of the forms of political thought under discussion: how authorities and administrators make judgements, the conclusions that they draw from them, the rectifications they propose and the impetus that "failure" provides for the propagation of new programs of government. (Miller & Rose 1990: 4)

From this viewpoint, efficiency is not so much an abstract universal property as it is a political claim couched in terms of the achievement of fairly specific political goals. Thus, historically the arguments of many of those proposing the establishment of such risk-management techniques as social insurance was that they would increase the efficiency of nations by improving the productivity of labour, and by reducing conflict generated by unemployment, poverty and other vicissitudes created by market relations. Such arguments prefigure those of Simon, Ewald and others. However, neither case in any simple sense is a factual representation of what welfarism is or was. It is, rather, a restatement of a political argument put forward initially in favour of welfarism and more recently (by the critical Left) against it (e.g. Gough 1984).

Again, such assumptions of welfare's efficiency are challenged by neo-liberal opponents in the political arena. For the neo-liberals, socialized actuarial developments have sapped the efficiency of the population. Proper efficiency will be achieved only by restoration of free-market relations and by the reassertion of individual initiative and entrepreneurialism.[4] Social insurances of all sorts, and all other devices that have removed the spur provided by the need to fend for oneself in open competition, must be stripped back and replaced by private arrangements.

This should not be taken to imply that neo-liberalism opposes actuarialism, for it accepts that individuals should manage risks. Rather, it implies that they should be prudent instead of relying on socialized securities. They should cover themselves against the vicissitudes of sickness, unemployment, old age, accidental loss or injury by making such private provisions as they see fit – including taking out the private insurances they can afford. In this fashion, risk-management techniques certainly play a vital role, but this is not the socialized actuarialism of Donzelot, Simon, Ewald and others. Better understood as *prudentialism*, it is a technology of governance that removes the key conception of regulating individuals by collectivist risk management, and throws back upon the individual the responsibility for managing risk. This is advocated by its supporters as "efficient", for individuals will be driven to greater exertion and enterprise by the need to insure against adverse circumstances – and the more enterprising they are, the better the safety net they can construct.

Market relations, risk and residual sovereignty

Simon's focus on an evolutionary model of power and its efficiency means that while the force of sovereignty is recognized, it appears as a technologically irrational anomaly – a throwback whose survival is explained in terms of the resistance of moral reactions to more efficient instrumental methods of control. Thus, "the state's effort to punish members of the underclass who commit crimes is one of the last traces of a commitment to share a community with them" (Simon 1987: 82). The focus of such approaches on the (presumed) politically pacifying effect of actuarialism, seems to blind these theorists to other possible relations between social security and political rationalities. In such models there is no recognition of the increasing severity and scope of the sovereign dispositions that have accompanied the changes in the delivery of welfare. As levels of imprisonment now surpass those extant for generations, and as the rationales for imprisonment increasingly tend towards the punitive and away from the correctional (especially in resurgent philosophies of "just deserts" and "truth in sentencing"), it is unsatisfactory to see actuarial forms of power as efficiently managing the population, and other forms (disciplinary and sovereign) merely as "surviving" or "persisting" in the face of a tide of actuarial power.

Attention to the political makes clear that explicit political rationales link the punitive and the actuarial in viable and socially dynamic arrangements. This point may be pursued, most clearly, in relation to criminal justice. Neo-liberalism's concerns with rational, responsible and free individuals lead it to a vigorous rejection of correctional and therapeutic programmes of criminal justice, and of the Keynesian, welfare-oriented concerns with links between crime, social deprivation and social justice. Overwhelmingly, crime, like welfare dependency, is understood in terms of the rational choice actor, which thinks in cost–benefit terms – weighing up the potential gains and potential costs or risks, and then acts. Criminal offending is understood to occur when the benefits of crime are perceived to outweigh the losses (see National Crime Prevention Institute 1986, Heal & Laycock 1986, Geason & Wilson 1989, Home Office 1990). Such rational choice criminals, like the abstract legal subjects explored by Pashukanis (1977) and Weber (1954), appear to be free and thus voluntary agents, free to act in a perfectly rational, self-interested fashion. They are free to commit crime or to act lawfully. By contrast, the actions of criminal offenders in Keynesian welfarism and its associated criminologies were determined by social and psychological causes, and as Foucault (1977: 252) made clear, thinking in terms of causation reduces the attribution of individual responsibility. Elimination of cause from the discourse of crime obviously restores responsibility, and this has its effects on legal sanctions. If individuals are rational choice makers and responsible for their actions, then therapeutic intervention becomes either mistaken (for there is nothing "wrong" with them), or an unwarranted interference akin to brainwashing (Van den Haag 1976). In neo-liberal discourse, the logical corollary of rational criminals, who are individually responsible for their actions, is a policy of punitive or "just deserts" sentencing. Confronted by a clear punitive cost of committing crime – unmuddied by the idea that the sanction will somehow be softened by therapy or retraining – potential criminals will be more likely to come down on the side of conformity.

Putting these points together, therefore, actuarialism must be understood in its place as a technology geared in different ways to specific kinds of political programmes. While Simon's model constructs a "struggle between risk and sovereignty", the policies of neo-liberalism reveal no such conflict. Both privatized actuarialism and punitiveness are consistent with a rationality of government based on responsible and rational individuals who take command of their own lives, and bear the consequences of freely-made decisions. The mistaken identification of actuarialism only with Keynesian social insurance, renders intelligible the "risk society" view that punitive and actuarial technologies are more or less incompatible. However, within a neo-liberal vision of responsible and rational individuals, the two technologies are systematically related to each other in a mutually supportive manner – albeit that contradictions inherent in the amalgam must be managed carefully. As a consequence, there is no inevitable expansion of the social field under the sway of actuarialism, nor inexorable movement towards a risk society.

Prudentialism

The past decade or more, has witnessed the partial transformation of socialized actuarialism into privatized actuarialism (prudentialism) as an effect of political interventions promoting the increased play of market forces. More specifically, this has involved three integrally related changes: the retraction of socialized risk-based techniques from managing the risks confronting the populace; their progressive replacement through the extension of privatized risk-based techniques; and the articulation of this process with the strategic deployment of sovereign remedies and disciplinary interventions that facilitate, underline and enforce moves towards government through individual responsibility.

While these processes have been outlined above in relation to crime control, they have become characteristic of many other areas of government. In the field of health, for example, the provision of publicly provided or subsidized medical treatment is downscaled, the scale and range of services provided by the State is narrowed, qualifying conditions for access to such services are made more rigorous and may also be allowed to become less attractive (e.g. long waiting lists for surgery). Reliance on publicly provided medicine is deterred, for example, by increasing the contributory payments, or by implying that it is immoral for the middle class to rely on public medicine, regardless of salary-indexing of contributions. This is paralleled by promotion of private health insurance and provision of private medical services, as both State and private sector voices stress the moral and rational basis for preferring private sector treatment. The rational and responsible self-interest of the medical consumers is thus relied upon to remove them from dependence on the public health services, *per medium* of a material and moral manipulation of the service environment.[5] At the same time, all manner of regimes and routines are promoted with respect to the care of the body. Whether commercially provided (weight-loss programmes, fitness centres) or State-funded (public endorsement of low fat diets, anti-smoking campaigns), a disciplinary regime of the body has been promoted, founded on the assumption that subjects of risk will opt to participate in a self-imposed programme of health and fitness.

Across this spectrum of developments, two closely related images recur – those of the responsible (moral) and of the rational (calculating) individual. The rational individual will wish to become responsible for the self, for (albeit via some neo-liberal manipulation of the environment) this will produce the most palatable, pleasurable and effective mode of provision for security against risk. Equally, the responsible individual will take rational steps to avoid and to insure against risk, in order to be independent rather than a burden on others. Guided by actuarial data on risks (e.g. on smoking and lung cancer; bowel cancer and diet, etc.) and on the delivery of relevant services and expertise (e.g. relative costs and benefits of public and private medicine), the rational and responsible individual will take prudent risk-managing measures. Within such prudential strategies, then, calculative self-interest is articulated with actuarialism to generate risk management as an everyday practice of the self. This is backed up by a moral responsibility, or duty to the self – or as Greco (1993) has termed it, a "duty to be well":

> Each individual acquires a personal preventative capacity *vis-à-vis* the event of his or her illness . . . If the regulation of lifestyle, the modification of risky behaviour and the transformation of unhealthy attitudes prove impossible through sheer strength of will, this constitutes at least in part *a failure of the self to take care of itself* – a form of irrationality, or simply a lack of skilfulness. (Greco 1993: 361)

As with health risks, so too with respect to crime risks. Prevention and risk management now become the responsibility of the victim. This view is by no means the construct of academic reflection but permeates crime prevention thinking at all levels. First, and most striking, the early liberal vision of the police force as an extension of the citizenry has been resurrected, but with a new emphasis on the disastrous consequences of Statist diminution of the responsibility of the public:

> The prevention of crime and the detection and punishment of offenders, the protection of life and property and the preservation of public tranquillity are the direct responsibilities of ordinary citizens. The police are given certain functions to assist the public to do its work but it simply cannot be left to the police. It is destructive both of police and public social health to attempt to pass over to the police the obligations and duties associated with the prevention of crime and the preservation of public tranquillity. These are the obligations and duties of the public, aided by the police and not the police occasionally aided by some public spirited citizens. (Avery 1981: 3, see also Hall 1986)

At broader political levels similar arguments are being presented in even more strident terms. Responding to news that crime rates in Britain have reached record levels, the then Prime Minister, Margaret Thatcher, "blamed a large portion of the crimes on the victims' carelessness. 'We have to be careful that we ourselves don't make it easy for the criminal', she said" (*Age* 28 September 1990). As with the duty to be well, not only does responsibility for crime-risk-management shift, but co-relatively the rational subject of risk takes on the capacity to become skilled and knowledgeable about crime prevention and crime risks.

As in the health field, State and private agencies take on the role of providing empowering knowledge and skills. Information is provided about local crime rates, about how to recognize suspicious persons, how to make the home and its contents secure, how to recognize and avoid high-crime-risk situations, about the value of insuring and marking property, and so on (O'Malley 1991). Such education, rather than being a perpetuation of State centralism, is provided in order to pass on the necessary skills for true autonomy, and to open the eyes of the public to the irrationalities of irresponsibility:

The general public's apathy about self-protection arises mainly from ignorance of the means of protection, and a perception that somebody else – "the Government" or insurance companies – bears most of the cost of theft and vandalism. The community is beginning to realize, however, that crime rates are rising despite increased penalties, that the judicial system cannot cope, and that it is the individual who eventually foots the bill for crime through increased taxes for expanded police forces and more jails, and through higher insurance premiums. (Geason & Wilson 1989: 9)

In this process, security becomes the responsibility of the private individuals, who through the pursuit of self-interest, and liberated from enervating reliance on the State, will participate in the creation of the new order. The emergent language of "working together against crime" and "partnerships with police" (concepts common in policing discourses in the United States, Australia, Canada and the UK), signal the changing relations of expertise between police and the public. The welfare model of dependence on State professionals is modified to one more in keeping with a nation of enterprising individuals. More than this, the prudent subject will invest resources in improving personal and property security – to be seen in the trend towards domestic use of private security agencies, the purchase of insurance and security devices (not only sophisticated versions of traditionally available locks and shutters, but hi-tech movement-sensitive alarms and lights, etc.). Reliance on the State, even for protection against crime, is not to be encouraged.

Rather than having a uniform level of security provided by the state, skilled and self-reliant individuals may now work with their peers in the "community" (arguably the voluntaristic and enterprising successor to the discredited "social"), make arrangements with "their" police to provide the services they require, and purchase the level of commodified security they deem appropriate to their specific needs.

Home-owners should insure their properties against burglary, and learn and implement the skills of securing the house against intruders. Prudent subjects should take out private superannuation rather than rely on State pensions to cater for their old age. Individuals should take active care of their bodies, purchase and deploy knowledge, products and skills to minimize health risks. The unemployed should retrain and acquire skills more in demand, in order to make themselves more marketable. The prudent subject of risk must be responsible, knowledgeable and rational. To rely on the State to deal with the harmful effects of known, calculable and individually manageable risks appears feckless and culpable.

Conclusions

Social technologies such as actuarialism undoubtedly have their own internal dynamics of development, but these are neither perfectly autonomous nor do they have intrinsic effects that follow automatically from their nature. Rather, the direction of development, the form in which they are put into effect in specific policies, their scope *vis-à-vis* that of other technologies, and the nature of their social impact are all quite plastic, and very much shaped by the nature of the programmes in which they are embedded. It is quite intelligible that risk-based techniques may be allied to political programmes of a socialized nature, through their discursive construction in terms of shared risk and the collective elements of insurantial techniques (Gordon 1991: 40). Conversely, it is equally clear that risk management may be articulated with an individualizing liberal or neo-liberal political programme through discursive construction in terms of rational choice actors.

It is not, then, intended to argue that a new order is emerging – that "risk society" is replacing "disciplinary society", or that "prudential society" is replacing "welfare society". However, risk management undoubtedly has become a much more important social technology than it was half a century ago. Correspondingly, it has become important to understand its nature and role as a technology of government. Within neo-liberalism (or more broadly, as Nikolas Rose would say, "advanced liberalism"), I have argued that actuarial techniques appear primarily in the specific form here described as prudentialism, and that as such they embody, and are aligned with, elements from other social technologies including the punitive and disciplinary. Prudentialism therefore does not involve merely a privatization of risk management. The management of risks through prudentialism involves shifts in many governmental relations, not least being that subjects are recast as rational, responsible, knowledgeable and calculative, in control of the key aspects of their lives. The constitution of the liberal subject as active and self-directive is linked to a change in the relations with authorities and professionals. Welfarism implies a subordination of the "client" to the professional service provider who has superior knowledge and status *and* who is empowered by the superordinate State or superior social standing. The prudential subject, by contrast, enters "partnerships" with public authorities (e.g. police), or becomes the "customer" – literally or figuratively depending on the degree of marketization of the service.

Not only the nature of the subject and of the technologies are changed in the move from welfare to prudentialism, for this transformation is itself intricately linked with a change in the conception of risk, often overlooked by those who envision risk management as unproblematically geared to security. Neo-liberal critics (e.g. Aharoni 1981) have perhaps captured the nub of the issue when they derogatively describe the Welfare State as "no-risk society". That is, for Keynesian welfarism, risk is regarded as a problem, as a product of pathology or incompleteness. Most risks, in some way or another, are regarded as pathologies, and scientifically guided government should eventually (or ideally) eliminate them or neutralize their effects. Unemployment and poverty appear as products of failures in market capitalism; crime is a product of personal pathologies, or of failures in the delivery of social resources and opportunities; poor health is in significant ways attributable to social inequalities in the distribution of diet, education, living conditions and health care. Social engineering can and should be directed to correct these problems and eliminate the risks they generate, not only because of the personal hardships they cause, and the systematic inefficiencies they are thought to create, but also because of their potential for creating social unrest (Gough 1984).

Contemporary liberal approaches to government adopt a rather different view. In the first place, as is argued by Aharoni, risk by no means is to be understood as indicative of an imperfectly governed world. Rather, risk is a source or condition of opportunity, an avenue for enterprise and the creation of wealth, and thus an unavoidable and invaluable part of a progressive environment. Without risk, wealth would not be created, innovation would be stultified, individuals would lose a spur to action and a crucial condition for generating responsibility. In this vision, the efforts of social engineers to eliminate risk have been a major contributor to the malaises of contemporary society. This is not to say that *all* risks are so conceived. Clearly, neo-liberalism would regard many *specific* risks as ones that can and should be prevented or minimized. But this is quite different to the social engineering vision of a society of universal security, "no-risk society", in which risk as such, ideally, should be eliminated. For neo-liberalism it is always necessary to ask "Which risk?" before deciding whether a constricting or a sustaining response is required.

For this reason the management of risk becomes the responsibility of neo-liberal governance only with considerable circumspection. On the one hand, this is because, as argued throughout, individuals should take responsibility for the management of risks, as part of their rational and responsible existence. On the other hand, it is because the definition of many risks as significant or insignificant, ideally, must also be devolved to the individual. To the extent that neo-liberal subjects confront risks, unmediated by interference from the State and social engineers (although, of course, provided with advice and information by such experts as police and the medical profession), then they will be moved to act on their own behalf. Those risks that will receive their attention will be the ones they identify as significant problems. The risk-management techniques they support – through personal advocacy and effort, or by purchase in the market place – will be the ones they define as the best available. And we can be sure of the efficiency of this process, because the success of the measures taken will be assessed in terms of the cost–benefit calculus of individuals who put their own resources and their own security on the line.[6] Prudentialism thus embodies a key technique for dealing with one of the central problematics of liberal governmentalities – defining the minimal parameters of State activity consistent with an ordered, prosperous and peaceful nation.

Notes

1. The use of the term "technology" broadly speaking refers to any set of social practices that is aimed at manipulating the social or physical world according to identifiable routines. The three principle forms identified by Foucault are sovereign, disciplinary and insurantial. "Techniques" here refer either to distinct forms of application, or to distinct components, of technologies. For example, the prison and the school, examination and the case record may all be thought of as techniques of the disciplinary technology.

2. For Foucault, it was the specific *combinations* of disciplinary and regulatory techniques that gave rise to "the four great lines of attack" in the modern politics of sex (1984: 146). Thus with birth control and the psychiatrization of perversions, "the intervention was regulatory in nature, but it had to rely on the demand for individual disciplines and constraints". On the other hand, the sexualization of children and the "hysterization" of women rested on the requirements of regulation (e.g. collective welfare) in order to obtain results at the level of discipline.

3. This is not to suggest that they are simply ingeniously constructed *de nova*. Many may come into existence more or less accidentally and are then refined, others are generated by drawing together disparate elements from other technologies, and so on. The process envisaged is one in which elements are drawn together pragmatically, and the ones that catch on do so because they work for present purposes at hand. The logic of growth is not therefore one of absolute efficiency, but of pragmatic appropriateness.

4. Gamble (1988: 40–41) comments on Friedmanesque economic visions in much the same tone that this chapter adopts towards assertions of absolute efficiency in crime management. Noting their claims that market solutions invariably are more efficient that governmental solutions, Gamble points out that the belief that economic propositions can be proven to be true is part of the political strategy used to discredit Keynesianism – rather than being a real foundation of such discrediting.

5. The obvious, if partial exception here is the (unrealized) proposal for a public health programme under the Clinton regime from 1993. However, it will readily be recognized that in that context, the process of downscaling public medicine and the promotion of private sector responsibility had been implemented considerably earlier. Clinton's reforms relate specifically to another generation of *political* problems. Such changes underline a general point in this chapter that politics is far more important than is implied by a focus on allegedly "given" effects of social technologies, and indeed, that the effects themselves are a matter of political negotiation rather than automatic consequence.

6. It may be argued that many important risks in everyday life could not be left to such a process. Crime control would be one of these, especially with reference to police. But as has been seen already, there is considerable scope for

increasing the role of prudential strategies here. Beyond the forms discussed in this chapter, it should be considered that, to the extent that the provision of expertise shifts towards the "customer" or to "partnership" models, so the determination of police priorities and practices in crime risk management is determined by the individuals who make up the "local community". These people direct police activities, and personally bear the costs and benefits of their preferred risk-management strategies. As Britain currently is witnessing, even a regime investing heavily in the politics of law and order is quite capable of subjecting the police to such neo-liberal practices (McLaughlen & Muncie 1993).

References

Abel, R. (ed.) 1982. *The politics of informal justice*. New York: Academic Press.

Aharoni, Y. 1981. *The no-risk society*. Chatham NJ: Chatham House.

Avery, J. 1981. *Police: force or service?* London: Butterworth.

Burchell, G., C. Gordon, P. Miller (eds) 1991. *The Foucault effect: studies in governmentality*. Hemel Hempstead, England: Harvester Wheatsheaf.

Castel, R. 1991. From dangerousness to risk. See Burchell et al. (1991), 281–98.

Cohen, S. 1979. The punitive city. Notes on the dispersal of social control. *Contemporary Crises* **3**, 339–63.

Cohen, S. 1985. *Visions of social control: crime, punishment and classification*. Cambridge: Polity.

Cuneo, C. 1986. Comment: restoring class to state unemployment insurance. *Canadian Journal of Political Science* **19**, 93–8.

Defert, D. 1991. Popular life and insurance technology. See Burchell et al. (1991), 211–34.

Donzelot, J. 1979. The poverty of political culture. *Ideology and Consciousness* **5**, 71–86.

Donzelot, J. 1991. Pleasure in work. See Burchell et al. (1991), 169–80.

Ewald, F. 1986. *L'état providence*. Paris: Grasset.

Ewald, F. 1990. Norms, discipline and the law. *Representations* **30**, 138–61.

Ewald, F. 1991. Insurance and risks. See Burchell et al. (1991), 197–210.

Foucault, M. 1977. *Discipline and punish: the birth of prison*. London: Peregrine Books.

Foucault, M. 1984. *The history of sexuality* vol. I. London: Penguin.

Gamble, A. 1988. *The free economy and the strong state*. London: Macmillan.

Geason, S. & P. Wilson 1989. *Crime prevention: theory and practice*. Canberra: Australian Institute of Criminology.

Gordon, C. 1991 Governmental rationality: an introduction. See Burchell et al. (1991), 1–52.

Gough, I. 1984. *The political economy of the welfare state*. London: Macmillan.

Greco, M. 1993. Psychosomatic subjects and the "duty to be well": personal agency within medical rationality. *Economy and Society* **22**(3), 357–72.

Hall, J. 1986. Burglary: the insurance industry viewpoint. In *Burglary: a social reality*, S. Mukherjee (ed.). Canberra: Australian Institute of Criminology.

Heal, K. & G. Laycock 1986. *Situational crime prevention*. London: HMSO.

Hogg, R. 1989. Criminal justice and social control: contemporary development in Australia. *Journal of Studies in Justice* **2**, 89–122.

Home Office 1990. *Crime, justice and protecting the public*. London: HMSO.

King, M. 1988. *How to make social crime prevention work: the French experience*. London: NACRO Occasional Paper.

La Fond, J. & M. Durham 1991. *Back to the asylum. The future of mental health policy in the United States*. Oxford: Oxford University Press.

McLaughlen, E. & J. Muncie 1993. The silent revolution. Market-based criminal justice in England. *Socio-Legal Bulletin* **8**, 5–12.

Miller, P. & N. Rose 1990. Governing economic life. *Economy and Society* **19**, 1–31.

National Crime Prevention Institute 1986. *Crime prevention*. Louisville: National Crime Prevention Institute.

O'Malley, P. 1991. Legal networks and domestic security. *Studies in Law, Politics and Society* **11**, 181–91.

Pashukanis, E. 1977. *Law and Marxism*. London: Ink Links.

Reichman, N. 1986. Managing crime risks: toward an insurance based model of social control. *Research in Law and Social Control* **8**, 151–72.

Scull, A. 1975. *Decarceration. Community treatment and the deviant. A radical view*. New York: Spectrum Books.

Simon, J. 1987. The emergence of a risk society: insurance, law, and the state. *Socialist Review* **95**, 61–89.

Simon, J. 1988. The ideological effects of actuarial practices. *Law and Society Review* **22**, 772–800.

Van den Haag, E. 1976. *Punishing criminals*. New York: Basic Books.

Weber, M. 1954. *Max Weber on law in economy and society*, Max Rheinstein (ed.). Cambridge, Mass.: Harvard University Press.

Chapter 10

Foucault, government and the enfolding of authority

Mitchell Dean

> . . . the diagnostic does not establish the facts of our identity by means of the interplay of distinctions. It establishes that we are difference, that our reason is the difference of forms of discourse, our history is the difference of times, that our selves are the difference of masks. (Foucault 1972: 131)

This chapter presents a way of reading Foucault's work as a critical, historical and political ontology of ourselves and our present. It suggests how this project differs from some apparently similar themes in the contemporary history and sociology of the self. Finally, it explicates the phrase "the enfolding of authority" – with the assistance of the work of Gilles Deleuze (1988, 1993, cf. Rose 1993, 1995, Dean 1994b) and with some reference to Heidegger – as a way of thinking about what emerges once the usual way of approaching identity formation has been displaced.

For a political ontology of ourselves and our present

The work of Michel Foucault lends itself, like any other body of historical and philosophical study, to conventional scholarly practices of commentary, exegesis, interpretation and criticism. We can bring our machines of truth, if one likes, to bear on his texts. I want to suggest, however, that there is a more fruitful and interesting way of approaching these texts, one captured by Deleuze's view of theory as a "toolbox" (Foucault & Deleuze 1977: 208), and Foucault's suggestion that his books be regarded as "experience books" rather than "truth books" (1991: 30–31). If we take this second approach, the contemporary legacy of Foucault – François Ewald has called the "*actualités de Michel Foucault*" (1994), Deleuze his "diagnostic" (1992) – might lie less in the interpretation text than in the specific uses to which his concepts, themes and analyses, can be put, their wilful reformation and deformation, and their insertion into different arguments and intellectual assemblages. We should be concerned not so much about the recuperation and integration of Foucault's work for philosophy, history or the social sciences, than for undertaking a form of analysis concerned with the limits and possibilities of how we have come to think about who we are, what we do and the present in which we find our selves. We can use Foucault to form or reform ourselves as philosophers, historians or sociologists, but we can also use Foucault to inaugurate a critical engagement with our present and to diagnose its practical potential and constraints. To invoke the language Foucault provided in relation to Kant (1986b), I would say that while certain institutional conditions might favour those who undertake an analytic of truth concerning Foucault, his own work suggests that we engage in the rather different work of a historical and political ontology of ourselves and our present.

To speak of a critical ontology of ourselves requires, however, an immediate qualification. First, what is at issue is a history of localized and heterogeneous ontologies that do not add up to either a single form of human being or a single present (Rose 1995). Nor is a "history of the present" about the emergence of a "modernity" that is a unity of discrete but interdependent elements (Dean 1994a: 51–2). There is rather a multiplicity of presents, a multiplicity of ways of experiencing those presents and a multiplicity of the "we" who are subjects of that experience. Secondly, these multiple ontologies are different ways of *thinking* about who we are, how we should act and how we should act upon ourselves. What is at issue here is not so much what human beings really are or have ˙come but how they think about who they are, and the consequences of ˙. What we seek to establish, then, is not a theory or even a history of g, but a history of truth, or a history of thought, given that thought is stricted to a philosophical or literary canon and that a part of such a of thought is to analyze its diverse "effects in the real", as Foucault ˙81: 10).

ˑucault, this critical ontology of our selves and our present can-ˑerstood in terms of a narrative of the triumphal or oppressive ate building and citizen formation after social liberals like T. (1963) or Marxist historical sociologists like Corrigan & ˀean 1994b). Rather than appearing as the prerogative of ate, concerns about conduct are voiced and pursued by a ˀthorities and agencies that seek to unify, divide, make

209

whole and fragment, our selves and our lives in the name of specific forms of truth. To understand the relation between authority and identity, if one likes, we should look beyond the global enwrapping of State formation and the moral regulation of individuals to the variegated domain in which what might be called "regimes of government" come to work through "regimes of conduct", a domain populated by the multiform projects, programmes and plans that attempt to make a difference to the way in which we live by a swarm of experts, specialists, advisers and empowerers.

These "authorities of truth" operate within and outside local, regional, national and transnational State bodies, demanding they take on or withdraw from their functions, act in new and different ways, form new relations with other bodies and other States, divide, compose and assemble themselves differently, and position themselves in certain networks and relays. They may pit one part of the State against another (the programme of a local or State women's health unit against those of the national Treasury) or enter into contestation with other authorities at other locales both within and outside the State. They may find ways of circumventing the network of State authority or simply ignoring it by establishing direct links between different specialists, sites and actors (e.g. the relation between AIDS activists and the laboratory). They may even seek to "empower" their constituency and clients so that they may participate in governmental programmes and even resist certain State authorities, such as the Community Action Programs initiated in the United States during the War on Poverty in the 1960s (Cruikshank 1994).

Our present is one in which we are enjoined to take care and responsibility for our own lives, health, happiness, sexuality and financial security, in which we are provided with choices that we are expected to exercise, and in which we might feel that there is a possibility of some greater freedom in the forms of life we can live, and be safe and prosper within. It is also one in which a multiplicity of authorities, movements and agencies comes into play, seeking to link up our freedom, choices, forms of life and conduct with an often uncertain mix of political goals, social aspirations and governmental ends. Within this cacophony of plans, programmes and policies concerned with our values, identities, lifestyles, hopes, fears, desires and relationships, with our capacities for self-reflection, critique, personal fulfilment and liberation, we might strain to discern the barely audible point first raised by Foucault's work, one that accounts for its novelty and great force and is doubtless in some danger of being lost again. He asked questions not about the true nature of our identity but about how we come to invest so much in all this talk about identity, self and subjectivity, how we have come to locate the truth of being in what we take to be deepest structures of our self (not only our sexuality, but also our memories and our childhood), and how authority comes to consti- tute, inscribe and invest itself in the different ways we produce true and false statements about who we are and what we should become.

Foucault's claim was not that personal life was necessarily political but that we need to analyze all the ways in which the conduct of government was linked to the government of conduct, as Jeffrey Minson has put it (1993: 5), such that the soul of the citizen is at stake in even the most mundane of governmental policies. He asked how we have come to problematize both our politics and our being in such a way that identity, subjectivity and self come to be hooked to questions of politics, authority and government.

Fragmentary selves into a fractured present?

Of course, Foucault is hardly alone in these concerns involving the forma- tion of identities, persons and their attributes and that others have produced far more detailed accounts of the dilemmas of the subject in contemporary social life. Indeed, there is no deficit of questions and authoritative answers about identity in recent social and cultural theory. Here I simply draw a composite sketch of how these themes are played out in recent discussions of late modernity, postmodernity or risk society. In so doing, I argue that a critical ontology of ourselves offers less an alter- nate substantive account of identity than a different style of analysis, one enunciated in somewhat less self-assured tones. My purpose is not to offer a critique of contemporary social theory but to suggest something of the ethos of studies of governmentality.

This ethos embodies a modesty closer to the work of certain historians, anthropologists and even empirical sociologists than much contemporary social theory. It seeks, in full knowledge of its own limits, to be meticulous, to respect dispersion and rarity, to grasp things in their admixture and impurity, to avoid the *a priori* and the dogmatic, and to be wary of global characterization, premature generalization, theoretical unification, politi- cal purity or the correct line. To bring this ethos to contemporary social and cultural theory is to engage the latter's concerns by means of what Osborne (1994) has called "principles of de-dramatisation". It is, in this sense, to continue the concerns of such theory without its will to represent world-historical epochs, conflicts, powers and processes, and without its godlike perspective over the destiny and attributes of humanity. In a practical sense, this means a suspension of the explanatory purchase of the key terms of such an account.

Our types of society, according to certain influential social theorists, are characterized by the end of the meta-narratives of reason and progress that accompanied the early stages of modernization, instanced by a loss of faith in the benefits of industrial efficiency, economic growth and scientific expertise. This is because the latter stages of modernization are organized around the production and distribution of risk as much as wealth (Beck 1989: 86–7). Late modernization brings a proliferation of industrial and technological hazards, their differential distribution among populations, and constant attempts at risk assessment and monitoring. We thus live in a "risk society" marked by an increasing publicity and awareness of threats posed by modernization for daily living, the attempt by individuals to control their own riskiness by the use of expert knowledges, and by the failure of the physical sciences to control or even accurately calculate risks of nuclear power, biochemical production or the threat to global ecology (Beck 1992a: 101–6).

The impact of risk culture on individual and collective conduct raises questions of trust in abstract systems and expertise and problematizes individual and collective security in ways that resonate with other general features of post or late modernity. Residual traditional, communal or regional bonds are undone by the relentless surge of globalization; solidarities of class, family and nation give way to a multiplicity of forms of life and the conscious adoption of lifestyles; new alliances between old class opponents emerge against schism-ridden citizen groups and social movements; conflict occurs over scientific knowledge and information; and the very notion of society collapses into particularized communities and differentially competitive regions and sectors. The net product of the forces constituting the present epoch make it one in which identities are either de-centred, dislocated, fragmented and placed in crisis (Hall 1992: 274–5) or, more subtly, subject to processes that, while offering opportunities for self-actualization, can also lead to fragmentation, insecurity and powerlessness (Giddens 1991: 187–201).

The new individualism, and its attendant existential anxiety and insecurity, are exacerbated and intensified by the mass media and advertising industry with their presentation of different and novel forms of life and their elicitation of consumer needs not only for material commodities but for the images attached and embodied in them, and for the lifestyles that they offer (Giddens 1991: 196–201). The legitimate search for authentic forms of life becomes subverted by the debased and commodified lifestyle that leaves genuine needs in a permanent state of dissatisfaction.

In short, the stable class, ethnic and gender identities characteristic of even early modernity have become undermined by forces liable to leave the subject in flux, fragmented and without a stable sense of anchorage in social networks or, more optimistically, open to the challenges of self-actualization and the formation of new forms of association and intimacy. Moreover, modernization takes on a "reflexive" character (Beck 1992b) that both turns on and overruns the forms of organization and identity characteristic of early modernization and provides forms of expert knowledge that can be appropriated by the subject in his or her own quest for self-identity. For each individual such identities are revealed to be the uncertain consequence of our previous choices and plans. Rather than something fixed, unified and relatively stable, they have become something to be worked on and worked out. Any sense of identity arises from a "reflexive project of the self" (Giddens 1991), in which the self emerges as something to be constructed and turned into coherent narrative and autobiography, as the subject of a political, personal or spiritual journey, with or without the help of the multiplying numbers of therapists, counsellors and other engineers of the human soul. A politics of identity or a life-politics, practised by ethnic and sexual minorities, feminists, Greens and others – according to this characterization of our present – thus becomes available through the fluidity, reflexivity and plurality of identity, the search for forms of life that will contribute to the goal of self-actualization, and as a means of contesting the identities constructed by experts, abstract systems and dominant groups.

How does a critical history of our selves and our present differ from this kind of account? First, we might note the concern for self-identity is neither as new nor as prolific as has been thought. Rather than an anxiety about self, identity or conduct being a general feature of a culture, epoch, society or civilization, it should be treated as something relatively rare, as arising in particular circumstances, at certain times, in specific locations and having particular purposes. It is bound up with conflicts of not only how to govern but who should govern and who has the right to govern. This work on self or identity is analyzable, then, not as a symptom of forces that have broken down traditional bonds, but through the specifically conceived topography of the person it employs, the questions it puts to aspects of conduct, the techniques it encourages, the "practices of the self" framing it, the populations it targets, the goals it seeks and the social struggles and hierarchies in which it occurs. This is what I take Foucault to mean when he suggests that his concern is with neither behaviour, ideas, societies, nor ideologies, but *problematizations* (1985: 11). Thus his analysis shows that the ethical problematizations posed by the ancient Greeks arise in particular domains of practice – e.g. the management of the health and life of the body, matters of marriage and the management of the household, matters of relations with boys who will be future citizens, and so on – rather than from a general theory or set of ideas about the nature of human being or from a global and necessary process of the social shaping of selves. Moreover, Foucault's researches into the "care of the self" of late antiquity and early Christian "hermeneutics of the self" suggest that many of the features held to be specific to the quest for self-identity in late modernity are part of the longer and more complex trajectory of techniques of the self. Thus we find the use of "autobiographical" techniques among Roman philosophical schools, including the keeping of notebooks, writing letters to friends, and mnemonic devices such as the nightly self-examination recommended by Seneca (Foucault 1988b). The point is not that we should erase all historical narratives of the self but that attention to particular practices of the self and the techniques that sustain them reveals awkward continuities for those seeking to claim the ruptural nature of the present.

We can use the work of historians of antiquity, such as Paul Veyne (1990) and Peter Brown (1992), to show how forms of ethical comportment and personality are implicated in different social hierarchies and crucial to social struggles (cf. Dean 1995a). Thus ethical practices and the forms of ethical personality they imply were crucial to the Christianization of the late Roman Empire. The (male) notables of the fourth century of the Eastern Empire were still initiated as late adolescents into a common culture of *paideia*, a form of grooming by which they asserted their own cultivation, communicated with others of their class, with governors and representatives of the emperor, and expressed their social distance from other classes (Brown 1992: 35–58). *Paideia*, which required the attainment of difficult skills, implied a conception of superior persons who combined discretion, self-restraint and justice in the activity of governing with a cultivation expressed as a "devotion to the muses". The central techniques of this educational practice were those of rhetoric, a training in highly formalized styles of speech that extended to voice modulation, breath control and deportment. The techniques of *paideia* provided the repertoire for the conduct of the complex and tension-laden practice of politics in the late empire and gave a certain gloss to the murderous intrigue around the emperor and his officials. These notables of the antique city were also thought to be possessed of particular attributes that they must display in relations to the plebs, including, most importantly, *euergesia*, the desire to show unfailing goodwill to one's city through acts of civic benefaction and ostentation manifest in the provision and restoration of public buildings, baths and stadia, and the giving of banquets, festivals and gladiatorial games (Veyne 1987b: 105–115, 1990). While this kind of activity was obligatory for those in public office, it sometimes proved ruinous to the giver. *Paideia* and *euergesia* together formed an ethical comportment of aristocratic civism that regulated the relations of the municipal notables with their superiors, their equals and their cities and citizens.

Such a set of techniques contrasts sharply with the emergent practice and conception of the person and community found in Judaism and early Christianity (Brown 1987: 253–85). This conception was also associated with an ethical injunction to give, but one that contrasted sharply with the culture of the antique city (Veyne 1990: 19–34). Rather than an ideal of the studious control of deportment, these communities worked with a conception of the human being that sought single-mindedness, simplicity, transparency to God and openness to others. Here, the material of this "profound and sombre scrutiny" was the "heart". These religious groups were concerned to root out the "zones of negative privacy" that contained dangerous opacities to both God and community (Brown 1987: 254). The efforts to combat this "double-heartedness" in early Christianity and the rise of practices of sexual renunciation, particularly among leaders, have specific purposes. They were concerned to maintain solidarity of a socially vulnerable group, to mark the status of church leaders within pagan society, and to create a public space for the Church. Moreover the claim to moral leadership of the Church in the fourth century was bound to the radical asceticism of the anchorite monks, rooted in the authority of the desert and the marginalized populations of the ancient economy, and in the claim, manifested in almsgiving, of the new Christian notable, the bishop, to be no longer a *philopatris* or "lover of the city" but a *philoptochos* or "lover of the poor" (Brown 1987: 292).

This work on ancient societies certainly shows the relativity of the contemporary desire for self-fulfilment or for self-identity. What is more important, it demonstrates the variety of conceptions of person and self within diverse "programmes of conduct", their dependence on different "regimes of practices" and techniques, their different and often competing constituencies, and their different social and political functions (cf.

Foucault 1981). Indeed, the rise of Christianity within the late Roman Empire is at least as much a struggle over different regimes of ethical comportment (*paideia* and single-heartedness), different forms of ethical personality (notable and bishop, philosopher and monk) and different ethical orientations towards the populace (*euergesia* and almsgiving), as a struggle of ideas, ideologies, religions or classes. These forms of comportment are far from disinterested ways of making up persons. They are the means in a struggle over who has the moral right to lead communities, over how wealth is best used and how best to govern.

Next, against a sociological model in which there is the assumption of a general form of the relation between society, its institutions and structures and the self and its personality, we start from the assumption that there is no natural, necessary or given mode of determination of selves and identities. Studies of governmentality are not concerned with a general figure of the self bound by a necessary social determination but with the more or less explicit attempts to problematize our lives, our forms of conduct and our selves found in a variety of pronouncements and texts, employed in a variety of locales, using particular techniques, and addressed to different social sectors and groups. Its raw material, then, includes books of manners and etiquette, catechisms, systems of military discipline, exercise and dietary regimens, treatises on erotic arts, lifestyle television programmes and magazine and newspaper columns, much popular psychological and sociological writing, and all types of "how to" texts concerned with success in work, business, school, money matters, child-rearing, marriage, love and sex. If we are to talk of processes of socialization as a general way in which "society" affects "individuals", then we must give an account of how this socialization is itself constructed, the historical forms it takes, the rationalities it deploys, the techniques, mechanisms, practices and institutions by which and in which it is proposed that we work on, divide, make whole, sculpt, cultivate, pacify, contain, empower and optimize not only our own lives, selves and conduct but the lives, selves and conduct of those over whom we claim some authority. Thus the real innovation of Jacques Donzelot's *The policing of families* (1979) was that it provided a hitherto-lacking analysis of the mechanisms by which the modern family was socialized without reference to the effect of general social processes on biological norms. To do so, it demonstrated how different families became variegated discretionary spaces in which their various members came to be entrusted with differential obligations and statuses specified by a range of medical, educational and welfare grids of perception, evaluation and intervention that, in turn, constituted particular bodies of expertise that were central to the constitution of various authorities (cf. Hodges & Hussain 1979, Hirst 1981, Minson 1985: 180–224). From this point of view, the problem with contemporary sociological accounts is that they are pitched at too general a level and propose a mysterious, even occult, relation between general social processes and events (e.g. globalization, postcolonialism, the emergence of postmodernity) and features of identity (fragmentation, fluidity, multiplicity, the desire for self-actualization, etc.).

We can say there is no single figure that can capture the form of the subject for a particular society or culture or even for the historical trajectory of forms of self in a civilization. The characterization of a fragmented postmodern subject ceaselessly reconstructing itself is an heir to a long historical and sociological heritage that has indeed tried to do just that. Notions of social and cultural types of individuals from the bourgeois individual and *homo oeconomicus* to one-dimensional man, the administered subject and fragmented self, are so many versions of this motif. In fact, this approach has one of its most recent ancestors in the writings of the Frankfurt school of the 1940s, particularly in the collective and individual writings of Horkheimer & Adorno (1972). Horkheimer, in his *Eclipse of reason* (1974: 128–61), provides something of a general history of the self in the West. Here a narrative is charted of the ebb and flow of individualism from tribal societies to late capitalism. It moves from a primitive pre-individuality living in the gratification and frustrations of the moment, through the model of the Greek hero, the flowering of individuality in the Hellenic city states with Socratic conscience and Platonic objective reason, and its retreat into Stoic resignation with the subjugation of the cities by the Roman Empire. This is followed by the investment of the individual with a unique and immortal soul in Christianity, and its secularization and humanization in the Renaissance, Reformation and Enlightenment. The "era of free enterprise" leads to an open proclamation of bourgeois individuality that proves to be evanescent under administered capitalism and mass culture with the arrival of what would later be called "one-dimensional man". In such an account there is a curious simultaneous historicizing and naturalizing of the individual or self. The self is a historical product, transformed through different phases of the historical development of features of society such as the division of labour and the forms of social domination. Yet it retains a general form throughout this trajectory as an entity that represses and instrumentalizes its own inner being and external nature in the interest of self-preservation. There is, then, a general form of subject underlying both the spurious unity of "the West" and the distinctive versions corresponding to each socio-cultural period.

This positing of a general form of the subject, whether for a particular epoch or for an entire civilization, is undermined, however, not only by its own implausibility but by the crucial work of recent cultural historians of private life and the work of other social thinkers such as Norbert Elias. The collective work of the historians of private life is exemplary in that, as Georges Duby notes (1987: viii), it remains conscious of the retrospective nature of reading over two millennia of European history in terms of a concept of personal existence barely a century old and that it seeks to avoid using these histories as evidence for a general history of individualism. Here, studies of education, marriage, slavery, religion, domestic architecture, notions of the sacred and the secret, and private belief – to cite some of the contents of the first volume (Veyne 1987a) – become so many occasions for an exploration of the myriad ways in different societies and at different times in which humans have carved out domains of private and public life, employing a vast array of techniques and means, to construct an existence for themselves and others made up of a bewildering variety of reasons and purposes. At their best, the work of the historians of private life shows how specific aspects of conduct and person were problematized, by various agents and authorities, among distinct populations, employing certain techniques, and with particular aspirations, goals and consequences. The danger with such cultural history, however, is that it is always at risk of viewing this multiplicity of concepts and practices as evidence of the quest of a universal subject seeking to give meaning to its activities or turning private life into the *telos* of civilization.

The work of Elias (e.g. 1978, 1982, 1983, Dean 1994a: 202–8) illustrates the very same point. His history of manners demonstrates the specificity of the aspects of conduct that are problematized in poems, songs and written treatises of manners (from table manners, nose-blowing, spitting, excretion, aggression, to relations between the sexes), the heterogeneous locale in which conduct is problematized (at the table, in the bedroom, in the street and market place, the castle on the feudal estate, the absolutist court), the diverse ends invoked (courtesy, civility), and the diverse groups addressed (the knights, the *noblesse de robe*, the *noblesse d'épée*, the clergy, the urban bourgeoisie and financiers) by very different authorities (secular, municipal, ecclesiastical, military). If genealogy is "grey, meticulous and patiently documentary" (Foucault 1986c: 76), the Elias of *The civilizing process* and *The court society* surely qualifies as a genealogist *par excellence*. However, Elias seeks to encapsulate this within a global thesis of the "civilizing process" in which there is an assumed fit between the rationalization of conduct and the development of the State, a concern ultimately with the sociogenesis of modern personality types. Moreover, he proposes a psychoanalytic mode of the moulding of persons through the regulation of drives by the social implantation of habits that later become unconscious mechanisms of constraint. Despite his genuine breakthrough in making the analysis of the mechanisms of self-moulding central to the historical–sociological enterprise, Elias – in both these moves – suffers the same problem as afflicts the social and cultural theorists of the Frankfurt school (cf. Bogner 1987). He assumes a general topography of the self that is shaped and moulded by civilizing processes to produce a definite form of the modern individual.

The aim of a critical ontology of our selves is not to provide an account of the genesis of the "modern" subject, or of its fragmentation in post-modernity, or even to align processes of "sociogenesis" with ones of "psychogenesis", as Elias might have put it (1978). Its aim, as Nikolas Rose (1995) has argued, is to understand how human beings came to be *thought of* and *characterized* as having a certain psychological interiority in which the determinations of culture could be inscribed, organized and shaped into a distinctive personality or character. Its point is to make intelligible how we came to understand ourselves as an essential innerness from which flows our thoughts, our expressions, our conduct and our emotions. Its objective is to show how this experience of personhood is given to us within the myriad ways we are made transparent to ourselves and others so that we might be rendered calculable and ultimately governable. The object of our studies of government is not the subject that is produced by specific governmental or ethical practices. It is the relation between the forms of truth by which we have come to know ourselves and the forms of practice by which we seek to shape the conduct of ourselves and others.

Finally, rather than posing the question of the relationship between politics and identity at the level of a general historical trajectory of the State and of the individual, we should turn our attention to the very situations in which the regulation of personal conduct becomes linked to the regulation of political or civic conduct. Two extraordinarily different examples of the interleaving of a problematization of personal existence and identity with political and governmental considerations will suffice here.

As a first example, simply note the advocacy and implementation of a so-called "active system" of the treatment of the unemployed in many

Organization for Economic Co-operation and Development (OECD) member countries (Dean 1995b). Here, the unemployed are rendered knowable as "job-seekers" who are required not only to agree to perform certain tasks (job search, retraining, undergoing counselling, joining self-help groups, etc.) in return for State allowances, but also to adopt a particular form of personal deportment and maintain a certain relationship to themselves encapsulated in the notion of active citizenship, a condition in which one is held to maintain self-esteem, networks of social obligation, life-skills, enthusiasm and motivation and avoid the dependency characteristic of an underclass (Gass 1988, OECD1988, Keating 1994). Here a loop, a doubling or a fold is established between the government of the unemployed and the way in which the unemployed learn to govern themselves, between the subject that is knowable and governable only in so far as it can know and govern itself, that double Foucault (1970: 312) had already called the "enslaved sovereign" in his discussion of *Las Meninas*. There is certainly a form of administratively guided asceticism at work here such that the regime of practices concerning the unemployed today is neither strictly a governmental regime nor an ethical regime but a hybrid assemblage of multiform dimensions.

As a second example, we can cite Foucault's own analysis (1985) of how a minority of men that were free and equal citizens in antiquity came to problematize their capacities of self-government as a consequence of their government of others in both the *polis* and *oikos*, as citizens and heads of households. In contrast to the government of the unemployed, here the problematization of one's own conduct is not a feature of being governed but of the exercise of authority over others. In short, to pose the question of politics and identity at the level of the State and the individual is both too general and empty. We must examine the specific problematization of identities that occur at the intersection of the way we conduct ourselves and the way we expect others to conduct themselves.

The enfolding of authority

The political ontology of our selves can be approached, in part, by a critical history of the ways in which human beings have sought to direct themselves and others as subjects of various kinds. Gilles Deleuze (1988: 100–101, Rose 1995) suggests that the Greeks, in their concern for self-mastery as a condition for civic power, "folded force", establishing a relation of forces to themselves, bending the outside through a series of practical exercises. He advances the fundamental idea of enfoldment in which interiority is not something other than the folds and the folding of the "peristaltic" movement of the outside. For the Greeks at least, self-mastery entails a project that already depends on the exercise of mastery over others in the household and in the city. The government of others here is a condition for the development of practices by which one seeks to act on oneself. In this sense one might speak of a folding of exterior relations of authority to sculpt a domain that can act on and of itself but which, at the same time, is simply the inside marked out by that folding, an Inside of the folding of an Outside (Rose 1995). In this example, the establishment of an interior domain is thus dependent on the enfolding of external authority.

Foucault's genealogies of ethics (1984: 352–7, 1985: 26–8, 1986a: 238–9) and punishment (1977: 16–31) also allow us to analyze governmental and ethical practices as just such practices of the enfolding of authority. The first aspect of such practices entails what I shall call the *governed substance or material*. This is the material part of ourselves that is to be surrounded and enfolded (Deleuze 1988: 104). It concerns what we seek to govern in ourselves and others, that which Foucault calls the "ethical substance" to be worked upon and over (e.g. the pleasures or *aphrodisia* in Greece, the flesh in Christianity, sexuality in contemporary liberation ethics). Moreover, it is that which, in his account of modern punitive practice, Foucault (1977: 17) had called the "substance of the punishable element" – the soul of the criminal rather than the criminal himself, a soul comprising all those circumstances, instincts, passions, desires and effects of environment or heredity that led to the commission of crime. The governed substance is a materiality drenched with thought. It is hence not a question of either a pure materiality or a pure ideality; it is both and at once. Thus consider the mundane practice of dieting. Here the material we seek to govern appears unequivocally material – the body and its intake of food. Yet we render aspects of the physico-chemical constitution of our bodies and food governable by a knowledge of blood cholesterol levels, or by calculations of the percentage of body fat or packets of energy called calories or kilojoules. We thus seek to act upon a materiality rendered governable through a grid of intelligibility and calculation, and various diets are adopted and become fashionable according to how they deploy and articulate such grids.

The second aspect of these practices of enfolding concerns what I shall call the work of government or the *governing work*. This refers to all the means, techniques, rationalities, forms of knowledge and expertise that are to be used to accomplish the enfolding of authority. It is a concern with how we govern, with the work we seek to perform on ourselves and others, or what Foucault called the self-forming activity or "forms of asceticism" (e.g. the employment of the various "techniques of the self" that comprise the Hellenistic and Christian cultures of the self such as dialogue, listening, meditation, prayer, training of memory, mortification rituals, diary-keeping, self-examination and, of course, confession). Similarly, the work of modern punishment, according to Foucault (1977: 23), comprises the totality of the means of supervision, management and normalization of the individual that together make up what he calls an entire "scientifico-legal complex".

Today, we are witness to a vast, newly articulated set of techniques and tactics that do this work of government and have implications for how we understand ourselves as governed or governors. Among them we find: new applications of contract between employee and employer in "enterprise agreements", between State agencies, community associations and professional bodies, and between bureaucrats and welfare recipients; techniques for the introduction of competition between public and private service providers in education, welfare and health, including privatization and contracting out; techniques for the minimization of risk and ensuring the safety and security of risky actions, places, individuals and populations; certain calculative technologies, such as the polymorphous employment of the audit, the devolved budget and cost accounting, to govern spaces and the individuals inhabiting and monitoring them; and all of those tactics that seek to effect the empowerment, consultation and participation of individuals and groups from the work of community development to the organization of quasi-autonomous non-government organizations or quangos (Castel 1991, Miller 1992, Rose 1993, Cruikshank 1994, Power 1994, O'Malley, this volume). Whether or not these sum into a distinctive set of programmes or formulae of government called neo-liberalism or advanced liberalism remains an open question, subject to the kind of empirical analysis dealt with in many of the chapters of this book. What is clear is that the arts of political invention remain extremely alive, and that government has come to increasingly depend on the deployment and assemblage of "relatively autonomized" powers, technologies, authorities, associations, institutions and persons. A history of the present, then, would be radically incomplete without an account of the way subjects are enjoined to exercise certain "practices of liberty" as a necessary component in practices of government (Foucault 1988a).

The third aspect of this analytic is that of the *governable subject*. This is concerned with what Deleuze calls (1988: 104) the "fold of the relation between forces according to a particular rule". This is, if one likes, the act of enfolding proper, where the rule acts as "snag" by which the "extended tissue is twisted, invaginated and doubled" (Deleuze 1988: 98). It concerns the "mode of subjectification" or "mode of obligation", with the position we take or are given in relation to rules and norms, with why we govern ourselves or others in a particular manner (e.g. to adjust the use of pleasures to our natural needs and status, to the right time and circumstances for the Greeks, to ward off sinfulness and submit to God's law in Christianity, to comply with an injunction to fulfil our potential in many contemporary liberation movements). Again, in the government of the criminal, the mode of obligation is determinable in so far as the criminal is judged by social workers, psychiatrists and other "extra-juridical" authorities to be delinquent, deviant or maladjusted, as one capable or incapable of normalization. What should be made clear is that there is no single mode of subjectification corresponding to an age, an epoch, an institution or even a single individual. We are obligated differentially according to different regimes of governmental and ethical practices. The same individual may find him- or herself obligated by various governmental–ethical regimes as citizen, mother, breadwinner, worker, entrepreneur, manager, health-conscious individual, consumer, taxpayer, juror, voter, patient, client, member of a neighbourhood or community, and so on.

A fourth set of questions concerns the *telos of government*, that is, the aim, end, goal or design, the plans into which they fit, the mode of being we hope to create, what we hope to produce in ourselves and others (e.g. to live a beautiful and noble life for the Greeks, to attain salvation through self-renunciation in Christianity, to emancipate and actualize the self for contemporary liberation movements and identity politics). The point can be made that, for Foucault, the *telos* of modern systems of punishment is not to be found in the history of criminal justice itself. Rather the *telos* refers to how the penalty is incorporated in a pattern of activities and knowledge leading to a specific matrix of ends, mode of being, or, as Max Weber (1970, 1985, Hennis 1983, Gordon 1987) would have put it in his sociology of religion, *Lebensführung or "conduct of life"*. The *telos* of punishment, then, is discipline itself, the new "political technology of the body" (Foucault 1977: 24) designed to operate on the body so that the subject will govern him- or herself as a docile and useful individual. It is the *telos* of punitive practices that authorizes the move beyond the history of punishment to that of discipline. Here, notions of a disciplinary society, far from being a totalizing description of a particular society, are simply the *telos* of such practices. One could say that we live in a world of multiple, interconnected and competing teleologies. If we suspend the attempt to provide a general characterization of society, culture and civilization, governed by a single principle, we can see how various programmes of conduct and regimes of practices have enfolded within them definite teleologies. Capitalist society, civil society, disciplinary society, the Welfare State, industrial or post-industrial society, risk society, modernity, postmodernity, the active society, the enterprise culture, the new contractualism, etc. may be viewed less as general characterizations of social and political relations and more as forms of codification of the diverse "effects in the real" of particular regimes of governmental and ethical practices and the prescriptions and programmes of conduct that invest and devolve from them. This is not to say that we cannot analyze the struggles, alliances and state of play in the competition between these multiple teleologies and the differential degrees of their realization and effectiveness. It is, however, to be forewarned about mistaking (explicit and tacit) *claims*, prescriptions and ethical ideals made on the basis of these regimes of practices for a kind of sociological realism.

We should note here that this schema reproduces the Aristotelian doctrine of the four Forms of Causality and suggests something of the later Heidegger. The reference to Heidegger reminds us of a particular feature of both governmental and ethical practices: their horizon is that of the "problematizations" of identity. Analysis begins with the questions raised by human beings about being. It seeks to define the conditions in which we are led to problematize what we are, what we can and should do, and the world in which we find ourselves. What is analyzed is not the empirically given behaviours or patterns of existing social relations but "the problematizations through which being offers itself to be, necessarily, thought – and the practices on the basis of which these problematizations are formed" (Foucault 1985: 11). What is at stake is not the social or psychological construct of the human subject, but the forms in which human being is problematized, interrogated and invested with meaning, within the frame of governmental and ethical practices. This captures Heidegger's formative insight that "the question of the meaning of Being must be *formulated*" (1978: 45), i.e. that the nature of being cannot be divorced from the questioning, interrogation or meaning of being. What we seek to examine, then, is not the way identities and selves are formed through a naturalistically conceived process of socialization, but the forms of interrogation, or questioning, of what we are and do within a horizon of historically specific and culturally given practices.

These practices of the enfolding of authority are also embedded within ways of revealing the totality of being. A full appreciation of the analytic of governmental and ethical practices inaugurated by Foucault prevents the empiricist reduction of the analysis of government to the instruments of rule, to questions of how authority is enfolded or implicated, to the *how* of government, as is sometimes said. The present analysis suggests at the least that *what* is governed, *who* is to be governed and *why*, are equally central questions. This is why we have emphasized questions not only of *ascetics* (the governing work), but also ones of *ontology* (the governed material), *deontology* (the governable subject) and *teleology* (the *telos* of government). Technologies of government, techniques of the self and of living, spiritual exercises, systems of manners and habits, should be analyzed not simply as instruments but as part of a frame (a *Ge-stell*, in Heidegger's sense) in which questions of who we are, of what our being is composed, of what we would like to become emerge, in which certain eventualities are to be avoided, and in which worlds to be sought, struggled and hoped for, and achieved appear. If I might put it this way: the study of the regimes of governmental and ethical practices and programmes of conduct is concerned to explicate or unfold that which has been implicated, complicated, replicated and duplicated in these regimes, i.e. the multiple, fragmentary and intertwined foldings that create spaces in which we live with our own doubles, and among doubles, and by which these doubles are folded together, under the authority of different forms of truth, to describe the lineaments of forms of life we are expected and expect to live.

References

Armstrong, T. J. (ed.) 1992. *Michel Foucault: philosopher*. Hemel Hempstead, England: Harvester Wheatsheaf.

Beck, U. 1989. On the way to the industrial risk society? Outline of an argument. *Thesis Eleven* **23**, 86–103.

Beck, U. 1992a. From industrial society to risk society. *Theory, Culture and Society* **9**, 97–123.

Beck, U. 1992b. *Risk society: towards a new modernity* (trans. M. Ritter). London: Sage.

Bogner, A. 1987. Elias and the Frankfurt school. *Theory, Culture and Society* **4**, 249–85.

Brown, P. 1987. Late antiquity. See Veyne (1987a), 235–311.

Brown, P. 1992. *Power and persuasion in late antiquity: towards a Christian Empire*. Madison: University of Wisconsin.

Burchell, G., C. Gordon, P. Miller (eds) 1991. *The Foucault effect: studies in governmentality*. Hemel Hempstead, England: Harvester Wheatsheaf.

Castel, R. 1991. From dangerousness to risk. See Burchell et al. (1991), 281–98.

Corrigan, P. & D. Sayer 1985. *The great arch: English state formation as cultural revolution*. Oxford: Basil Blackwell.

Cruikshank, B. 1994. The will to empower: technologies of citizenship and the war on poverty. *Socialist Review* **23**(4), 29–55.

Dean, M. 1994a. *Critical and effective histories: Foucault's methods and historical sociology*. London: Routledge.

Dean, M. 1994b. "A social structure of many souls": moral regulation, government and self-formation. *Canadian Journal of Sociology* **19**(2), 145–68.

Dean, M. 1995a. A genealogy of the gift in late antiquity. *Australian Journal of Anthropology* **5**(3), 320–29.

Dean, M. 1995b. Governing the unemployed self in an active society. *Economy and Society* **24**(4), 559–83.

Deleuze, G. 1988. *Foucault* (trans. S. Hand). Minneapolis: University of Minnesota Press.

Deleuze, G. 1992. What is a *dispositif?* See Armstrong (1992), 159–68.

Deleuze, G. 1993. *The fold: Leibniz and the Baroque* (trans. T. Conley). Minneapolis: University of Minnesota Press.

Donzelot, J. 1979. *The policing of families* (trans. R. Hurley). London: Hutchinson.

Duby, G 1987. Foreword. See Veyne (1987a), vii–ix.

Elias, N. 1978. *The civilizing process*, vol. I: *The history of manners* (trans. E. Jephcott). New York: Urizen.

Elias, N. 1982. *The civilizing process*, vol. II: *State formation and civilization* (trans. E. Jephcott). Oxford: Basil Blackwell.

Elias, N. 1983. *The court society*, (trans. E. Jephcott). Oxford: Basil Blackwell.

Ewald, F. 1994. Actualités de Michel Foucault. In *Foucault: the legacy*. Queensland University of Technology, conference abstracts.

Foucault, M. 1970. *The order of things: an archaeology of the human sciences* (trans. A. Sheridan). London: Tavistock.

Foucault, M. 1972. *The archaeology of knowledge*, (trans. A. M. Sheridan Smith). London: Tavistock.

Foucault, M. 1977. *Discipline and punish: the birth of the prison* (trans. A. Sheridan). London: Penguin.

Foucault, M. 1981. Questions of method. *Ideology and Consciousness* **8**, 3–14. Republished in Burchell et al. (1991), 73–86.

Foucault, M. 1984. On the genealogy of ethics: an overview of the work in progress. In *The Foucault reader*, P. Rabinow (ed.), 340–72. New York: Pantheon.

Foucault, M. 1985. *The use of pleasure* (trans. R. Hurley). New York: Pantheon.

Foucault, M. 1986a. *The care of the self* (trans. R. Hurley). New York: Pantheon.

Foucault, M. 1986b. Kant on revolution and Enlightenment. *Economy and Society* **15** (1), 88–96.

Foucault, M. 1986c. Nietzsche, genealogy, history. In *The Foucault reader*, P. Rabinow (ed.), 76–100. London: Penguin.

Foucault, M. 1988a. The care of the self as a practice of freedom. In *The final Foucault*, J. Bernauer & D. Rasmussen (eds), 1–20. Cambridge, Mass.: MIT Press.

Foucault, M. 1988b. Technologies of the self. In *Technologies of the self: a seminar with Michel Foucault*, L. H. Martin, H. Gutman, P. H. Hutton (eds), 16–49. London: Tavistock.

Foucault, M. 1991. *Remarks on Marx: conversations with Duccio Tombadori* (trans. R. J. Goldstein & J. Cascaito). New York: Semiotext(e).

Foucault, M. & G. Deleuze 1977. Intellectuals and Power. See Foucault (1977b).

Gass, J. 1988. Towards the "active society". *OECD Observer* **152**, 4–8.

Giddens, A. 1991. *Modernity and self-identity*. Cambridge: Polity.

Gordon, C. 1987. The soul of the citizen: Max Weber and Michel Foucault on rationality and government. In *Max Weber, rationality and modernity*, S. Whimster & S. Lash (eds), 293–316. London: Allen & Unwin.

Hall, S. 1992. The question of cultural identity. In *Modernity and its futures*, S. Hall, D. Held, T. McGrew (eds), 274–316. Cambridge: Polity.

Heidegger, M. 1978. *Basic writings*, D. F. Krell (ed.). London: Routledge & Kegan Paul.

Hennis, W. 1983. Max Weber's "central question". *Economy and Society* **12**(3), 135–80.

Hirst, P. Q. 1981. The genesis of the social. *Politics and Power* **3**, 67–82.

Hodges, J. & A. Hussain 1979. Review article: La police des familles. *Ideology and Consciousness* **5**, 87–123.

Horkheimer, M. 1974. *Eclipse of reason*. New York: Continuum.

Horkheimer, M. & T. Adorno 1972. *Dialectic of enlightenment* (trans. J. Cumming). New York: Continuum.

Keating, P. 1994. Working nation: policies and programs. Canberra: Australian Government Publishing Service.

Marshall, T. H. 1963. Citizenship and social class. In *Sociology at the crossroads and other essays*, 67–127. London: Heinemann.

Miller, P. 1992. Accounting and objectivity: the invention of calculating selves and calculable spaces. *Annals of Scholarship* **9**(1/2), 61–86.

Minson, J. 1985. *Genealogies of morals: Nietzsche, Foucault and Donzelot and the eccentricity of ethics*. London: Macmillan.

Minson, J. 1993. *Questions of conduct: sexual harassment, citizenship and government*. London: Macmillan.

OECD 1988. *The future of social protection*. OECD Social Policy Studies No. 6. Paris.

Osborne, T. 1994. Sociology, liberalism and the historicity of conduct. *Economy and Society* **23**(4), 484–501.

Power, M. 1994. *The audit society*. London: Demos

Rose, N. 1993. Government, authority and expertise in advanced liberalism. *Economy and Society* **22**(3), 283–99.

Rose, N. 1995. Authority and the genealogy of subjectivity. In *De-traditionalization:*

authority and self in an age of cultural uncertainty, P. Heelas, P. Morris, S. Lash (eds). Oxford: Basil Blackwell.

Veyne, P. (ed.) 1987a. *A history of private life*, vol. I: *From pagan Rome to Byzantium*, (trans. A. Goldhammer). Cambridge, Mass.: Belknap Press.

Veyne, P. 1987b. The Roman Empire. See Veyne (1987a), 5–234.

Veyne, P. 1990. *Bread and circuses: political pluralism and historical sociology*, (trans. B. Pearce). London: Allen Lane.

Weber, M. 1970. Religious rejections of the world and their directions. In *From Max Weber: essays in sociology*, H. H. Gerth & C. W. Mills (eds), 323–59. London: Routledge & Kegan Paul.

Weber, M. 1985. *The Protestant ethic and spirit of capitalism* (trans. T. Parsons). London: Unwin.

Chapter 11

Revolutions within: self-government and self-esteem

Barbara Cruikshank

What breach of order is it possible to commit in solitude? (Gustave de Beaumont & Alexis de Tocqueville 1964: 72)

Some feminists have criticized Gloria Steinem's best seller, *Revolution from within: a book of self-esteem* (1992), for calling a feminist retreat to personal life from the collective political front. Deidre English's (1992: 13) reservations about Steinem's book are typical: "What is disturbing is to see the empowering therapy supplant the cause. The strategic vision of social revolution here has all but been replaced with a model of personal recovery." Echoing Tocqueville, critics ask how it is possible to challenge the existing order from a solitary position. Is it possible to wage a real "revolution from within"? Critics are afraid that feminism is going the way of Steinem's self-esteem movement and trading in collective action and confrontation for the solitude of self-reflection, the political for the personal.

I argue here that there is nothing personal about self-esteem.[1] In fact, what is remarkable and of political importance about Steinem's book is not where she directs her revolutionary subjectivity – to the personal or political fronts – but that she turns self-esteem into a social relationship and a political obligation. Self-esteem is not merely a misbegotten strategy for women's liberation as Steinem's critics charge. The self-esteem movement is more than that; it is a movement that does not leave politics and power as they were, but seeks to constitute a "state of esteem", a new politics and a new set of social relations. The self-esteem movement, spearheaded by the California Task Force to Promote Self-Esteem and Personal and Social Responsibility in 1983, promises to deliver a technology of subjectivity that will solve social problems from crime and poverty to gender inequality by waging a social revolution, not against capitalism, racism and inequality, but against the order of the self and the way we govern our selves.

Steinem's book is only a small part of the self-esteem movement made up of a whole range of experts, policy and social service professionals, and grass-roots activists. California Assembly Bill 3659, which established the Task Force to Promote Self-Esteem and Social and Personal Responsibility, states that the social problems we face today have become ungovernable and seriously threaten democratic stability (California Task Force 1990b: 102). "Government and experts cannot fix these problems for us. It is only when each of us recognizes our individual personal and social responsibility to be part of the solution that we also realize higher 'self-esteem'"(California Task Force 1990a: vii–viii). This is a social movement premised upon the limits of politics and the Welfare State, the failures of American democracy and upon the inability of government to control conflict; it is a "revolutionary" movement seeking to forge a new terrain of politics and a new mode of governing the self, not a new government. In short, the question of governance becomes a question of self-governance in the discourse of self-esteem.

Liberation therapy

Personal fulfilment becomes a social obligation in the discourse of self-esteem according to an innovation that transforms the relationship of self-to-self into a relationship that is governable (California Task Force 1990a: 22). Self-fulfilment is no longer a personal or private goal. According to advocates, taking up the goal of self-esteem is something we owe to society, something that will defray the costs of social problems, something that will create a "true" democracy. Hence, the solution to the current "crisis of governability" is discovered in the capacity of citizens to act upon themselves guided by the expertise of the social sciences and social service professionals.

A key finding reported by the California Task Force (1990a: 4) is as follows:

> Self-esteem is the likeliest candidate for a *social vaccine*, something that empowers us to live responsibly and that inoculates us against the lures of crime, violence, substance abuse, teen pregnancy, child abuse, chronic welfare dependency, and educational failure. The lack of self-esteem is central to most personal and social ills plaguing our state and nation as we approach the end of the twentieth century.

Hardly a simple shot in the arm, self-esteem is a kind of "liberation therapy" that requires a complete re-orientation to social problem-solving, as well as the mobilization of an effort compared by advocates to landing on the moon, the discovery of the atom, and it calls for the mobilization of "every Californian" (California Task Force 1990a: vii). These scientific innovations carried the burden of social stability, but the new science of the self places the hope of liberation in the psychological state of the people, especially poor urban people of colour to whom most of the "social problems" listed above are attributed.

Self-esteem is a practical and productive technology available for the production of certain kinds of selves, for "making up people", as Ian Hacking (1986a) might put it.[2] Self-esteem is a technology in the sense that it is a specialized knowledge of how to esteem our selves, to estimate, calculate, measure, evaluate, discipline, and to judge our selves. It is especially, though not exclusively, a literary technology.[3] A "self" emerges out of confrontation with texts, primarily, or with the telling and writing of personal narratives, a practice Steinem refers to as "bibliotherapy". We can learn and perform "bibliotherapy" upon ourselves or join any of the numerous agencies, associations and programmes set up to "enhance" self-esteem that are catalogued along with books and scholarly articles included in the bibliographic materials compiled by the California Task Force and in Steinem's book; compiling research is tantamount to delivering therapy.

One of the goals of the self-esteem movement is to elicit the participation of as many people as possible and that means hearing their personal stories and struggles with their lack of self-esteem. California legislator John Vasconcellos claims that his efforts to establish the California Task Force to Promote Self-Esteem and Personal and Social Responsibility grew first out of his own "personal struggle despite repeated successes and achievements in my life – to develop my own self-esteem". Secondly, his commitment to building self-esteem came from his experience with the State's budget that spent "too little, too late [on] efforts to confine and/or repair our fellow Californians, whose lives are in distress and disrepair" (California Task Force 1990a: ix). Similarly, Steinem links her personal lack of self-esteem to her role in the feminist movement and links her commitment to self-esteem to the limits of politics.

Self-esteem programme goals include getting clients to write and tell their personal narratives with an eye to the social good. Narratives bring people to see that the details of their personal lives and their chances for improving their lives are inextricably linked to what is good for all of society. Steinem (1992: 29) insists that requiring teenage girls, for example, to write down their personal narratives, their feelings about teenage pregnancy and so on, can result in the prevention of teenage pregnancy. The girls construct a self to act upon and to govern in the process of writing.

Self-esteem is a way to subject citizens in the sense of making them "prone to" or "subject to" take up the goals of self-esteem for themselves and their vision of the good society. Thus we make our selves governable by taking up the social goal of self-esteem. As Foucault (1988: 146) explained, "through some political technology of individuals, we have been led to recognize ourselves as a society, as a part of a social entity, as part of a nation or of a state". A link is established between the individual's goal of achieving self-esteem and the social goal of eliminating child abuse, crime and welfare dependence. Those who undergo "revolution from within" are citizens doing the right thing; they join programmes, volunteer, but most importantly, work on and improve their self-image. At all times, self-esteem calls upon individuals to act, to participate. "The continuation and future success of our democratic system of government and society are dependent upon the exercise of responsible citizenship by each and every Californian" (California Task Force 1990b: 102).

Self-esteem is a technology of citizenship and self-government for evaluating and acting upon our selves so that the police, the guards and the doctors do not have to. This relationship to our selves is directly related to citizenship because, by definition, "Being a responsible citizen depends on developing personal and social responsibility" (California Task Force 1990a: 22). Individuals must accept the responsibility to subject their selves, to voluntarily consent to establishing a relationship between one's self and a tutelary power such as a therapist, a social worker, a social programme, a parenting class or what have you. Consent in this case does not mean that there is no exercise of power; by isolating a self to act upon, to appreciate and to esteem, we avail ourselves of a terrain of action, we exercise power upon ourselves.

Those who have failed to link their personal fulfilment to social reform are lumped together as "social problems", are diagnosed as "lacking self-esteem" and are charged with "antisocial behaviour". Society needs protection from those who lack self-esteem, according to advocates. Obviously social science is the foremost expert on the needs of society, along with social workers and other professionals: philanthropists, policy experts, public health professionals and politicians, to name a few. Tutelary power is placed in the hands of all those who speak for the interests and concerns of society at large, for example, in *The social importance of self-esteem* (Mecca et al. 1989), a volume dedicated to promoting the wellbeing of society.

I do not mean to underestimate the blatantly coercive and punitive measures taken by legislators, social workers and other professionals under the guise of liberation therapy. Very often, for example, women, say battered women, are coerced by the courts into participating in therapeutic programmes that aim at "empowerment". Mothers caught up in the juvenile court system are often forced to "graduate" from parenting courses, group therapies and the like before the custody of their children is secure. Foster care is an institution that is easily made into a coercive apparatus for preparing mothers to become the kind of mothers deemed appropriate by society, by legislation, by philanthropists. The threat of taking children away is a primary tool of coercion.

But just as often, women are convinced to participate in their own "empowerment" without threats. Governance in this case is something we do to our selves, not something done to us by those in power. Nikolas Rose shows us that governing subjectivity is not consistent with centralized power:

> Rather, government of subjectivity has taken shape through the proliferation of a complex and heterogeneous assemblage of technologies. These have acted as relays, bringing the varied ambitions of political, scientific, philanthropic, and professional authorities into alignment with the ideals and aspirations of individuals, with the selves each of us want to be. (Rose 1990: 213)

I am suggesting here that we have wildly underestimated the extent to which we are already self-governing. Democratic government, even self-government, depends upon the ability of citizens to recognize, isolate and act upon their own subjectivity, to be governors of their selves. The ability of citizens to generate politically able selves depends upon technologies of subjectivity and citizenship that link personal goals and desires to social order and stability, which link power to subjectivity (see Foucault 1983).

The line between subjectivity and subjection is crossed when I subject my self, when I align my personal goals with those set out by reformers – both expert and activist – according to some notion of the social good. The norm of self-esteem links subjectivity to power; it "binds subjects to a subjection that is the more profound because it appears to emanate from our autonomous quest for ourselves, it appears as a matter of our freedom" (Rose 1990: 256).

The call for self-government and democracy is extended away from political institutions and economic relations by the self-esteem movement; the political goals of participation, empowerment and collective action are extended to the terrain of the self. Steinem turns around the feminist slogan, "the personal is political", claiming that "the political is personal". Nikolas Rose has shown how contemporary technologies of subjectivity (like self-esteem) promise a certain kind of freedom:

> . . . not liberation from social constraints but rendering psychological constraints on autonomy conscious, and hence amenable to rational transformation. Achieving freedom becomes a matter not of slogans nor of political revolution, but of slow, painstaking, and detailed work on our own subjective and personal realities, guided by an expert knowledge of the psyche. (Rose 1990: 213)

The liberation promised by self-esteem originates within the relation of self-to-self but is not limited to the self. Indeed, self-esteem is advocated as a strategy for the democratic development of the individual and society; it outlines a whole new set of social relationships and strategies for their development under the expert tutelage of "liberation therapists".

Constituting a state of esteem

The California Task Force to Promote Self-Esteem and Personal and Social Responsibility was charged by the State legislature with compiling existing research on the relationship between "self-esteem" and six social problems: "chronic welfare dependence", alcoholism and drug abuse, crime and violence, academic failure, teenage pregnancy and child abuse. Neil Smelser, a sociologist and member of the task force, admits the failure of social scientists to identify the lack of self-esteem as the cause of social problems. "The news most consistently reported, however, is that the associations between self-esteem and its expected consequences are mixed, insignificant, or absent" (Mecca et al. 1989: 15).

Despite the fact that a "disappointing" correlation was found between the lack of self-esteem and the social problems listed, the task force forged ahead, calling for increased funding for further research.[4] Task force members and the social scientists involved did not diagnose, empirically discover or even describe an already existing malaise and its cure. Instead, the social scientists devised methods to measure what was not there: the focus of research was on the *lack* of self-esteem and its (non-)relation to social problems.

The task force included in its final report the following quotation from Professor Covington who claims that self-esteem

> . . . challenges us to be more fully human. In addition to being an object of scientific investigation and also an explanation for behavior, self-esteem is above all a metaphor, a symbol filled with excess meaning that can ignite visions of what we as a people might become. (California Task Force 1990a: 44)

From the "discovery" of an absence of the thing, social scientists have created a tangible vision of a "state of esteem". Here the social sciences can be seen as productive sciences; the knowledges, measurements and data they produce are constitutive of relations of governance as well as of the subjectivity of citizens. In devising the methods for measuring, evaluating and esteeming the self, social science actually devises the self and links it up to a vision of the social good and a programme of reform. In short, social scientists have helped to produce a set of social relationships and causal relations where there were none before.

Social science has been instrumental in generating a self capable of self-governance, but it is a decidedly unscientific enterprise. In the end, social scientists themselves eschew the importance of evidence:

> Our purpose is to build a *prima facie* case for the importance of self-esteem in the causation of violent crimes. Public policy does not wait for final proof in other realms . . . We see no need to be defensive about advocating the importance of self-esteem. (Scheff 1990: 179)

The obvious question is why social science is a necessary member of a coalition for building a *prima facie* case for self-esteem. If the case is to be built *prima facie*, why call for more funding to gather evidence in the form of social science research? The answer lies, I think, in the productive capacities of social scientific research. It is this that produces the subject, as one who lacks self-esteem, and it is social science research that sets the terms for telling the truth of that subject. Finally, it falls to social science research to establish policy measures to regulate the subject according to that truth. In a turn of phrase taken from Pierre Bourdieu, from professing a faith in self-esteem for its liberatory properties, experts have turned self-esteem into a profession (cited in Rose 1990: 256).

Social service providers and researchers will earn high salaries from the self-esteem movement and new programmes are proliferating. "Empowerment" and "self-esteem" are almost mandatory in mission statements and grant applications for non-profit agencies. But self-esteem advocates are not merely the poverty pimps of the 1990s (although there is certainly plenty of evidence for that characterization).[5] It is a mistake to focus solely on the immediate economic and professional interests of service providers. Programme directors and researchers may profit from the advances of the self-esteem movement, but that does not fully explain why or how people come to understand themselves as lacking self-esteem. It is equally partial to characterize self-esteem programmes as obscuring or neglecting the "real" underlying causes (e.g. poverty, sexism, racism) of the lack of self-esteem. Self-esteem is not conceived on the level of ideology; it is not a ruse, a panacea, a cynical plot; it is a form of governance.

Again, despite the failures of social scientists to discern any scientific relationship between violence and self-esteem, a correlative (if not causal) relationship worked its way into law. I quote here from Assembly Bill No. 3659 which established the California Task Force (1990b: 104):

The findings of the Commission on Crime Control and Violence Prevention included scientific evidence of the correlation between violent antisocial behavior and a lack of self-esteem, to wit: "A lack of self-esteem, negative or criminal self-image and feelings of distrust and personal powerlessness are prevalent among violent offenders and highly recidivistic criminals."

The task force adapted the model of the Commission on Crime Control for their own "citizens' effort" to secure funding for further research and took from the field of criminology its methods of applying and organizing knowledge.

It is significant, of course, that the new technology of self-esteem is produced in part out of methods devised for the prevention of crime and the punishment and supervision of criminals. It is also important to remember that the language of empowerment and self-esteem emerged out of social movements. Liberation is clearly tied to discipline in the discourses of self-esteem in more ways than I can chronicle here where I mention just two.

First, so-called "welfare dependency", alcoholism and teenage pregnancy are pathologized and criminalized alongside violence, child abuse and illegal drug use. This move is accomplished by relating the "low self-esteem" of the welfare recipient, for example, to the failure of welfare recipients to act politically, to participate in their own empowerment, to engage their self in fulfilling the social obligation of "responsible citizenship". According to the report, welfare recipients are not fulfilling their responsibilities to society because of their lack of self-esteem, a deficiency demonstrated by their being on welfare in the first place.

Secondly, the knowledge originally applied to the government, control and reform of criminals and "antisocial behaviour", is now applied throughout the social body: the overt use of technologies of surveillance and control in the field of criminality are displaced by the technology of self-government applied to welfare recipients and alcoholics. From analyzing the causes of the bloody Attica Prison riot (a decline in the self-esteem of guards who were not consulted before their powers were reduced), reviewers leap immediately to the policy implications of that analysis for relationships between clients and staff, doctors and patients, teachers and students, parents and children (Scheff 1990: 192–3). The whole of society and all its designated "social problems" become the location for the deployment of this new technology of subjectivity. A whole society of esteemed, estimated, quantified and measured individuals can replace a citizenry defined by their lack of self-esteem.

According to the California Task Force, the "social vaccine" must be applied at all levels of society: family, work, government; all areas of society must be integrated by the principles of self-esteem, personal and social responsibility:

> In the twenty-first century every government level in the state and each of its programs are designed to empower people to become self-realizing and self-reliant . . . Every citizen (and noncitizen as well) recognizes his or her personal responsibility for fully engaging in the political process, and he or she recognizes the possibility for positively affecting every other person in every situation and relationship. (California Task Force 1990a: 12)

The mixture of future and present tense notwithstanding, the discourse of self-esteem is aimed at constituting a just and democratic society. To get there, rather than revealing our opinions and persuading others to act with us in concert, "self-esteem has to do with our reputation with our 'selves'". Constituting a state of esteem has nothing to do with traditionally conceived public life and speech. Today, a state of esteem can be founded upon the inner dialogue between self and self.

From the prison cell to the whole of society, individuals in isolation can act to bring about a social and democratic revolution. As Steinem puts it:

> self-esteem plays as much a part in the destiny of nations as it does in the lives of individuals; that self-hatred leads to the need either to dominate or to be dominated; that citizens who refuse to obey anything but their own conscience can transform their countries; in short, that self-esteem is the basis of any real democracy. (Steinem 1992: 9–10)

Given the possibility of thus aligning political power and personal empowerment in the self, we can return to Tocqueville's question about the possibility for resistance to the established order in isolation.

A new science of politics

From Foucault and from feminism we have learned how individuals come to understand themselves as the subjects of sexuality and gender, respectively. Similarly, I am arguing that individuals learn to recognize themselves as subjects of democratic citizenship and so become self-governing. As with technologies and discourses of sexuality and gender, it is possible to give a history of the fabrication of citizen-subjects and of their relation to the social order. But what Foucault and feminism have not elaborated, Alexis de Tocqueville took as a guiding question, namely: Why do these forms of power, citizenship and subjectivity emerge only with democracy? How does governance become a question of self-governance in a democracy?

The capacities of citizens to govern their selves as well as the conditions of self-government underwent dramatic changes in the transition from Republican to Democratic government in the Jacksonian America that Tocqueville visited. The 1830s marked the birth of mass democracy, the social as a sphere of government and the development of social science, and the demise of the republican public sphere.[6] Moreover, the difficulties that Tocqueville encountered in distinguishing despotism and democracy reveal that self-government not only entails the exercise of subjectivity, but also the subjection of the self.

Ostensibly, democracy liberated political subjects, transforming them overnight into political citizens. A society in which a citizen is subject to the rule of another is, *ipso facto*, not a democracy. Tocqueville (1961a: 62) permanently enlivened the argument for local and decentralized government when he distinguished citizens from subjects: "Yet, without power and independence, a town may contain good subjects, but it can have no active citizens." The democratic citizen who participates directly in government, in self-rule, thereby avoids subjection. However, the line between the subjectivity of the citizen and their subjection was not so clear Tocqueville discovered; by the time he finished the second volume of *Democracy in America*, he seemed unable to distinguish either democracy from its tendencies towards despotism, or the subjectivity of the masses from their subjection.

Both despotism and democracy relied upon isolated and powerless citizens, according to Tocqueville. Under *despotism*, subjects were simply unfree and isolated. In a *democracy* under conditions of equality, citizens are isolated and made powerless by the freedom granted to each singly; while they are free, they are relatively powerless as isolated individuals. Hence, the power of numbers became the *sin qua non* of democratic power and stability. In order to exercise self-government, citizens must act in concert and combine forces to wield any power and guard against the tendency of democracies towards despotism.

However, the same democratic conditions – individual equality and individual freedom – made combining numbers very difficult.

As in ages of equality no man is compelled to lend his assistance to his fellow-men . . . every one is at once independent and powerless. These two conditions, which must never be either separately considered or confounded together, inspire the citizen of a democratic country with very contrary propensities. (Tocqueville 1961b: 352)

Getting independent citizens to participate and take an interest in the life and wellbeing of society was no small task. In a chapter titled "That the Americans combat the effects of individualism by free institutions", Tocqueville insists that local and associational freedoms – political freedoms – are the only guards against despotism because they ensure the capacity of citizens to actively govern themselves by providing the training and the taste for freedom.

Yet the features of despotism and democracy led citizens to neglect their political freedoms that, from disuse, were rendered powerless against despotism.

> Equality places men side by side, unconnected by any common tie; despotism raises barriers to keep them asunder: the former predisposes them not to consider their fellow-creatures, the latter makes general indifference a sort of public virtue. (Tocqueville 1961b: 123)

Tocqueville recognized that while the police and the State can prevent action with outright domination and force, they cannot produce the active co-operation and participation of citizens. Democratic governance relied upon a productive rather than a repressive form of governance (see 1961b: 91). To govern a democracy, Tocqueville called for a "new science of politics" (1961a: lxxiii). Democratic participation was not clear-cut or naturally occurring, it was something that had to be solicited, encouraged, guided and directed. Hence, the new science of politics must develop technologies of citizenship and participation.

Isolated in their freedom from one another, individuals required an artificially created solidarity, namely, a science of association. "In democratic countries the science of association is the mother of science; the progress of all the rest depends upon the progress it has made" (Tocqueville 1961b: 133). Even the legal recognition of associations, previously considered a dangerous source of disorder, was not enough to ensure democratic order if citizens could not be led to exercise their political freedoms; the capacity of citizens to exercise self-government itself had to become a matter of government.

In short, the threat of despotism and disorder did not come from the unruly, but from the indifferent citizens, the apathetic (ibid.: 124). "Citizens who are individually powerless, do not very clearly anticipate the strength which they may acquire by uniting together; it must be shown to them in order to be understood" (Tocqueville 1961a: 140). Citizens had to be made to act; they must first know how to get together, to amass themselves to act in concert, and second, they must desire to do so. The former could be accomplished through the science of association; the latter was a matter of what Tocqueville called "enlightened self-interest", or "interest rightly understood":

> When men are no longer united among themselves by firm and lasting ties, it is impossible to obtain the co-operation of any great number of them unless you can persuade every man that his private interest obliges him voluntarily to unite his exertions and the exertions of all the others. (Tocqueville 1961b: 162)

Persuading citizens to tie their self-interest and their fate to society voluntarily was the key to stability without the use of force.

The republican preoccupation with civic virtue – overcoming one's
self-interest to take up the common interest – was replaced, according to
Tocqueville, by the discipline that led to actions incited by "enlightened
self-interest". Democratic political action is further distinguished by a
"general rule" that links citizens to society:

> The principle of interest rightly understood produces no great acts
> of self-sacrifice, but it suggests daily small acts of self-denial. By itself
> it cannot suffice to make a man virtuous, but it disciplines a number
> of citizens in habits of regularity, temperance, moderation, fore-
> sight, self-command; and, if it does not lead men straight to virtue
> by the will, it gradually draws them in that direction by their habits.
> (Tocqueville 1961b: 147)

Tocqueville learned about discipline and enlightened self-interest from
his study of prisons. As others have pointed out, Tocqueville learned that
prison discipline could "make up" good citizens even if it could not produce virtuous men.[7] However, we must not make too much of the prison
as a model for democratic government.[8] The prison may serve as a perfect model for despotism, but not for democracy. The task Tocqueville set
himself was to discover those aspects of democracy that could be mobilized against despotism, despite the similarities between the two forms of
governance.

Both democracy and despotism were completely new forms of governance in that neither were distinguished by any particular set of institutions. Tocqueville claimed that neither despotism nor democracy was a
form of government so much as a kind of society. The condition of democratic equality and individual isolation led to contradictory propensity of
democratic citizens, on the one hand, to become ungovernable in their
independence, and on the other hand, to wholly submit in powerlessness
to any authority powerful enough to command them.

> I am persuaded, however, that anarchy is not the principal evil
> which democratic ages have to fear, but the least. For the principle
> of equality begets two tendencies: the one leads men straight to
> independence, and may suddenly drive them into anarchy; the
> other conducts them by a longer, more secret, and more certain
> road, to servitude. (Tocqueville 1961b: 345)

Tocqueville's new science of politics, then, is not concerned with political institutions, but with preserving democratic freedom and the power of citizens within the realm of the social.

The ties that citizens must cultivate are not political, but social (associational); their fabrication marks the dislocation of the political, the State, and the emergence of "the social" in the nineteenth century alongside the birth of the social sciences. Associations – organized to build bridges, develop the arts and sciences, to do business – were useful for cementing the individual citizens' desires and goals to a vision of what is good for society. With no apparent coercion or centralized State action, voluntary associations ensured a united citizenry and a stable society.

Democracy entailed the transformation of politics from an activity dependent upon a conception of public (as opposed to private) life, to a matter of social life and the life of society. For democracy to meet the requirement of getting individuals to act together in concert as citizens, Tocqueville initially sounded a common republican theme:

> As soon as a man begins to treat of public affairs in public, he begins to perceive that he is not so independent of his fellow-men as he had at first imagined, and, that, in order to obtain their support, he must often lend them his co-operation. (Tocqueville 1961b: 124)

However, in a mass democracy, as opposed to a republic, a single public sphere could not extend far enough to impress upon all the citizens their need of each other to maintain stability. Republican self-government was understood to be a part-time activity taking place within the restricted public sphere and over matters of public (shared) importance; freedom and politics were located in the restricted public sphere. In a democracy, on the other hand, democratic freedom and hence the activities of self-government underwent a despacialization and were then located in associations and in the capacities and actions of individuals. The capacity of citizens to be self-governing in a republic depended upon institutions that disappeared under the conditions of democracy. Tocqueville claimed that the legislators of American democracy knew that a single public sphere could not extend the awareness of mutual dependence upon an isolated citizenry. Hence, the whole of society had to be governmentalized and venues constructed for citizens to take care of organizing and governing themselves.

The legislators of America . . . thought that it would be well to infuse political life into each portion of the territory, in order to multiply to an infinite extent opportunities of acting in concert, for all the members of the community, and to make them constantly feel their mutual dependence on each other. (Tocqueville 1961b: 125)

Multiple public spheres for the exercise of citizenship were developed beyond the States, counties, cities and other geographically based spheres. These new spheres were civil, racial, professional, economic and social. By politicizing or governmentalizing as many areas of social life as possible, by multiplying as far as possible the number of public spheres, citizens were held responsible for the promotion of social stability.

Still, what was it that distinguished democracy from despotism? The answer does not lie in politics or institutions, but in the relationship of the individual to society. Again, Tocqueville (1961a: 66) was struck by the absence of visible official governmental powers and actions in America. Moreover, he was dumbstruck and terrified by the invisible governance to which citizens were subject:

the species of oppression by which democratic nations are menaced is unlike anything which ever before existed in the world . . . I seek in vain for an expression which will accurately convey the whole idea I have formed of it. (Tocqueville1961b: 380)

What Tocqueville called "despotism", for lack of a better expression, he describes as a condition of holding society – its interests, privileges, wisdom and power – above the individual.

The idea of intermediary powers is weakened and obliterated; the idea of rights inherent in certain individuals is rapidly disappearing from the minds of men; the idea of the omnipotence and the sole authority of society at large rises to fill its place. (ibid.: 349)

Powers of government then, are transferred from the government and from the individual onto society at large; society is granted "the duty, as well as the right . . . to guide as well as to govern each private citizen" (ibid.: 348).

We have traditionally understood Tocqueville to be holding out the threat of the tyranny of the majority or society writ large as a threat to the subjectivity, actions and independence of individuals. However, for Tocqueville, democratic government is not a question of pitting the individual citizen *against* collective society. Society has no agency or power of its own to wield. The dangerous tendency in a democracy is not towards tyranny, visible forms of domination or forced conformity, but towards an invisible and gentle subjection. The tutelary power of associations, which could lead citizens to exercise their subjectivity and to act upon their enlightened self-interest, could also lead citizens into complete subjection. "Every man allows himself to be put in leading-strings, because he sees that it is not a person or a class of persons, but the people at large that holds the end of his chain" (Tocqueville 1961b: 383). Citizens obey the call of society at large and are self-guided, without chains, without force, they quietly place themselves in the hands of society and mobilize themselves in society's interest.

Tutelary power is easily combined with outward forms of political freedom because it is society at large, not a class or a tyrant placing citizens in chains. That which stands above is society. The individual citizen was not pitted against the majority but was artificially linked to the majority by discipline and association. The distinction between despotism and democracy rests on the degree to which tutelary powers act for individuals rather than guiding them to act for themselves. "The proper object therefore of our most strenuous resistance, is far less either anarchy or despotism, than apathy which may almost indifferently beget either the one or the other" (Tocqueville 1961b: 432). It is upon the small and daily routines of social life that self-government depends.

> Subjection in minor affairs breaks out every day, and is felt by the whole community indiscriminately. It does not drive men to resistance, but it crosses them at every turn, till they are led to surrender the exercise of their will. (Tocqueville 1961b: 383)

Conclusion

Tocqueville overestimated the tendency of democracies towards despotism because he underestimated the successes of the social sciences, social reformers and their development of the social.

Beaumont and Tocqueville (1964: 80) found prison reformers in the United States a bit overzealous: "Philanthropy has become for them a kind of profession, and they have caught the *monomanie* of the penitentiary system, which to them seems the remedy for all the evils of society." Today, self-esteem is our reformers' *monomanie*. It is an innovation in the means of governing a democratic society.

Self-esteem is but one in a long line of technologies of citizenship. Democracy is entirely dependent upon technologies of citizenship that are developed, to list only a few examples, in social movements, in public policy research, sciences of human development, and as is well documented, discourses of "republican motherhood".[9] The constitution of the citizen-subject requires technologies of subjectivity, technologies aimed at producing happy, active and participatory democratic citizens. These technologies rarely emerge from the Congress; more often, they emerge from the social sciences, pressure groups, social work discourses, therapeutic social service programmes and so on. Their common goal, nevertheless, is to get citizens to act as their own masters.

They begin with the acknowledgement that democratic government is limited in its capacity to govern. Democratic government is one that relies upon citizens to voluntarily subject themselves to power. Here is the State of California saying go ahead and democratize the family, the workplace, the schools:

> Sometimes we feel that if we create democracy in the home, work place or school, we will undercut someone's authority and encourage irresponsibility. In fact, democracy works well only when we all exercise self-discipline and personal and social responsibility. (California Task Force 1990a: 37)

The goal is to deepen the reach of tutelary powers intended to enhance the subjectivity of citizens.

Of course, not everyone can be vaccinated and those who lack self-esteem will abuse, haunt, rob, reproduce and otherwise bring ill-health back upon the social body. Self-esteem means about as much as "positive thinking" meant in the 1970s and "empowerment" meant in the 1980s, and "enterprise" will mean in the 1990s. We are not entering the age of an all-powerful therapeutic state, or a state of complete subjection for we are still citizens. Yet thousands of people now define their lack of power and control in the world as attributable to their lack of self-esteem. Needless to say, Gloria Steinem is spokeswoman for one of the largest feminist associations, NOW, and today she attributes the failures of her political career and the feminist movement to her lack of self-esteem.

More importantly, a State government document like the one I have considered here does not create citizen-subjects by itself. Discourse is not literally constitutive. Nor do the therapists, mothers and politicians who vaccinate citizens with self-esteem bear the responsibility for creating citizen-subjects. Self-esteem is but one in a long line of technologies that avail citizens of themselves. Self-rule remains essential to democratic stability, I argue here, and so the relationship of self to self is a political relationship, although one that is more dependent upon voluntarily applied technologies of selfhood than upon coercion, force or social control engineered from above.

Self-esteem advocates, including Steinem, do not recognize the extent to which personal life is the product of power relations. Steinem fails to realize the extent to which personal life is governed and is itself a terrain of government. The "inner voice" that she teaches us to listen to is the voice of pure and unmediated self-knowledge. She assumes that women have a natural subjectivity that is hindered or repressed by power, rather than shaped and constituted by power. Steinem fails to grasp the difficulty of distinguishing subjectivity from subjection.

Self-esteem is a social movement that links subjectivity and power in a way that confounds any neat separation of the "empowered" from the powerful. Most importantly, the self-esteem movement advocates a new form of governance that cannot be critically assessed by mobilizing the separation of public from private, political from personal. Too much is left out by critics of the self-esteem movement who continue to think of power and resistance in paired opposition: individual and collective, public and private, political and personal. What these criticisms omit, I contend, is the extent to which the self is (like inequality, poverty and racism) not personal, but the product of power relations, the outcome of strategies and technologies developed to create everything from autonomy to participatory democratic citizenship. External powers act upon the terrain of the self, but we also act upon ourselves, particularly according to models of self-help, like the self-esteem movement. To use the words of Hacking (1986b: 236): "[Critics] leave out the inner monologue, what I say to myself. They leave out self-discipline, what I do to myself. Thus they omit the permanent heartland of subjectivity." We might add that they leave out self-government, how we rule ourselves.

Tocqueville attributed to the general "equality of conditions" shared by American citizens the greater role in generating stability. What has become evident since is that even in a society deeply divided by inequalities of race, class and gender, political stability is relatively secure and overt resistance is rare. While the absence of open conflict is notable, social science that proposes a lack of something – lack of resistance, a social movement, a consciousness of race, class or gender, a lack of self-esteem – is productive science.

I have outlined here a history of the present "state of esteem". That history shows how self-governance is an invention of, and crucial to, modern democracy. My claims about modern democratic forms of power help us to understand how, for example, poor single mothers on welfare who are enrolled in self-esteem programmes become subjects even as they are subjected to forms of power and government. The failure of a women's movement united across race, class, gender and sexuality is due as much to the means by which we are "empowered" as to any "lack of self-esteem".

Notes

1. Nikolas Rose (1987) offers a compelling account of the limitations of feminist critique based on the public/private division that has influenced my arguments here.

2. Consider, for example, the following publication titles included in California Task Force (1990b): Stewart Emery, *Actualizations: you don't have to rehearse to be yourself* (New York: Irving Publications, 1980), Morris Rosenberg, *Conceiving the self* (Melbourne, Fla.: Robert E. Krieger Publishing Co. Inc., 1979), Virginia Satir, *People making* (Palo Alto, California: Science and Behavior Books, 1988).

3. For a discussion of the political and constitutive nature of narrative strategies, see Nancy Armstrong (1987); Carolyn Kay Steedman (1986); and for a study of narrative across social scientific, journalistic and fictional discourses, see Anita Levy (1991).

4. The statement I allude to reads: "One of the disappointing aspects of every chapter in this volume (at least to those of us who adhere to the intuitively correct models sketched above) is how low the association between self-esteem and its consequences are in research to date" (Mecca et al. 1989: 15). Notice that although no association is ever established, self-esteem is here linked to "its consequences".

5. For a compelling and insightful account of the economic interests of the middle class in service provisions to the poor, see Theresa Funiciello (1990). Although Funiciello fails to see that the social services are a form of governing the poor, she does clearly articulate the relationship between the social science professions and income redistribution. "What became the profession-

alization of being human took off, bloating under government contracts. For every poverty problem, a self-perpetuating profession proposed to ameliorate the situation without altering the poverty" (Funiciello 1990: 38).

6. Denise Riley (1988: esp. 44–66) points to the tangled history of women's citizenship and the emergence of the social as a sphere of governance and science.

7. The disciplinary origins of democratic citizenship in the United States are elaborated in Thomas Dumm's (1987) reading of Alexis de Tocqueville & Gustave de Beaumont. Also, see Roger Boesche (1987: especially 229–59).

8. As Peter Miller (1987: 201) put it: "Carceral power opened up the entire fabric of society to a normalizing regulation, but it no longer provides the exclusive model."

9. For an overview of "republican motherhood", see Gwendolyn Mink (1990).

References

Armstrong, N. 1987. *Desire and domestic fiction: a political history of the novel*. Oxford: Oxford University Press.

Beaumont, G. de & A. de Tocqueville 1964. *On the penitentiary system in the United States and its application in France*. Southern Illinois University Press.

Boesche, R. 1987. *The strange liberalism of Alexis de Tocqueville*. Ithaca, New York: Cornell University Press.

California Task Force to Promote Self-Esteem and Personal and Social Responsibility 1990a. *Toward a state of esteem: the final report*. California Department of Education.

California Task Force to Promote Self-Esteem and Personal and Social Responsibility 1990b. *Appendixes to "Toward a state of esteem"*. California Department of Education.

Dumm, T. 1987. *Democracy and punishment: the disciplinary origins of the United States*. Madison, Wisconsin: University of Wisconsin Press.

English, D. 1992. Review in *New York Times Book Review*, 2 February.

Foucault, M 1983. The subject and power. In *Michel Foucault: beyond structuralism and hermeneutics*, 2nd edn, H. Dreyfus & P. Rabinow (eds). Chicago: University of Chicago Press.

Foucault, M. 1988. The political technology of individuals. In *Technologies of the self*, L. Martin et al. (eds). Boston, Mass.: University of Massachusetts Press.

Funiciello, T. 1990. The poverty industry: do governments and charities create the poor? Ms. (November/December).

Hacking, I. 1986a. Making Up People. In *Reconstructing individualism: autonomy, individuality, and the self in Western thought*, T. Heller, M. Sosna, D. Wellberg (eds). Palo Alto, California: Stanford University Press.

Hacking, I. 1986b. Self-improvement. In *Foucault: a critical reader*, D. C. Hoy (ed.). Oxford: Basil Blackwell.

Levy, A. 1991. *The other woman: the writing of class, race and gender, 1832–1898*. Princeton, New Jersey: Princeton University Press.

Mecca, A., N. Smelser, J. Vasconellos (eds) 1989. *The social importance of self-esteem*. Berkeley: University of California Press.

Miller, P. 1987. *Domination and power*. London: Routledge & Kegan Paul.

Mink, G. 1990. The lady and the tramp: gender, race, and the origins of the American welfare state. In *Women, the state, and welfare*, L. Gordon (ed.). Madison, Wisconsin: Wisconsin University Press.

Riley, D. 1988. *"Am I that name?" feminism and the category of "women" in history*. Minneapolis: University of Minnesota Press.

Rose, N. 1987. Beyond the public/private division: law, power, and the family. *Journal of Law and Society* **14**(1), 61–76.

Rose, N. 1990. *Governing the soul: the shaping of the private self*. London: Routledge.

Scheff, T., S. Retzinger, M. Ryan (eds) 1989. Crime, violence, and self-esteem: review and proposals. See Mecca et al. (1989).

Steedman, C. 1986. *Landscape for a good woman: a story of two lives*. London: Virago.

Steinem, G. 1992. *Revolution from within: a book of self-esteem*. London: Little, Brown.

Tocqueville, A. de 1961a. *Democracy in America*, vol. I. New York: Schocken Books.

Tocqueville, A. de 1961b. *Democracy in America*, vol. II. New York: Schocken Books.

Chapter 12

Foucault in Britain

Colin Gordon

The British reception of Foucault's work has been difficult and uncertain. Difficult because no other contemporary case demonstrates so strikingly the obstacles that can intrude themselves between a French thinker and a British public. Uncertain because largely translated, widely read, often discussed (but mainly within the younger theoretical Left), Foucault's work has been received in silence by the great majority of his academic peers and contemporaries, whether philosophers, historians or sociologists.

This silence among the scholarly opinion-forming class sometimes doubtless signifies mistrust and rejection, but also, and perhaps more fundamentally, a reticence and perplexity. Reading one of the polemics on the misdeeds of "structuralism", or of Parisian "Nietzscheanism" and "nihilism", one might be tempted to conclude that all this is less a matter of the reception, friendly or unfriendly, of Foucault's ideas than of the relentless circulation of a certain number of received ideas about him. But it might be truer to say that there are no received ideas here about Foucault: there are many people who know who Foucault is, but have difficulty in knowing what they should think about him.

Within this unclaimed terrain of opinion, anyone who dislikes Foucault can say more or less what they please about him, and some commentators have made extensive use of this freedom. His admirers, conversely, have been free to enjoy the non-authorized status of their enthusiasm and to put the Foucauldian tool-kit to work as an engine for change within their political culture. The secondary literature on Foucault and the expanding body of work produced over the last few years under his inspiration includes some useful, worthwhile work. Rather than carrying out a detailed review of this here, however, I would like to enquire into the reasons underlying the commoner attitudes of unease and malaise that manifest themselves in this area. Why do many of the British appear to have a particular difficulty in appreciating, in understanding, and even, one might be tempted to say, in perceiving Foucault?

I

It is hard to think about what Foucault was without employing the notion of the intellectual, a title that he himself was ready to assume in a categorical and impassioned way. Foucault explained his own understanding of this term several times, and it is perhaps not certain that all his remarks on the subject coincide in an identical image. Here I would like to consider a group of his writings that develop what are surely some fundamental elements of his ideas on the intellectual's function: these are his discussions of the Kantian question: "What is Enlightenment?" In his "Chronology" that prefaces the new edition of Foucault's shorter writings, Daniel Defert indeed records that, from 1978 on, Kant's opuscles on history became a constant element of Foucault's reading (Defert 1994).

Foucault takes the answers that Mendelssohn and Kant gave to this question in the pages of the *Berliner Monatsschrift* as marking the beginning of a new modern genre of what he calls "philosophical journalism". He sees this as involving the emergence for the first time as a topic within the field of philosophical thought of the question of the present, the question of what we are and who we are in our quality as beings who live and inhabit a contemporary moment. In his preface to the English translation of George Canguilhem's *The normal and the pathological*, Foucault writes that "it would no doubt be necessary to study why this question of Enlightenment had, without ever disappearing, a different destiny in Germany, France and the Anglo-Saxon countries" (Foucault 1989: 10). On Germany and France, he adds some remarks that emphasize, notably, his own sense of indirect kinship with the Frankfurt school and his interest in the work of Max Weber. I do not know if Foucault ever elaborated on the same theme with regard to English-speaking culture.

It would have been all the more interesting to know his views on this, because there are good grounds for contending that the idea and tradition of Enlightenment have never existed among the British, at least not in the narrow sense of the term. Similarly, and more notoriously, the French idea of the intellectual, as the designation of a role, a status or a mode of conduct, has never been fully naturalized into British culture. To find in British history the equivalent of a "question of Enlightenment", it would first be necessary at least to modify or complicate the terms of the question, so as to retrace within this national culture the outlines of a different framework of modernity, a different figuration of thought, experience and time. We will see that some of Foucault's analyses can help us to define this figuration: making this connection may help at the same time to throw light on some British perceptions of Foucault.

In *The philosophy of the Enlightenment*, a book that Foucault praised at the time of its French translation in 1966, Ernst Cassirer traced one side of the ancestry of Kantian critique back to some Scots and English writers on morals and aesthetics (Cassirer 1951). In his lectures at the Collège de France in 1978, Foucault drew attention to an element of critical thought in the Scots creators of political economy: Smith's thought could be viewed as a "critique of state reason", which, in Kantian manner, demonstrated to political power the ineluctable limits of its capacity to know. Furthermore, far from taking a neo-Marxist view of political economy as a long-lived tradition of ideological complacency, Foucault sees in it an unquiet, vigilant and problematizing style of thought.

During roughly the same years in the 1970s, English-speaking authors were developing analyses of the origins of liberalism that are sometimes close to Foucault's. Albert Hirschman, in *The passions and the interests*, shows how the spirit of capitalism was in a certain sense summoned up in advance to help avert the prospect of political disorders and civil wars by inducing more peaceable and reasoned styles of individual conduct (Hirschman 1977). In *The machiavellian moment* Pocock explores this same problematic in terms of the difficulties posed during the early modern period by the republican notion of civil virtue (Pocock 1975). Pocock describes the eighteenth-century beginnings of a new secular self-awareness of society. The writings of Defoe invite the age to accept "that in a commercial society, the individual's relation to his *res publica* could not be simply civic or virtuous" (ibid.: 436). There is no neat pre-established harmony between the civic and the commercial domains.

> The dominant paradigm for the individual inhabiting the world of value was that of civic man; but the dominant paradigm for the individual as engaged in historical actuality was that of economic and intersubjective man, and it was peculiarly hard to bring the two together. (ibid.: 466)

> If indeed capitalist thought ended by privatizing the individual, this may have been because it was unable to find an appropriate way of presenting him as citizen. "Bourgeois ideology", which old-

fashioned Marxism depicted as appearing with historical inevitability, had, it seem, to wage a struggle for existence and may never
have fully won it. (Pocock 1975.: 461)

Pocock resembles Foucault by underlining the lucid, self-aware tone of
these early modern debates.

> The Augustan journalists and critics were the first intellectuals on
> record to express an entirely secular awareness of social and eco-
> nomic changes going on in their society, and to say specifically that
> these changes affected both their values and their modes of per-
> ceiving social reality (ibid.: 461).
> To this extent, "England was too modern to need an Enlighten-
> ment and was already engaged on the quarrel with modernity
> itself" (ibid.: 467).

Too modern to need an Enlightenment . . . One might begin to see here
the basis of the frequent sceptical disdain of the British for the notion of
the intellectual (a term that Pocock seems to me to be using in a deliberately artificial way in the above-cited passage). The British non-creation
of the role of the intellectual forms part, no doubt, of a classic topos of
historical sociology: the cunning and flexible process of interweaving of
old and new classes, status groups, estates and powers, whose overall
result was to render redundant, in British society, the continental role of
the heroic literary figure whose powerless culture challenges a despotism
that despises and excludes it.

If the Augustan age did not invent the intellectual, then no doubt this is
because it invented something else, namely public opinion. In his fine
book on Hume, Didier Deleule (1979) notes the existence in Britain of a
connection between journalism and philosophy that passes via the refusal
of a militant critical ideal: "In a way, the attitude of neutrality adopted by
Hume in politics is a continuation, in the philosophical sphere, of the
enterprise which Addison and Steele had begun in journalism from 1711
onwards." Addison had argued in *The Spectator* against the invocation of
"an old Greek law forbidding any citizen to remain neutral and to observe,
in the role of a disinterested spectator, the divisions of his country": Hume,
in similar spirit, writes that "public spirit should, it seems to me, oblige us
to love the mass of the nation" (Deleule 1979: 324–5). A man of encounters, a subtle connoisseur of passions, interests and opinions, a non-
conformist conservative, the Humean thinker assumes, through the

practice of an engaged detachment, a public vocation as the craftsman of compromises. This is not "philosophical journalism", then, but a common cause and task that philosopher and journalist may share.

This open space of opinion, this British *Öffentlichkeit* (also studied, prior to Pocock and Deleule, by the young Habermas) constitutes an essential part of the Kantian conception of *Aufklärung*. But is it not precisely a trait of this German *Aufklärung*, in its status as project, that the said *Öffentlichkeit* remains as yet no more than a potentiality, a normative unrealized wish, such that it becomes the thinker's and the intellectual's vocation to function in his own person as the precarious vessel, the provisional bearer of this universal possibility? In an actually existing *Öffentlichkeit*, on the other hand, the roles are constructed and allocated differently.

II

The commentaries on the Anglo-Scots beginnings of modern liberalism that Foucault presented in his 1978–9 Collège de France lecture on "governmentality" attach a special importance to the notion of civil society (Foucault 1991). Like Pocock, Foucault sees, underlying the uses of this term, an aporia concerning political individuality. Empiricist philosophy rethinks the individual as a subject of interest, which is impossible to identify with the subject of law postulated by doctrines of political sovereignty. The new understanding of the social and economic interplay of interests postulates a "dialectic of spontaneous multiplicity", a "non-totalizable multiplicity", incompatible with the unitary principle of totalization of wills assumed by doctrines of juridical sovereignty. Foucault sees Adam Fergusson's history of civil society as sketching a way of coming to terms with this problem. The Scots thinkers' conception of civil society is an act of political invention, the instrument or correlate of a new technique of government. "Civil society" no longer means for them, as it did for Locke, the political dimension of society. Instead it signifies the denser, fuller and more complex reality of the collective environment in which men as economic subjects of interest must be located, in order to govern them. The problem of the foundation of power is dissolved, or rather dispersed, into a space of historical immanence. Men effect their division of economic and political labour through a natural and spontaneous historical process; the dialectic of interests causes society to ceaselessly unmake and remake itself, through a dynamic of "self-sundering unity"; passing historically through its successive forms of organization, governmental rationality participates in the corresponding transformations of society in general.

Foucault speaks of civil society as a "transactional reality", as a vector in the "common interplay of relations of power and that which continually escapes their grasp". This way of considering the British experience of modernity seems full of promise. That experience can then be seen as being produced through an interplay of invention and (real or postulated) nature, characterized by a political culture moulded upon a schematism of social becoming, and, at the same time, a political critique of society conducted in the name of society.

As Pocock points out, modernity was from early on being perceived in Britain as accomplished fact rather than intention; as problem rather than project. This very problem has become a national tradition, not to say archaism; the relation with the new clothes itself in a language that pre-exists its object; hence the very English taste, which one should be careful not to take too much at face value, for a certain vein of nostalgic prophecy. Equally significant is the long trend towards the disconnection of philosophy and history. In Britain, the silence of philosophers concerning history enters in some sense, into the definition of national happiness. In the present century, British philosophy has rejected the "Continental" themes of the "crisis of philosophy" and the "philosophy of the crisis". Critique, as practised by British thinkers, is more likely to address a decay of society than the defeat or betrayal of reason.

In his commentary on the "question of Enlightenment" in Kant, Foucault indicates a way of thinking the present that is as distant as most British thought from speculative philosophy of history. This Kantian intellectual posture is one that might be termed a vertical reflexivity: its radicalism, as a consciousness of the present, has the character of an encompassing downward overview, whether with the intention to capture, to embrace or to escape. In British culture since Hume, however, one finds something different, a horizontal reflexivity that places itself on the same footing as the world it observes. This seems to have among its consequences the production of an intellectual atmosphere where the genealogical approach finds few takers. One is not likely to arrive at Nietzsche – this might have been Foucault's view – without having first travelled via Kant.

An objection to this line of reasoning immediately arises. For, using the terms of our discussion, one might argue that there are as many "British" as "Continental" elements in Foucault's own intellectual personality. Whatever may have been written about the theme of the "carceral society" in *Discipline and punish* (the critics' equivalent in Foucault of the "iron cage" theme in Weber studies) (Foucault 1977), Foucault is someone who abstained (more so than some British thinkers) from the genre of apocalyptic genealogies. He did not care for the role of Cassandra. In his rereading of Kant, as in many of his later public statements, Foucault can be credited with a certain prudent concern to de-dramatize. In an interview with Gerard Raulet, he criticizes his own former Nietzschean tendency to read the present always in terms of crisis, break, dawn or completion. We need, he suggests, a more modest and circumspect time-sensibility; we should regard our present as "a time like any other, or rather a time which is never entirely like any other" (Foucault 1988a: 36).

A number of Foucault's views and position fit well with Didier Deleule's intellectual profile of Hume. For Hume: "nothing is fatally determined, everything is possible; the real, as an accomplished form of the possible, does not carry the prestige of an entelechy, but is first and foremost a contingent product" (Deleule 1979: 360). In 1984, Foucault says to Dreyfus and Rabinow: "My idea is not that everything is bad, but that everywhere there is danger, which is not exactly the same thing. If everything is dangerous, then there is always something for us to do" (Foucault 1986: 343). From the history of his recent past, Hume draws out an act of invention. He valorizes political concertation as a work of creation. "The revolution of 1688 represents a real innovation, it manifests the inventive power of the human mind" (Deleule 1979: 332). "Behind the coalition of parties and the triumph of moderation over the spirit of faction, lies something which must properly be called an intellectual collaboration" (Deleule 1979: 336). Foucault, although clearly reluctant to subscribe to Habermas's normative conception of political consensuality, emphasizes, in his 1983 discussion with R. Bono on contemporary health policy, the importance of efforts to conceptualize new mechanisms for collective arbitration of resources and needs (Foucault 1988b).

One is dealing here, of course, with a complex thought in constant evolution. I do not mean to imply that Foucault's complexity was too much for British intelligences, blocking recognition of his thoughts' more kindred and acceptable elements. To be sure, one may still hope that a better knowledge of Foucault's later work and writings will improve the chances of fruitful discussion. But one must also take into consideration other, persistent factors that have long pushed British critics in the direction of unilateral and active simplification.

III

As we know, Foucault's work involves a particular way of making history and philosophy interact and overlap. British culture in general is little accustomed to frequent these borderlands. Foucault's French friends have been known to express regret that his philosophical enterprise did not find as understanding a contemporary audience among his historian contemporaries as one might have wished. As a British observer, I am tempted to say that they do not have much to complain about. In comparison with the British situation, the relative richness of the relations between the historical and philosophical sectors of French thought in his time was one of the factors that most helped to make Foucault's thought possible and to ensure its welcome in France. Foucault makes the point himself when writing in the preface to *The archaeology of knowledge* about the affinity and convergence between the archaeological procedure and the concepts of structure and series employed by the *Annales* School (Foucault 1971). Another important and little-noticed indicator is the welcome Braudel gave in *Annales* to *Histoire de la folie*, a book he saw as admirably executing Lucien Febvre's programme for a "history of mentalities" (Mandrou 1962). Some have thought this a case of well-meant mistaken identity. I am not so sure. "History of mentalities" did not always or necessarily connote that bland and anodyne genre that it is nowadays common to scorn. In his very interesting book entitled *Le discours et l'historique*, Gerard Mairet pointed out that Febvre's *La religion de Rabelais* contains an archaeology of the thinkable: a study, that is, of the limits, in a given period, of possible thought and the thought of the possible (Febvre 1942, 1968). It was Febvre who said that we need historians with a philosophy training. Foucault was repeating Febvre's own words when, in a debate with some historians, he drew a contrast between a history centred on problems and a history centred on periods. It was Febvre, again, who focused attention on thresholds of discontinuity in the history of the sciences. Working within such a tradition, it is not surprising that Foucault was able to form such a fruitful friendship with the historian Paul Veyne, that Veyne's *Bread and circuses* could provide – as Foucault testified – a model of method for his researches on governmental rationality (Veyne 1990 [1976]), or that Veyne in return was afterwards able to take up and put to work Foucault's notion of a history of truth. If "governmentality" is doubtless short for "governmental rationality", can it not also be paraphrased as "mentality of government"?

Foucault and Deleuze are heirs of a generation of philosophers who established the history of thought as a task worthy of philosophers: together with the leading role played by the school of historical epistemology, one should also acknowledge the importance of the historians of systems of philosophical thought: Bruhier, Alquiu, Gouhier, Hyppolite, Gueroult. Against this background it is easier to see how so many young left-wing French philosophers came in the 1970s, sometimes by way of Althusserianism, to write a history of knowledges, powers and revolts.

In Britain there was nothing like this. Among philosophers, history of philosophy had, and to a large extent still has, the status of a lightweight, semi-popular didactic genre. As proof of this one may take Bertrand Russell's highly successful pot-boiler and the equivalent works by his successors. British or other English-speaking philosophers seldom trouble about philological exactitude in the reading of past philosophers. Analytical philosophy doubtless does not lack its own kind of rigour, but it is a chronic, argumentative rigour, and not a rigour of system. Even when English-speaking philosophy of science pays attention to the history of concepts, this is usually done for the purpose of illustrating an argument. The attempt Foucault makes to introduce a strictly historical pluralization into the problematic of rationality, even the coining of such a term as the "historical *a priori*", is liable in this culture to arouse the double suspicion of historicism and irrationality. At these points, the empiricist temperament is quickly irritated.

Conversely, British historians of ideas and mentalities have generally tended not to look to philosophers for an input to their method of working. Within the New Left, this non-dialogue developed into a family quarrel when the (then) Althusserians Barry Hindess and Paul Hirst asserted that Marxism, the science of history, had no need to deal in the class of narrative romances produced by the professional historians (Hirst 1985). Edward Thompson's rejoinder in *The poverty of theory* expressed equal and opposite doubts about the value of Althusserian and other French intellectual innovations, including the work of Foucault (Thompson 1978). Here one can remark that the concurrent reading in Britain on Foucault and other new French producers of "theory" generated a certain number of misguided amalgamations. However, one may also feel that the determination of many British commentators (along with French Sartrians) to categorize Foucault under the heading of a "structuralism" presumed by definition to be anti-historical (or at any rate opposed to any history with a human face), may have had the effect of reinforcing a very British barrier of incommensurability between history and philosophy, thus consolidating a division of labour in the exercise of suspicion. For the historians, Foucault could be taken as a theorist, and thereby as a despiser of experience and the human; for philosophers, he could be taken as a Nietzschean relativist, and thereby as a despiser of truth.

But the motives of such reactions cannot be grasped without considering some traits of British political culture, and particularly of its Left. The British Left has played with full conviction the game of the social that we mentioned above, the game of a critique of society in the name of society allied to the invocation of a deeply rooted, popular and constitutive sociability. This style doubtless fits the political strength of the Labour Movement and the role taken in the present century by the trade unions as partners in a governmental system. Its intellectual signature is the manner in which (to the disgust of at least one English Marxist) historical sociology, the discipline *par excellence* of an unquiet liberalism, is displaced in Britain by social history, the vehicle of an assured social democracy. If one wanted to speak of Left "intellectuals" in Britain during the past few decades, the title would usually go, not to philosophers or political scientists, but to historians or literary thinkers like E. P. Thompson, Richard Hoggart or Raymond Williams. One reason why the term is not much in favour here is perhaps because, within this national Left, "intellectuals" like to think of themselves as Gramscian "organic" intellectuals, living in an imaginary consubstantiality with popular being and committed to the task of recovering or recreating, out of the existing residues of a "common experience", the true democratic elements of a "common culture" (Williams 1961).

In its best moments, this ethos conveys an impressive sense of solidity, or of what Weber meant by "personality". And yet when one looks at what allows this culture to call itself a Left, more problematic features emerge. For after all, if one is a Marxist then British history is the history of a long defeat, a perverse singularity. The bourgeoisie is seen, in this narrative much cultivated by the British New Left, as having betrayed its own historic destiny and the proletarian future, by timidly allying itself with aristocracy and landed property (Anderson 1992). Preferring the corrupt pursuit of social distinction over its capitalist vocation, the spineless British bourgeoisie made itself responsible at once for the secular deterioration of the national economy and the permanent blockage of the class struggle. This diagnosis, redolent of frustration, led on to some scarcely scientific paths of compensatory reasoning. On the one hand, there was a new version of the thesis of the "Norman yoke": the search in social memory, beyond and against the trickery of the Whig settlement, for ancient Puritan virtues and the lost will to invent an "other republic".

(The reverie of an exceedingly long, specifically English march towards socialism acquired a strong, curiously durable hold on socialist imaginations during the Stalinist post-war years of the British Communist Party.) On the other hand, as a supplement to the analyses of classical Marxism, there was the extravagant edifice of a "theory of the State", the highly coloured portrait of a British monster-State complete with its ideological and repressive apparatuses, its imperial monarchic baubles and servilities, its elites, spies and secrets.

As is well known, Foucault openly abstained from the theory of the State (in the sense, as he put it, of abstaining "from an indigestible meal") and was inclined to make fun of what he called a tendency, shared by the Left, towards "State-phobia". This abstention may have seemed more shocking to Left opinion in Britain than in France. But perhaps it was not the real need for a theory or history of the State that was at issue here (for this was a kind of theory that most people were keener to talk about than to actually practise). Foucault's real fault in the eyes of the British Left lay not so much, one suspects, in his insufficient aversion to the State, as in his unwillingness to take the side of society against the State.

This aspect of Foucault's social sensibility perhaps merits attention. Among the critical discourses of his time, Foucault avoided the garrulous genre of social critique that tells us that we live badly and that even narcissism is not what it used to be; as well as the rancorous vein of sociology that dissects the mean aspirations and resentments of *petit-bourgeois* humanity. At the same time, Foucault showed a certain attitude that offended the sensibilities of some English-speaking moralists: an attitude, not so much of contempt, but of mistrust for the social bond. Consider the theme running through Foucault's work, from *Histoire de la folie* (1961) to "La vie des hommes infâmes" (1977) and "Le désordre des familles" (Farge & Foucault 1982): the history of "lettres de cachet", of obsequious appeals by humble families under the *ancien régime* to solicit from royal power the social elimination of their more disorderly and disreputable members. *Histoire de la folie* traces, as the practical correlate of emerging practices of normalization from the *ancien régime* to the Revolution and beyond, the continuing history of a social practice of denunciation. A certain kind of historical material, which reappears in passages of *Discipline and punish*; a conception of power, outlined here and there, in which all are in virtual conflict with all; an acute sensitivity to contemporary residues and recurrences in French society of the Pétainist collaboration; a clear refusal, finally, to recognize in civil society – as defined by Left or Right – a principle of good opposable to the evil of State: taken together, all of this seems to have been obscurely perceived within the British Left as carrying implications contrary to their national and political morals. (One might add that, if a biographer were seeking to understand the consequences of Foucault's homosexuality either for the orientation of his work or for its reception, then this would be a good place to look.)

Some of these ideas, further developed in work (translated into English from 1978 on) by friends of Foucault including Jacques Donzelot, Robert Castel, Giovanna Procacci and Pasquale Pasquino, seemed, nevertheless, to a minority in the British Left, to offer a new critical and analytical grasp on that reality that these writers dubbed "the social" – meaning, approximately, the all-encompassing collective universe of the twentieth-century Welfare State – that was both more effective and more provocative than neo-Marxist theories of ideology or social control. These analyses made possible a reading of the "social" as the terrain, the objective and even the invention of a series of governmental techniques and knowledges (Burchell et al. 1991). Admittedly, this current of work, which was not originally designed to address British historical subject matter, was perhaps not to prove a perfect ready-made formula for explaining everything about our own political culture: there would surely be a whole additional effort needed to explain the quality, mentioned above, of the English social as *naturans* as well as *naturata*, the complex anchoring (and contestation) of social techniques and institutions in sociabilities and (counter-)conducts (Rose 1985, Miller & Rose 1986, Burchell et al. 1991).

But political rejections of Foucault's philosophy often had more stubborn and radical grounds than this: objection not to an insufficiency of its results, but to the reprehensible implications of the whole enterprise. The commonest objections of the orthodox Left add up to a consistent, if unwieldy set of complaints: Foucault's lack of a theory of the subject; his lack of an analysis (or a non-scandalous analysis) in terms of class; his lack of a strategic doctrine of resistance; his lack of a normative vision of society; his lack of an anthropology. To this may be added the philosophers' and historians' critiques of Foucault as a relativist or a theorist, the reproach for the double lack of a fundamentalism of value and of a principle of identification. These critics no doubt understood Foucault perfectly well when he said that "the guarantee of freedom is freedom", and "perhaps what is important today is not to discover what we are, but to refuse what we are". For the *New Left Review*, this amounted to a refusal of "any collective construction of a new form of social identity" – and, consequently, of any possibility of a progressive politics. In a similar spirit, the philosopher Charles Taylor summed up a whole climate of suspicion by his criticism of Foucault's "impossible attempt to stand nowhere" (Taylor 1986).

Some critics went so far as to say that Foucault had no right or reason, given his principles, to concern himself with the defence of rights, his politics being capable of grounding nothing more than a spontaneism of gratuitous acts. All this English-speaking criticism took little concern – for lack, in part, of factual information – of the actual concerns and meanings of Foucault's public actions and utterances. Possibly these actions belonged, in any case, to a quite important aspect of French political life that the British and Americans understand poorly: a type of democratic civic spirit that places little faith in the goodness of society. Tocqueville, wondering over "the source of this passion for political liberty", concluded that the question must in some senses necessarily remain unanswered: "do not ask me to analyze this sublime taste: it is one which can only be experienced". The British, feeling less obliged to treasure the rarity of such a sentiment, perhaps tend more to think they can and should know where the passion for liberty comes from or (if they belong to the German-influenced Left) what is its foundation.

During the 1980s, this tendency takes on such a marked aspect in some English-speaking countries as to give the impression of a crisis of critical culture: a tensing in the face of a reality subconsciously felt to undo all militantism: a need for moral stiffening that betrays the inward, empirical suspicion that spontaneity is now anything but revolutionary. At the same time, the dogmatic basis of the official Left began to migrate from class fundamentalism to philosophico-anthropological fundamentalism.

This new tone of strident Enlightenment, this aggressive normativity to be heard among the Anglo-Saxon Left's critics of Foucault – this 1980s Habermas effect, in other words – may not offer the best possible way to understand our present, nor indeed the best basis for any kind of "collective construction" to be undertaken in the public sphere. It reminds one more of the language of the policing action undertaken a few years earlier, in the homeland of *Aufklärung*, to eliminate from the public service (including universities) those who were judged "not to feel at home" on the "footing of basic liberal-democratic order". As Foucault remarked, there might be grounds to beware here the possible transformation of the Enlightenment ideal into a new kind of McCarthyism.

Most of all, one should question here the peremptory presumption that demands, at any price, a normative founding of identity as the basis of any morally respectable form of political consciousness. Why not, on the contrary, acknowledge, in what has been called an "attempt to stand nowhere", a quest – highly compatible with certain Anglo-Saxon values –

for truths that do not depend on the place where one stands? Habermas himself came to recognize something like this (his admirable obituary notice being perhaps his only intelligent comment on Foucault, and perhaps significantly the one comment based on a direct personal encounter) when he writes of the "tension" in Foucault between the acute moral sensibility of the intellectual and the "almost serene" reserve of the scholar's quest for objectivity (Habermas 1986a). In a similar vein, one may read, in the fine obituary that Foucault himself wrote for his friend Philippe Ariès, a morality very well attuned to British experience. Here, invoking the name of Max Weber, Foucault praises the virtue of confronting an identity made from personal heritages and choices – values, a style, a mode of life – with the hazards of thought and knowledge; through such encounters, loyalty to self can lead to a changing of the self – on condition that this change is a kind of work (Foucault 1974). Some such tempered conduct of identity and non-identity might be the best way of responding to the present necessity of our own culture to practise a form of the virtue that Foucault termed "inventive fidelity".

IV

Some of Foucault's main political ideas have lost none of their challenging force or pertinence over the past decade. Moreover, some of them seem to be being received, though how much of this can be specifically counted as a "Foucault effect" is difficult to measure.

One of the key sources for Foucault's later political thinking still remains inaccessible in English or French; this is his 1976 Paris lecture course, exploring notions of struggle as a principle of historical intelligibility, and the genealogy of notions of historical struggle as the bases of political action. The opening lectures in this series were translated on their own some years ago, and led some to suppose, wrongly, that Foucault was here not only exploring or experimenting with, but unequivocally endorsing a Nietzschean metaphysic of war, will and struggle. In fact the overall implication of this genealogical foray, with its troubling rapprochement of the class and race struggle theories of the nineteenth century, comes, in its implicit conclusions, far closer to the message that the militant ideal (at any rate, in many or most of its known Western forms) is the surest of roads to nihilism. Foucault after the mid-1970s did not become apolitical or politically quietist, but his politics became, in a very acute and aware sense, a "morale de l'incomfort".

Foucault's other main later political idea was that the Left – more specifically, socialism – needs and lacks an art of government, while in recent decades its adversaries have developed and practised, to relatively impressive effect, precisely such an art – namely, neo-liberalism. What Foucault said to his Paris audiences in 1978 and 1979 was, almost in so many words: you cannot hope to contest successfully for electoral victory if you cannot show that you know how to govern; at present, although you have hardly noticed this, others have acquired a more convincing claim than you to possess such knowledge.

The simplest part of this idea is one that, although more and more perceptibly in the air, has still not become entirely commonplace. Electability may depend on many factors, but one of these is certainly the perceived capacity to govern; such a capacity is, on the whole, more likely to be recognized where there is evidence of some distinct conception of how to govern, and indeed of what governing is. Foucault's work points out the linkage between such knowledges and arts, in the modern West, and certain problems of conduct (governing as the "conduct of conduct"). The contemporary question of government that candidates for its exercise have to address is and remains, perhaps ever more transparently, what it was for Pocock's early modern Britons, the problem of prescribing rules of the game for a society of individuals in a world where the civic and the commercial strata of individuality fail to harmonize.

The questions that it seems to me are posed by, or should be posed about, Foucault's intellectual legacy in this area have to do with the value of identity and the nature of collective identity. It has seemed to me that what Foucault teaches us is to know that we do not know what we are. This is not a universally pleasing message, but it is also one that can be readily misunderstood. This is one question that perhaps becomes clearer with the benefit of a decade's hindsight and against the agenda of questions our own time puts to itself. Foucault's thought is sometimes classed among the causes of a cultural malaise called "post-modern blankness", a sort of collective personality deficit characterized by an absence of moral identity or personality, of values or passions. This latter syndrome – admittedly one that ageing and disgruntled cultural critics are always prone to diagnose in their own times and periods – more or less tallies with the set of charges that the conservative New Left was bringing in the 1980s against Foucault and other Parisian practitioners of "logics of disintegration". Looking back at Foucault's life and career in the light of his recent biographies, one has a clear impression of intellectual unquiet and mobility, indeed of a capacity for radical philosophic doubt. Yet, equally clearly, one does not have the impression of incoherence of character or absence of moral personality. Foucault may well have been, as it were, a role model in doubt about what we are, but not in doubt about who we are. If we (the British, perhaps, more than most) have problems about the latter question, Foucault is not the cause or symptom of those problems.

Thanks partly to Foucault's influence, questions of identity are currently being promoted to the status of a subgenre of theory, but perhaps one that sets itself too restricted an agenda. Reading recent writings grouped under this heading, one has the impression that the subgenre would be better entitled "theory of difference". Difference itself is a proper object of study and so are those movements and struggles based on some specific (ethnic, gender or sexual) difference. Difference is, in a valid and justifiable sense, a major contemporary source of identity. The question is whether it can be a sole or sufficient source. Here I find myself grudgingly in agreement with the view represented in recent debates by Richard Rorty, to the effect that some degree of explicit adhesion to a more universal principle of collective identity (or equivalent set of collective values) may be a necessary precondition for some forms of effective political action within a democratic state. (The extent to which the *de facto* meaning of "universal" and "collective" is assumed here to be "national" is a more problematic and troubling point.)

The belief in the need to meet such a condition seems, at least, to be well founded in so far as it corresponds, in Foucault's vocabulary, to a prerequisite for a rationality of government. The argument would run as follows: a practice of government entails a consistent conception of both the conduct of governing and the conducts of the governed, and requires that the governed are able and prepared to recognize themselves in this representation of their conduct. That representation covers the conduct "of all and of each": individual existence, reciprocity and interaction. The game of government, like all the regimes and *dispositifs* that Foucault describes, is not something given of necessity and forever; some – notably the English – have imagined a society without government; the game of government is, however, given to us as a contingent historical *a priori* unless and until we replace it by (or transform it into) a different game, and it is given in the form of a more or less stable or perishable repertoire of practices, techniques and concepts. Government entails, or is liable to require, periodic acts of both political and moral reinvention. This is the collective or public aspect of what Foucault called, in the individual sphere, the "aesthetics of existence": moral practice in the absence of categorical codes founded in an anthropology or a theology.

The current leader of the British Labour Party appears to take the view that a statement of position about the conduct of all and of each from the point of view of government is a necessary step in demonstrating the capability of a Left party to govern. An initiative of this nature does indeed seem timely and necessary. As Foucault said, quoting Baudelaire, one has no right to despise the present. Our own generation has, perhaps, as much talent for moral invention as any other. The present may be a good moment to use it.

References

Anderson, P. 1992 *English questions*. London: Verso

Burchell, G., C. Gordon, P. Miller (eds) 1991. *The Foucault effect: studies in governmentality*. Hemel Hempstead, England: Harvester Wheatsheaf.

Cassirer, E, 1951. *The philosophy of the Enlightenment*. Princeton, New Jersey: Princeton University Press.

Defert, D. (ed.) 1994. *Michel Foucault: dits et écrits*, vol. I. Paris: Gallimard.

Deleule, D. 1979. *Hume et la naissance de libéralisme économique*. Paris: Aubier Montagne.

Farge, A. & M. Foucault 1982. *Le désordre des familles*. Coll. Archives, Gallimard/Juillard, Paris.

Febvre, L.1942, 1968. *Le problème de l'incroyance au 16e siècle. La religion de Rabelais*. Albin Michel.

Foucault, M. 1961. *Folie et déraison: histoire de la folie à l'âge classique*. Paris: Plan.

Foucault, M. 1971. *The archaeology of knowledge* (trans.A. Sheridan). London: Tavistock.

Foucault, M. 1974. Obituary, Philippe Ariès. *Nouvel Observateur* (17 February), 56–7.

Foucault, M. 1977. *Discipline and punish* (trans. A. Sheridan). London: Allen Lane.

Foucault, M. 1978. La vie des hommes infâmes. *Les Cahiers du Chemin* **29**, 12–29.

Foucault, M. 1986. *The Foucault reader*. P. Rabinow (ed.). London: Penguin.

Foucault, M. 1988a. Critical theory/intellectual history. See Kritzman (1988), 17–46.

Foucault, M. 1988b. Social security. See Kritzman (1988), 159–77.

Foucault, M. 1989. Introduction. In *The normal and the pathological*, G. Canguilhem. New York: Zone Books.

Foucault, M. 1991. Governmentality. See Burchell et al. (1991), 87–104.

Habermas, J. 1986a. Foucault's lecture on Kant. *Thesis 11* **14**, 4–8.

Habermas, J. 1986b. Taking aim at the heart of the present. In *Foucault: a critical reader*, D. Couzens Hoy (ed.), 103–8. Oxford: Basil Blackwell.

Hirschman, A. O. 1977. *The passions and the interests*. Princeton, New Jersey: Princeton University Press.

Hirst, P. 1985. *Marxism and historical writing*. London: Routledge & Kegan Paul.

Kritzman, L. 1988. *Michel Foucault: politics, philosophy, culture*. London: Routledge.

Mandrou, R. 1962. Trois clefs pour comprendre la folie à l'époque classique. With a note by F. Braudel. *Annales ESC*: 761–72.

Miller, P. & N. Rose (eds) 1986. *The power of psychiatry*. Cambridge: Polity.

Pocock, J. G. A. 1975. *The machiavellian moment*. Princeton, New Jersey: Princeton University Press.

Rose, N. 1985. *The psychological complex*. London: Routledge & Kegan Paul

Taylor, C. 1986. Foucault on freedom and truth. In *Foucault: a critical reader*, D. Couzens Hoy (ed.), 69–102. Oxford: Basil Blackwell.

Thompson, E. P. 1978. *The poverty of theory*. London: Merlin.

Veyne, P. 1990 [1976]. *Bread and circuses: historical sociology and political pluralism*. London: Penguin.

Williams, R. 1961. *Culture and society 1780–1950*. London: Penguin.

Index

INDEX